OUT OF THE SHADOWS

Out of the Shadows
The Life of Lucy, Countess of Bedford

Lesley Lawson

hambledon
continuum

Hambledon Continuum is an imprint of Continuum Books
Continuum UK, The Tower Building, 11 York Road, London SE1 7NX
Continuum US, 80 Maiden Lane, Suite 704, New York, NY 10038

www.continuumbooks.com

First published 2007

Quotations form Daphne du Maurier, *Golden Lads: A Study of Anthony Bacon,
Francis and their Friends* (London: Victor Gollancz, 1975), reproduced by kind
permission of Curtis Brown Group Ltd, London, on behalf of the estate of
Daphne du Maurier, copyright © Daphne du Maurier, 1975.

British Library Cataloguing-in-Publication Data
A catalogue record for this book is available from the British Library.

ISBN 978 1 84725 212 8

Typeset by Pindar New Zealand (Egan Reid), Auckland, New Zealand

Contents

In memory of my mother

Preface

With one eye on posterity John Donne promised Lucy, Countess of Bedford to 'show future times/What you were' and for well over four hundred years that promise has been faithfully kept. Generations of readers have discovered Lucy in the lines Donne wrote for and about her. But Donne's poetry tells only part of Lucy's story and for modern audiences she remains a shadowy and elusive figure.

In her own time however Lucy was anything but shadowy. Born into a highly ambitious Elizabethan family, she lived through the reigns of three monarchs. As an enthusiastic and well informed supporter of the arts she was a patroness and friend to John Florio, Samuel Daniel, John Donne, Ben Jonson, Michael Drayton and John Dowland, among others. Attractive, educated, cultured and charming she rose to become one of the most important female courtiers during the reign of James I. She forged an especially close relationship with James's queen, Anna, and the power and influence this connection bought enabled her to further the fortunes of her friends and family. Lucy was a prominent and successful public figure but her private life was not always glittering or straightforward and she encountered reversals, illness and heartbreaking loss. Her story provides a rare insight into the preoccupations and actions of a remarkable woman who lived in quite remarkable times.

Acknowledgements

This book has been a long time in the making and it could not have been completed without a great deal of help and support which I am very pleased to acknowledge.

Writing is a solitary activity but it is also collaborative and my understanding of Lucy and the times in which she lived has been enriched by the work of writers and researchers in the fields of history, literature, medicine and the visual arts. Their work, acknowledged in the notes and bibliography, has been thought provoking and informative and made this book much better than it would have otherwise been. Access to manuscripts relating to Lucy and Edward held at Woburn Abbey was made available to me by the kind permission of the Duke of Bedford and the Trustees of the Bedford Estates. I would like to thank the Woburn Abbey archivist Mrs Ann Mitchell for her assistance. I am also grateful to the staff of the Essex Record Office for their help.

Martin Sheppard first believed that Lucy's story was worth telling and then waited, very patiently, for it to evolve. Ben Hayes, my editor at Continuum, has been a constant source of enthusiasm and support. Thanks are also due to Tony Morris and Slav Todorov. Tom Adair has been coerced into discussions about Lucy for longer than he probably cares to remember and bravely agreed to be the first reader of this book. I am indebted to him both for his stoicism and for his critical eye. Sarra Manning kindly helped me to the realisation that sometimes the most important thing to do is get words down on paper. Finally, I would like to thank my husband Steve for letting Lucy into the house because without his generosity this book would never have been written.

In biography you have your little handful of facts,
little bits of a puzzle, and you sit and think and fit
'em together this way and that, and get up and throw
'em down, and say damn, and go out for a walk.

R.L. Stevenson, *Letter to Edmund Gosse*

Beginnings

What a Mother I have lost I need not tell yow,
that know what shee was in hirselfe & to me.

LUCY, COUNTESS OF BEDFORD

In the darkened room of a large house Anne Harrington prepared to give birth. A former maid of honour to Queen Elizabeth I, Anne was a woman of high rank married to a wealthy man but neither her social status nor her money could insure her against the physical risks of Elizabethan childbirth. Anne had made careful arrangements for her confinement: laying in a copious store of new white linen and engaging the best attendants for the birth, but both she and her unborn child faced exactly the same dangers as any other woman of the time. Surrounded and supported by the women she had chosen to attend the birth, Anne awaited her time. As her labour progressed she alternated between pacing the room to stimulate contractions and lying on a specially constructed bed while bracing her feet against a piece of wood placed there to assist her in pushing out her baby. Between contractions her midwife encouraged her to drink potions brewed from roses, lilies and cyclamen to ease the pain and speed the delivery. Perhaps Anne remembered her last birth experience some eleven years earlier in 1570 when her first child, a son named Keilway, had arrived to bless the lives of herself and her husband only to die within the first year of his life. In another part of the house Anne's husband, John, did some pacing of his own. Firmly excluded from the female domain of the birth room he was reduced to walking and waiting. Both husband and wife anxiously awaited the arrival of the infant, who, after a long period of childlessness, would publicly symbolize the fruitfulness of their marriage. A child was a blessing from God, and Anne and John Harrington were godly people who longed to be called parents. In due course their hopes were fulfilled. A baby 'swallowed, and smothered in a red sea'[1] of blood slipped into the world and the household rejoiced and thanked God for the safe arrival of a daughter.

The exact place and date of the birth are unknown but the baby was christened at St Dunstan's, Stepney, on 25 January 1581. The high risk of infant mortality in the period meant that christenings tended to take place soon after birth so the baby was probably born in the week prior to the ceremony. On a chilly day in late January, John and Anne Harrington stood inside St Dunstan's and watched as the friends they had chosen to act as the godparents for their daughter – and who customarily took the place of the parents at the baptism ceremony – solemnly promised to raise the child in the ways of God. After the service the proud parents, their baby, and friends gathered in the nearby family house to celebrate the baptism with a party. Anne and John would have provided sweetmeats and drink for their guests and accepted gifts on behalf of their daughter. In her cradle, oblivious to all the celebrations taking place around her, lay the child, newly named Lucy after her paternal grandmother.

Lucy Harrington had the good fortune to be born into a well-connected family that could claim kinship with royalty as well as with key members of the Elizabethan political and literary elite. If one looked far enough back the Harringtons could trace their descent from the Bruces, the ancient kings of Scotland through Bernadus de Brus who settled in Exton in the time of Edward II. The family had been based for successive generations in the gentle rolling countryside of Rutland, the smallest county in England, and although country dwellers they were highly ambitious. Lucy's father John Harrington, born in 1539 or 1540, was the eldest son of Sir James Harrington and his wife Lucy, née Sidney. Sir James and Lady Lucy had eleven children – three sons and eight daughters – and every one of the Harrington daughters married well, their respective spouses being either members of the landed gentry or soldiers. While the daughters of the family were embarking on marriage their brothers were being prepared for public life. During the early 1560s 'many heads of land-owning families were ... sending their sons to the universities, where many of them would be deeply affected by the influence of their puritan tutors'.[2] There is no evidence that John Harrington studied at either Oxford or Cambridge, although his younger brother, James Harrington, appears to have attended Christ's College, Cambridge, around 1594 or 1595.[3] Despite what appears to be a gap in his education in 1558 John Harrington followed the same route as many young men of his generation by entering the Inner Temple to study law. The legal training he received there prepared him for future involvement in local politics in a variety of roles that included serving as a Justice of the Peace and eventually as a Member of Parliament.

John Harrington's mother was the daughter of Sir William Sidney of Penshurst and the family therefore shared kinship with one of the most well-known literary families of the time. John Harrington was first cousin to Philip Sidney, a soldier and renowned poet, his brother Sir Robert Sidney and their sister Mary, Countess of Pembroke, a leading patroness of poets and herself a writer. This blood tie with the Sidneys was important to the Harringtons and was to prove especially so for Lucy who developed close relationships with several of her Sidney relatives.

Moreover, the links the Harringtons had with the Sidneys commanded the respect of their contemporaries, often being mentioned in writing addressed to members of the family.

Another prominent relative – coincidentally bearing the same name as Lucy's father – was John Harrington of Kelston, a poet and a godson to Queen Elizabeth. The exact relationship between the two Harringtons is unclear. Harrington of Kelston referred to his relative from Exton as a 'cousin' but the relationship was not that close. On another occasion John Harrington of Kelston told King James that he and John of Exton were 'bothe branches of the same tree'.[4]

In 1573 John Harrington of Exton married Anne Keilway, the only child of Sir Robert Keilway and his wife Cecily, née Bulstrode. Sir Robert had been appointed to the position of surveyor-general of the courts of wards in 1546 and he held the post until his death in 1581. It was probably while John Harrington was studying at the Inner Temple that the marriage to Anne was arranged. On her marriage Anne bought the properties of Minster Lovell in Oxfordshire and Combe Abbey, located a few miles north of Coventry in Warwickshire, as a dowry but being the only child of a father with extensive estates and a great deal of money, these properties formed only a part of a considerable estate which Anne would inherit on the death of her father.

As an eldest son John also stood to inherit a number of substantial properties in the Rutland area including the 'most daintily seated' house of Burley-on-the-Hill and Exton Hall, which lay barely a mile away.[5] There was also a family house in Stepney.[6]

It is impossible to account for the movements of John and Anne Harrington in any detail but they appear to have spent considerable periods of time at Combe Abbey, especially before 1592, when the Rutland properties passed to John on the death of his father. A former Cistercian monastery set in 500 acres of land and surrounded by woods, Combe had, over a period of time, been converted into a beautiful house through the efforts of Sir Robert Keilway and his industrious son-in-law. Considerable sums of money were lavished on creating a comfortable interior. The wood-panelled rooms were richly decorated with tapestries and there were beautifully carved staircases and polished wooden floors.

For John and Anne Harrington life was busy. There were vast lands to be managed, houses to be maintained and myriad public duties to be fulfilled. In the early-to-mid 1580s the Harringtons were 'vertuous parents' engaged in caring for their daughter and taking an active role in the society in which they lived.[7] As the years passed John became a man of considerable local power and influence. One of his most important relationships was with the Dudleys who were the pre-eminent family in the West Midlands. He exchanged gifts with and extended hospitality to Robert Dudley, Earl of Leicester, a great friend and favourite of Queen Elizabeth. Leicester availed himself of John Harrington's hospitality when he stayed at Combe Abbey for a few days in August 1585 and enjoyed some hunting: buying arrows for his crossbow and taking possession of two new birds of prey.[8] But John Harrington shared more than a passion for hunting with Leicester. Harrington was a staunch Protestant and sympathetic to Leicester's Puritan position. Although some of Leicester's contemporaries questioned the Earl's sincerity in matters of religion, the political results of his stance were plain to see. In the court and the Privy Council, Leicester and his likeminded friends pushed for diplomatic and military intervention in support of Protestants abroad, particularly in the Netherlands. John Harrington became caught up in Leicester's Puritan 'rationale' that 'purchased and cemented the friendship of the sober, religious gentlemen coming to the fore in local government and in politics ... in East Anglia and the Midlands'.[9] Firmly committed to the cause of international Protestantism, John Harrington served under Leicester in the Netherlands in 1585. When, a year later, Sir Philip Sidney died from the wounds he received in battle at Zutphen, John Harrington was an assistant mourner at one of the most impressive funerals England had ever seen. John was related to Philip Sidney, but he was also close to Leicester who had arranged the lavish funeral to take centre-stage as part of a 'major propaganda exercise'.[10] When, in 1586, Mary, Queen of Scots was being transported to Fotheringhay Castle in Northamptonshire, John Harrington was one of the men chosen to accompany her as she moved through the county of Warwickshire.

Leicester died in 1588 and John Harrington was an assistant mourner at his funeral which was held in early October. The chief mourner at that funeral was Robert Devereux, Earl of Essex, and Essex was assisted by Philip Sidney's brother, Sir Robert Sidney.

John Harrington also enjoyed the patronage of Elizabeth's influential Lord Treasurer, William Burghley, Lord Cecil. Relations between Harrington and Burghley were sufficiently close in later years for John Harrington of Kelston to find the two men discussing matters of religion together while taking the waters at Bath:

> I have been to visit at the house which my Lord Treasurer dothe occupy at the Bathe, and found him and another cripple together ... Sir John Harrington, of Exton ... My lord doth seem dead on one side, and my cosen on the other, though both in their health were ever *on one side*. It gave me some comfort to hear their religious discourse, and how each did despise his own malady and hold death in derison.[11]

For six years Lucy remained the only child of the family as John and Anne gave a great deal of thought as to how she should be raised and lavished care and attention upon her. It is easy to imagine Anne as the doting mother who 'delights to heare / Her early child mis-speake halfe utter'd words'.[12] The Harringtons believed passionately in education and considered it important for female as well as male children. They were not of the view, as were some of their contemporaries, that 'to make women learned and foxes tame had the same effect – to make them more cunning'.[13] Instead, John and Anne embraced fully the humanist ideas about education that had swept through Europe a generation earlier. Education was considered important because it served the ends of God. As part of his civic duties John had, along with his brother James, been actively involved in fostering educational reforms in Rutland. In 1587 the two Harrington brothers became the governors of the grammar schools and hospitals of Oakham and Uppingham, which lay within the county. When John's aunt, Lady Frances Sidney, Countess of Sussex, died early in 1589 she named him as one of the executors of her will and together with the Earl of Kent he used her bequest of £5,000 to establish the Puritan Cambridge college of Sidney Sussex. By 1594 Harrington and Kent had been granted a licence to erect the college and in a personal capacity John gave money, land, paving stones and plate to the new establishment. The geographical origins of John Harrington and the Earl of Kent were clearly reflected in the statutes of the college, which gave preference to students from the counties of Rutland and Kent. John was also instrumental in getting his nephew, James Montagu, appointed as Master of the college.[14] Sidney Sussex was to provide the university education for the Harrington heir, John, who entered it as a fellow-commoner in 1607.

Anne Harrington's commitment to education, especially insofar as it furthered religious ends, was demonstrated in later years by her paying for a small library to be built in the parish church of Oakham, which lay close to Burley, and by her provision of texts: about 200 Latin and Greek folios 'consisting chiefly of Fathers, Councils, School-men, and Divines' for the use of the vicar of the church and the neighbouring clergy.[15] The library and books were a precious gift: 200 folios was a considerable number for the period and they were not just any books; each had been carefully personalized. The folios were 'curiously', or carefully bound, their covers decorated with gilded fretwork knots, known as 'Harringtons Knots', and the identity of their donor made clear by printed labels pasted onto the title pages which read: '*Ex Dono Dominae Annae Harringtonae Baronessae*'.[16] The creation of such beautiful objects by the addition of knots and labels reflected how strongly Anne felt about them, but they also carried another meaning, because their physical appearance was intended visually to reflect the beauty of the knowledge contained within their pages. These books exemplify how meaning in the period was often transmitted through visual images. Such images could take many forms (the most obvious being drama) but equally the visual image might be a carving, a tapestry, or even an individual's choice of a particular costume or dress. Whatever form the image took, the intention was to convey meaning in a coded way. How to decipher such meanings was a skill that was learned early. So, as she played in the rooms of her various homes, surrounded by a wealth of ornate embroideries, tapestries and carvings, Lucy absorbed lessons from what her relative Philip Sidney had called 'speaking picture[s]'.[17] As a child she learned to decipher the meanings painstakingly stitched into the embroidery on cushions and wall hangings that depicted the tales of biblical and classical figures and scenes from the natural world. She discovered that meanings could be contained in something as simple as a strawberry flower – denoting virginity – or perhaps a pelican, which symbolized Christ. What Lucy learned in her childhood about the power of the visual image found its most potent expression years later in her two great gardens – at Twickenham and at Moor Park – in which the choice and arrangement of every flower, plant and tree was suffused with meaning.

In 1587, there was another addition to the Harrington family, a daughter named Frances. As yet a baby wrapped in swaddling clothes crying in her cradle, Frances would in her turn be well grounded in religion and learning at home as too would Lucy's other sibling, John, the long-awaited son and heir who was born in 1592. The Harringtons participated actively in the education of Lucy, Frances and John, but they needed the expertise of specialist teachers. John Harrington was determined to educate his children to the same level as the offspring of his more socially prominent contemporaries, and by this means enable them to achieve leading roles at court. To that end he sought advice on educational matters from men like Anthony Bacon, who was an authority on French matters, and a friend of the educationalist and essayist Montaigne. Bacon often responded to John's requests by recommending tutors to him, and nowhere was the need for such specialist tuition more important than in the acquisition of foreign languages. A knowledge of foreign languages was prized by humanist educators because they were viewed as a source of 'inestimable treasures' and capable of providing 'unspeakeable contentation of the minde' for those who learned them.[18] More pragmatically, languages were essential prerequisites for social and political advancement. The tutors in households of the time were often Protestant refugees from the Low Countries who sought sanctuary in England from religious persecution in their own countries. Such men were taken into sympathetic households as an act of Christian charity and to provide an education for the children of the house. A number of these men combined their teaching duties with more erudite projects. Spending their days inculcating their students they devoted the time left to them to translating foreign texts into English. Many of the most treasured works of European literature became accessible through the efforts of these men. Others pursued different interests and produced language manuals, or conversation books for those who wished to improve themselves by learning a foreign tongue. The printers and booksellers of London – at Ludgate, at Blackfriars and in the maze of streets that lay in the shadow of St Pauls – stocked large numbers of books that tempted their customers to broaden their linguistic horizons by tutoring them in foreign languages appropriate to their day-to-day concerns. So, the London man about town might purchase a book from a Huguenot printer and bookseller like Thomas Vautrollier and learn how to say 'bring me a clean pair of socks' in Italian, Latin and French merely by scanning and committing to memory the phrases laid out in parallel columns within a conversation book:

Porgimi anco	Vdones dato	Baille moy	Giue me
vn paio di	itidem mundos,	de's chauffons	a cleane
scarpetti di tela		bla[n]cs,	paire of
monde,			sockes[19]

This type of comparative approach to language learning was based on the methods advocated by the humanist educator Juan Luis Vives and was probably the means by which Lucy, Frances and John were introduced to foreign languages. The conversation books covered subjects such as getting up in the morning, washing and dressing, going to school, going to an inn and eating a meal. But these books had functions that went beyond merely acquiring a new language. The French books in particular made 'strong attempts … to establish the relationship between the teaching of the language in question and the practical inculcation of protestant piety and civility'.[20]

In 1583, when she was barely two years old, Lucy received her first literary dedication. A Protestant refugee from France, Claudius Holyband, who also went under the pseudonym Desainliens, dedicated a book called *Campo di Fior or else The flourie field of foure languages* to her. Holyband's dedicaton of a language text to a toddler who had not yet mastered her mother tongue was clearly a proxy dedication. He was in fact offering the fruits of his labours to her parents, who had given him a place in their house and encouraged his endeavours. That Holyband chose to dedicate his work to Lucy suggests he clearly understood how important she was to her parents and how much such a gesture would please the Harringtons. Indeed, in the dedication her name is closely followed by that of her father. In dedicating his work to 'the yong gentle-woman Mistris Lvce',[21] Holyband was, at a stroke, celebrating Anne and John's educational ambitions for their daughter and approving their methods while paying them a fulsome compliment through their child. Holyband further reported that John and Anne were 'vertuous parents' and commented on 'the goodwill they beare to learning'.[22] It was clearly important to the Harringtons that their children understood their lessons fully and did not behave like trained parrots able to regurgitate words but comprehend nothing. That Lucy did not fall into this unfortunate category is clear from comments made by John Florio. Florio compiled an Italian-English

dictionary called *A Worlde of Wordes*, which he published in 1598 and dedicated
jointly to Lucy and the Earls of Rutland and Southampton. In the dedication
Florio complimented Lucy on her ability with languages:

> ... by conceited industrie, or industrious conceite, in Italian as in French, in French
> as in Spanish, in all as in English, understand what you reade, write as you reade, and
> speake as you write; yet rather charge your minde with matter, then your memorie with
> words ...[23]

According to Florio, as an adult Lucy was fluent in Italian, French and Spanish
and most important of all she could think in these languages, rather than just fill
her 'memorie with words'. As a linguist Florio clearly considered Lucy's ability
with languages to be an admirable achievement, but this view was not universally
shared. John Harrington of Kelston expressed his unease about women learning
languages in a characteristically witty epigram:

> You wisht me to a wife, faire, rich and young,
> That had the Latine, French and Spanish tongue.
> I thank't, and told you I desir'd none such,
> And said, One Language may be tongue too much.
> Then loue I not the learned? yes, as my life;
> A learned mistris, not a learned wife.[24]

While it might be diverting for a man to bandy foreign words about with a lady
with whom he was having a romantic liaison, he usually looked for quite different
qualities when choosing a wife. A learned woman was not always a guarantee of
domestic harmony, whereas a large dowry and the ability skilfully to manage a
household were highly prized.

Growing up in an aristocratic household Lucy's education would have
included being read to from books written in English and in the foreign languages
she was expected to master. The task of reading was usually undertaken by
women living in the household, and the kind of book to be read dictated the
social rank of the woman who did the reading. Her sister Frances was read to in
French by her tutoress, and there is no reason to suppose that Lucy was treated
any differently. Reading aloud in this way assisted in the acquisition of translation
skills and in refining pronunciation. This latter ability was especially important
for a woman who would be expected to converse fluently and gracefully with
foreign dignitaries visiting the court. In her diary Anne Clifford, a friend and
relative of Lucy, revealed female reading habits which were probably similar
to those enjoyed by the Harrington daughters.[25] Within her household Anne
Clifford was attended by two women of high rank and these women read aloud
to her from the Bible, Philip Sidney's *Arcadia* and Edmund Spenser's *The Faerie
Queene*. On occasion Anne would be read to from the Bible and other devotional

texts by lower-ranking serving women. However, when a text considered to be learned – such as Montaigne's essays or Augustine – was to be read, a manservant was called upon to do the reading.

Lucy's education also included the acquisition of skills deemed womanly and the arts needed to assume a place in the social life at court. Among the skills to be learned was needlework. Industriously plying a needle was considered a proper and godly occupation for a woman. Slowly and painstakingly Lucy stitched emblematic flowers and patterns on cushions and samplers for another generation to interpret. Learning to sew was not without its pitfalls, and for many women it was a torment that brought no better result than bleeding fingers. Yet for others embroidery became a lifelong pastime. Between being read to, singing psalms and playing cards Anne Clifford found time to take up her needlework, reporting that she had finished work on an 'Irish Stitch Cushion' and just over a week later recording that she had begun work on another.[26] Embroidery was often offered as a gift to a friend or a relative, but the patterns created in embroidery were also closely linked in the early modern mind with other activities that involved the creative manipulation of blank spaces. In his treatise on gardening published in 1659, Sir Hugh Plat promised not to 'trouble the Reader with any curious rules for shaping and fashioning of a *Garden* or *Orchard* ... Every Drawer or Embroiderer, nay, (almost) each Dancing Master, may pretend to such niceties'.[27] For Plat the gardener, 'Drawer', 'Embroiderer' and 'Dancing Master' all inhabited the same design domain; it was only the medium in which they worked that differed. This relationship between working at a piece of needlework and participating in a dance was echoed by Sir John Davies in his poem on dancing. Davies took the view that:

> ... when you sew your needles point advaunceth,
> And makes it daunce at thousand curious straines
> Of winding rounds, whereof the forme remaines,
>   To shew, that your faire hands can daunce ...
>   Which your fine feet would learne as well as they.[28]

So, just as Lucy learned to sew she also learned to dance under the tutelage of a dancing master. Dancing had the advantage of providing the individual with 'good presence in and addresse to all Compaynes since it disposeth the Lims to a Kind of Souplesse ... and Agillity'.[29] As a physical skill, dancing was also related to the etiquette of public deportment, of knowing 'how to come in and goe out of a Roome where Company is, how to make Courtesies handsomly, according to the ... degrees of persons ... encounter[ed]'.[30] Good dancing was a highly prized accomplishment and depended upon a combination of expert tuition and a pair of legs fit for the task. Some unfortunate souls possessed legs which were simply 'nott shaped for dauncing' while others, such as George Villiers, the

Duke of Buckingham, had legs so shapely they attracted the admiring glances of King James.[31] Lucy was described by her contemporaries as a 'dancing Dame' and in later years she became an accomplished performer in court masques.[32] This ability was of considerable importance, because dancing 'was an integral part of the spectacles organized for the important state occasions: visits by foreign princes or ambassadors, wedding celebrations ... and entries by the ruler'.[33] But the significance of court dancing went well beyond its social and ceremonial functions and merged with early modern ideas of the divine. The steps dancers took upon the floor were carefully choreographed and created the same kinds of geometric patterns as those found in formal gardens. Just as gardens were considered to produce a 'moral effect on those who walked through them', so too the dance worked an effect upon its participants.[34] The shapes created in both dance and in the garden 'such as the square (traditionally a symbol of earth and its elements), the circle (a symbol of heaven and divinity), the regular polygons, and the triangle (a symbol of fire) – had to sustain complex astrological and magical-esoteric connotations'.[35] But above all else, dance was something in which the whole universe participated, from the humblest plant to the highest sphere of heaven:

> See how those flowers .../
> As oft as they the whistling wind doe heare,
> Doe wave their tender bodies here and there;
> > And though their daunce no perfect measure is,
> > Yet oftentimes their music makes them kis ...
>
> But why relate I every singular?
> Since all the worlds great fortunes and affaires
> Forward and backward rapt and whirled are,
> According to the musick of the spheares:[36]

In addition to learning social skills necessary for assuming a role at court, Lucy's education included practical instruction on how to run a household. As a girl she learned to manage a house by observing her mother as Anne went about her domestic duties. Rising early was considered a laudable spiritual virtue and for the women of the household an early start to the day enabled them to fulfil their religious duties and then begin the housework. As aristocratic women, neither Anne Harrington nor Lucy were expected to do any physical work within the house, but they were fully involved in supervising the servants who did. The houses occupied by the Harringtons were large and employed vast numbers of people to run them, and those people in their turn had to be managed. Everything, from the cleaning of the house, the provision of food, the management of the dairy and the spiritual welfare of one's servants was the responsibility of the mistress of the house.[37]

Much time was taken up in visiting and receiving friends and such 'hospitality was not only the expression of obligatory reciprocity, but also an opportunity for conspicuous display'.[38] When, in later years, Lucy paid a visit to her friend Jane Bacon, no expense was spared in the provision of food. In the week that Lucy stayed with Jane, the amount of money spent on food was double the normal amount for the household, and Jane earned a gentle rebuke from her sister for her over-generous entertainment of Lucy, telling her 'you should not lose so much of your precious time of entertaining and enjoying so honourable a personage'.[39] Lucy often encouraged Jane and her husband, Nathaniel, to visit her and the invitation invariably included the couple's children. So Lucy suggested that Jane should come to London, telling her:

> I should be glad yow wold resolve to bring vp yo[u]r children, & famele because I thinke itt wold be best for them & yow: but if on the sodain yow cannot accommodate yo[u]r selfe with a convenient house for them all, yf itt please yow to lett mee have yo[u]r companie heare while yow are providing yourself with a convenient dwelling for your whole company yow shall do mee a very great pleasure ...[40]

As a child Lucy would have travelled with her parents to visit and stay with friends and relatives, just as those same friends and relatives would have come to visit and stay with the Harringtons. Through these visits Lucy developed relationships with members of her extended family and family friends, taking her place within a social network which would support and sustain her when the time came for her to assume adult duties and responsibilites.

In 1603, long after she had left childhood behind, Samuel Daniel published an epistle to Lucy in which he drew an analogy between her sex and imprisonment, claiming that: 'And no key had you else that was so fit / T'vnlocke that prison of your Sex'.[41] In using the imagery of prisons and locks Daniel was creating poetry out of the sights that formed part of his everyday existence. Doors, locks and keys were of great importance in early modern England. From the nursery chamber to the stables, household inventories of the period meticulously recorded the presence, and absence, of locking doors. On occasion visiting dignitaries were sufficiently impressed by the doors they observed to comment upon them. The Venetian ambassador to London, Giovanni Carlo Scaramelli, reported back to the Doge that Hampton Court had no less than 'one thousand eight hundred inhabitable rooms ... all of them with doors that lock'.[42] The locked door could mean imprisonment, exclusion, safety, or, more simply, the entrance to a sequestered space, and these associations frequently emerged in the drama and entertainments of the period. In Massinger and Field's play, *The Fatal Dowry*, one character is at pains to reassure another that the 'doore's lockt, yet for no hurt to you, But priuacy'.[43] The need to explain that a door was locked on grounds of 'priuacy' and not for 'hurt' illustrates how close these functions were and how easily they might intersect. Privacy lay close to imprisonment, and personal safety might depend on excluding others.

According to Daniel's epistle, Lucy had done something quite extraordinary: she had managed 'T'vnlocke' her place of confinement and the key to this particular lock was her learning. What makes Daniel's poetry such a valuable insight into this aspect of Lucy's character is that he was himself employed as a tutor whose pupils included Lucy's cousin William Herbert, third Earl of Pembroke, and Lady Anne Clifford. If he had so chosen, Daniel could easily have selected another image with which to compliment Lucy, perhaps her piety, maybe her beauty. Yet he selected an analogy that, in effect, changed her sex. This idea of sexual change should not be confused with the most famously unsexed female of the period, Lady Macbeth, whose appeal – 'unsex me here'[44] – is a chilling plea for dehumanization. Rather, the change in Lucy suggested by Daniel's verse was a great compliment in a period that considered the male to be the superior of the two sexes. Daniel's identification of learning as a specifically male preserve is also present in John Florio's dedication of his *A Worlde of Wordes* where he wrote of how:

> Italians saie ... Wordes they are women, and deeds they are men. But let such know that ... wordes and deeds with me are all of one gender. And though they were commonly Feminine, why might not I by strong imagination ... alter their sexe?[45]

Samuel Daniel and John Florio were brothers-in-law – Daniel having married Florio's sister – and both men were closely linked to Lucy and the Harrington family in the late 1590s and early-to-mid 1600s. According to Daniel, Lucy broke free from the prison of her sex through learning. The imagery of the manly and learned woman is deeply embedded in the work of Florio, particularly in his prose work called *Second Frutes*, which was published in 1591. The final chapter of the work took the form of a discussion between two gentlemen, Pandolpho and Siluestro on the nature of women and love. Pandolpho viewed women as 'the errours of nature ... the cause of infinite calamities'[46] while Siluestro argued that a difference exists between vulgar love and heavenly love.

Siluestro made a clear distinction between the sexuality of 'wanton Venus' and 'Vesta or Iuno in their wiue-like chastitie, or Diana or Minerua, or the nine Muses in their maidenly modestie'.[47] Earthly women who conformed to the virtues of this latter group – be it in matters of chastity or modesty – were likened to these goddesses. The privileging in Florio's work of martial goddesses like Juno and Athena was part of an iconography which assigned the qualities of 'the chaste and armed woman, beautiful but ... masculine of soul'[48] to female dedicatees and patronesses. As well as being represented as Athena or Juno, the learned woman was sometimes presented as an Amazonian figure or as an exemplary Roman matron. It has been argued that while such imagery seems to confer real power on the woman to whom it was attached, very often this power amounted to nothing more than a 'tokenism that utilises her not as the source of any general educational or political changes in the training and employment of women, but as an icon of cultivation and "manly" virtue'.[49]

The cult of the learned woman was recognized by, and fully comprehensible to, Lucy's contemporaries including other educated women. Her relative, Lady Mary Wroth, was of the view that Lucy 'excelled her sexe so much, as her perfections were stiled masculine'.[50] With the benefit of historical hindsight it could be argued that a learned woman like Lucy did not effect any tangible educational or political changes for her sex, yet such momentous changes are a great deal to ask of a single woman in any age. Furthermore, the structure of Jacobean society meant that 'aristocratic and royal women were at the nexus of conflicting demands of class and gender; political, factional and familial allegiances [which] overcame any simplistic sense of gender solidarity and also bring into question the validity of looking for an uncomplicated early modern proto-feminism'.[51] What Lucy did do was serve as a powerful focus for both male and female writers. She played an integral part within lively and varied networks of professional and non-professional writers and she understood very clearly the role of virtue that writers encouraged her to assume. And she took her identification with virtue seriously. Indeed, the major crises in her life were marked by a profound loss of confidence and great soul searching over how truthfully she considered herself conforming to that ideal.

Lucy's life was strongly shaped by her upbringing in a religious household that revered learning and set a strong patronage example. As one contemporary writer put it, having been born into such a family she had no choice but to emulate the patronage practices of her parents, because the 'Wombe that bare thee, made thy noble Breast / abound with Bountie, yer thou knew'st thy Fate'.[52] By the mid 1590s the next phase in the Harrington plan for Lucy was marriage. John and Anne must have had very high hopes that through marriage their beautiful and educated daughter would achieve the social advancement they so ardently desired. But the unusually strong bond between Lucy and her parents meant that whether he liked it or not her future husband would gain not just a bride but the bride's parents as well.

2

Marriage

Put on your wedding garments ...
The Bridegroome stayes to entertaine you ...
Let all your roabes be purple scarlet white,
Those perfit colours purest Virtue wore

AEMILIA LANYER, *SALVE DEUS REX JUDAERORUM*

In the early months of 1591, Anne Russell, Countess of Warwick, the aunt and guardian of Edward, third Earl of Bedford, began trying to arrange a marriage for her nephew. It would take the determined and tenacious Anne nearly four years to find Edward a bride worthy of his rank and status, but where Edward was concerned nothing was ever quite straightforward. The Earl's formative years were blighted by illness and death. His mother had died, either giving birth to him or soon afterwards. His father, Sir Francis Russell, finding himself unable to care for his newborn son, had sent the baby to live in the household of his grandfather, the second Earl of Bedford.

By all accounts Edward was a sickly child. Recovering from one bout of illness he soon contracted another complaint, and his anxious grandfather feared that the little boy would not survive childhood. Yet survive he did. As he grew older Edward continued to be dogged by health problems, but these did not prevent him receiving the usual education of an aristocratic male of the period, which included spending time as a page and student in the stern and strongly religious household of the Earl of Huntingdon. Then, in 1585, Edward's life suddenly changed. On 27 July his father was killed in a skirmish on the border between Scotland and England. This misfortune was quickly compounded by the death of his grandfather the following day.

With both his grandfather and father dead, the thirteen-year-old Edward inherited a title and extensive properties that included land and houses in Covent Garden, Buckinghamshire, Northamptonshire and Bedfordshire. But by law Edward was a minor. He could not legally transact business on his own estates until he reached the age of twenty-one.[1] The orphaned Edward was made a ward of the crown and the running of his affairs became the responsibility of William Cecil, Lord Burghley. Burghley was an extremely powerful man in his prime. He was the Lord Treasurer and a trusted adviser to Queen Elizabeth.

One of his more lucrative official roles was as Master of the Wards, a position that allowed him shrewdly to control the lives of the titled minors who were placed in his care by the Queen and the courts. As Master of the Wards, Burghley busied himself arranging marriages and conducting business transactions on behalf of his charges. This was often of considerable financial benefit to himself. Edward was the ward of Burghley for a year. In 1586 the Queen transferred responsibility for him to his aunt and uncle, Ambrose, Earl of Warwick, and Anne, Countess of Warwick. The change in guardian probably came about at the instigation of Anne, who sought to put an end to Burghley's control over her nephew's affairs. Anne did not possess power like Burghley, but she was a lady-in-waiting to Elizabeth and as such a woman of considerable influence. As a lady-in-waiting, Anne occupied a position that fell somewhere between a servant and a friend to the Queen. Her duties brought her into daily contact with Elizabeth, and she became attuned to the swiftly changing moods of her royal mistress. She could judge precisely the right time to ask a favour of Elizabeth or deliver a letter on behalf of a third party. Correspondence from the period makes it clear that Anne used the power she possessed intelligently and worked hard at the court to promote the interests of her friends.

When the time came for Anne to find a bride for Edward, Burghley was the first person she approached. On 6 March 1591, a friend of Anne's, Roger Manners, wrote to Burghley. Manners told Burghley that he had recently been visiting Anne who had mentioned that she was very keen for Edward to marry Lady Elizabeth Vere, Burghley's granddaughter. According to Manners, Anne was 'desirous to know if his Lordship approves' of such a match.[2] Burghley did not approve. For some time he had intended that his granddaughter should marry one of his wards, Henry Wriothesley, the third Earl of Southampton.

But even Burghley, Master of the Wards and, as such, marriage broker in chief, did not always have everything his own way. The Earl of Southampton did not want to marry Elizabeth Vere and played for time. He told Burghley that he was too young to make such an important decision and that he needed the 'respitt of one yere to answere'.[3] Even after a year in which to make up his mind, and despite immense pressure from Burghley, Southampton did not marry Elizabeth. In 1595 Elizabeth Vere was married to the Earl of Derby. Edward was passed over as a suitor twice: first in favour of Southampton and then of Derby. He was to meet similar disappointment over Katherine Bridges, the wealthy daughter of Lord Chandos. Katherine instead became the mistress of the Earl of Essex.

As an experienced courtier, accustomed to helping others achieve their ambitions, Anne's inability to arrange something as commonplace as a marriage for her nephew must have caused frustration and not a little anxiety. By the middle of 1594 Edward was still unmarried, but with no bride in sight. Despite his title and connections there was clearly a problem with him. Another of Burghley's granddaughters, Lady Bridget Manners, provided some clue as to what the problem might have been. In July 1594 Bridget's attendant, Mary Harding, wrote to Bridget's mother proposing that the Lady Bridget should marry Lord Wharton, a widower with children. Mary refers to Bridget's uncle, Mr Manners, in connection with the choice of spouse for Bridget:

> If your Ladyship ask Mr Manners his advice, he will speake stryghte of my Lord of Bedford, or my Lord Southampton. If they were in her choice, she [Bridget] saith, she would choose my Lord Wharton before them, for they be so younge, and fantasticall, and would be so caryed awaye.[4]

Roger Manners had been closely involved in Anne's attempts to pair Edward off with Elizabeth Vere. It is therefore not surprising that one of the men he proposed for Bridget was Edward. But Mary claimed Bridget would rather marry Wharton, a widower with children, than either Southampton or Bedford. In part, Bridget's alleged willingness to saddle herself with the children of another woman and become a second wife may have been due to wounded pride. At the time the court was buzzing with the rumour that Burghley had offered Bridget to Southampton as a bride, but that Southampton had promptly declined. Southampton's refusal of Lady Bridget was bold. He had already prevaricated in the matter of Lady Vere, and in rejecting yet another of Burghley's granddaughters he ran the risk of provoking the Lord Treasurer's wrath. Bridget's indifference to both Southampton and Bedford may also have been due to the fact that she had secret marriage plans of her own, which she was unwilling to jeopardize. In loudly protesting that Bedford and Southampton were 'younge, and fantasticall' Bridget may have been throwing both her family, and her fellow courtiers, off the scent of her impending clandestine marriage by simply speaking the truth.

In calling Bedford and Southampton 'fantasticall', Bridget was not paying them a compliment. She was dismissing them as extravagant, fanciful, capricious and eccentric,[5] accusing them of possessing qualities that were the opposite of the order and stability to which Elizabeth society so ardently aspired. Southampton had something of a reputation as a rash and petulant youth. Aspersions about his character had already been publicly aired in a poem – written by an employee of Burghley's and probably at the Lord Treasurer's request – in which Southampton was unflatteringly compared to the mythological character Narcissus. For Elizabethans, the Narcissus myth, which told the story of a youth so completely self-obsessed that his life ended in total destruction, illustrated in the most graphic possible way the folly of the self-lover.

Bridget's further claim, that Southampton and Bedford could be 'caryed awaye', hints at the giddy impetuosity of the pair, so wrapped up in their private enthusiasms that they ignored the consequences their actions might have on others. On a minor level Edward got so 'caryed awaye' while out hunting that complaints were made about his thoughtless behaviour. A youth behaving badly was one thing, but in later years the recklessness of Bedford and Southampton led them both to act inappropriately with serious personal consequences.

In the early 1590s Bedford and Southampton were in attendance at the court but they also formed part of the glittering social circle surrounding the flamboyant figure of Robert Devereux, Earl of Essex. This group was bound by firm friendship and strong marriage ties, many of which flowed from kinship with Sir Philip Sidney, the Elizabethan war hero and poet. Sir Philip Sidney's widow, Frances, had married the Earl of Essex, while Essex's sister, Lady Penelope Rich, had been the female subject of Sir Philip's sonnet sequence *Astrophel and Stella*, her name being concealed under the pseudonym 'Stella'. Sidney's younger brother Robert, who was a close friend of Southampton, also belonged to the group. So too did the Earl of Rutland, who had married Philip Sidney's daughter. This group shared aspirations and interests. They dreamed of a new golden age when England would once again be renowned for its military greatness and foreign conquests. They were enthusiastic supporters of poets and musicians. They frequented playhouses, drank, gambled and dined. Essex himself penned poetry and Southampton became the patron of Shakespeare.

While Edward socialized, Anne of Warwick continued to work on his behalf. After many false starts and much fruitless negotiating, she had at last succeeded in finding a bride for her nephew. The Earl of Bedford was to marry Mistress Lucy Harrington. The Harringtons were not unknown to Anne of Warwick. From 1588 to 1590 John Harrington had been the keeper of Kenilworth Castle for Anne's husband, Ambrose Dudley, the Earl of Warwick. Furthermore the Harringtons had the right religious credentials to satisfy the Puritan stance of the Warwicks and also honour the memory of Edward's grandfather, the great Puritan Earl Francis Russell, who had been a leading force in the movement and had corresponded privately with Calvin. It is quite possible that the marriage was encouraged, if not brokered, by Cecil. By helping to pair off his former ward, he would have assisted Anne of Warwick and simultaneously satisfied the social aspirations of the Harringtons, who were part of his patronage network. Socially the Harringtons were not quite a match for the Bedfords, but Anne probably felt that she could not delay any longer. Lucy came from a highly respectable family, had a dowry of £3,000 and the former Keilway property of Minster Lovell, which obviously proved acceptable. Furthermore, as contemporary writings made clear, marriage was considered an effective way to calm down rash young men like Edward: 'we have ty'd you … in wedlock fast, / … let the bonds of Matrimonie hold you'.[6]

Edward was twenty-one, but Lucy was only thirteen. Although she was legally entitled to marry, the incidence of child wedlock was in steep decline, as parents chose to delay giving their daughters in marriage until they were more mature. John and Anne Harrington's decision to allow Lucy to marry so young may have stemmed from their feeling that the chance for her to marry into such a prestigious family as the Bedfords represented an opportunity too good to refuse. By marrying Lucy to Edward, John and Anne Harrington had allied their daughter 'to one, that for a grandfather, for a father, for two uncles, & three or foure auntes, may compare with most men in England'.[7]

On 13 December 1594, Lucy and Edward were married at the church of St Dunstan's on Stepney Green. The church records note that 'The right honorable Edward Erle of Bedford and M[istress] Luce daughter to Sr John Harrington Knight married'.[8] The Bedford wedding was the last ceremony to be conducted that year and the three lines the clerk of the church devoted to recording it indicates the social importance of the Earl and his new Countess, contrasting as they do with the brisk one-line entries afforded to the socially anonymous couples who were married in the same month. But one Elizabethan marriage custom made less distinction of rank: the ritual teasing, usually of a ribald nature, which followed a wedding. A newly married couple were subjected to being undressed and put to bed by well-wishers, encouraged to drink large quantities of sack-posset (thought to possess aphrodisiac properties) and closely questioned about their sexual activity the morning after the wedding. Lucy and Edward's marriage took place on the eve of St Lucy's Day, which was considered to be the shortest day of the year, and the long hours of wintry darkness may have provided rich material for jokes about the newly wedded couple spending time locked in one another's arms undisturbed by intrusive daylight. In a poem written to celebrate his own wedding, the poet Edmund Spenser recounts how eagerly he anticipated the approach of night when he might finally lie with his new bride, his chief concern being that the frogs outside the bedroom window might spoil their enjoyment:

> Now welcome night, thou night so long expected, / ...
> Spread thy broad wing ouer my love and me,
> that no man may us see, / ...
> Ne let the'unpleasant Quyre of Frogs still croking
> Make us wish theyr choking.[9]

Lucy and Edward may have had many hours of darkness in which to consummate their marriage but the irony was that, like the saint whose name she shared, Lucy probably remained a virgin for some months after her wedding. At thirteen she was legally entitled to marry, but physically she was still immature. She was probably not yet menstruating and therefore unable to fulfil one of the primary roles of a wife, which was to conceive and bear children because 'In Paradice God *Mariage* first ordain'd, / That lawfully *kind* might be so maintain'd'.[10] After the ceremony the wedding party made its way back to the Harringtons' Stepney house and the couple perhaps lay together, still fully clothed, on a bed in a chamber in the presence of the people who had arranged the match – Edward's aunt and John and Anne Harrington – to give the union an air of authenticity.[11] But Lucy probably returned to her parents' household soon after the wedding, only returning to Edward when it was felt she was capable of embarking on childbearing.

Lucy's change in status, from Mistress Harrington to the Countess of Bedford, was keenly noted by one Londoner, the poet Michael Drayton. In 1593 Drayton had dedicated a poem called *Matilda* to Lucy. At the time there was no way he could have foreseen that she would marry an earl, but when she did he must have counted himself most fortunate. As a professional writer dependent for his livelihood on the generosity of patrons, Drayton would have had high hopes, for although he had already addressed poetry to the Harringtons, he knew too that Lucy would become a member of a social group to which important literary benefactors like Southampton and Essex belonged. A few months after the Bedford wedding, in early 1595, Drayton dedicated another poem to Lucy, entitled *Endimion and Phoebe*. It is no coincidence that this work follows exactly the same new poetic form Shakespeare had used in his *Venus and Adonis*, which he had dedicated to the Earl of Southampton. Drayton's hopes of bounty, and his awareness of the power Lucy had acquired through her marriage, were carefully embedded in the language he used in dedicating *Endimion and Phoebe* to her. He was deferential and flattering: Lucy was addressed as a 'Great Ladie' of 'the most pure and finest tempred spirit' – and he went on to speak of how she had 'rain'st ... sweet golden showers' upon him.[12] The reference to 'golden showers' was a polite euphemism for money. Drayton had received some kind of payment from Lucy for *Matilda* and he obviously hoped that his new poem would generate more. But there is also a secondary meaning in the language Drayton used which would have been evident to a contemporary reader like Lucy. The 'golden showers' were a direct allusion to the Danae myth, which told of how the king of the gods, Zeus, visited his lover Danae in a shower of gold. In his dedication, Drayton inverted the myth so that Lucy was raised to the status of a powerful deity, while he assumed the passive feminine role. He was hoping that Lucy would, metaphorically speaking, favour him as Zeus favoured Danae. But he was also acknowledging just how much power she has acquired through her marriage; as the new Countess of Bedford she had become strong enough to overturn the normal hierarchy of the sexes.

Marriage to Edward brought about significant changes in Lucy's life. Though for a time she probably returned to the calm and steady routines she had known since childhood in her parents' house, this was soon replaced by an entirely different way of life. Her new home in London was Bedford House, which had been built for Edward in the early 1590s and was situated on the north side of the Strand. According to contemporary reports, the house was very large and had a spacious yard located in front of it for the reception of coaches and at the rear a beautiful garden. A booklet written by Richard Brathwait in the early 1600s outlined in detail the employees required to ensure the smooth running of an earl's household. According to Brathwait a vast army of people – a steward, a treasurer, a chaplain, yeomen of the wardrobe, footmen, cooks, kitchen boys, musicians, drummers, laundresses, chambermaids, coachmen, wagoners, gardeners and more – would have been needed to run Bedford House.[13] The house was convenient for the life Edward and Lucy led, with the Strand running straight down to the court at Whitehall and the close proximity to the river providing easy access for travel to the theatres that lay on the south bank of the Thames. Bedford House was surrounded by other residences of the nobility. Burghley owned the property next door, and Essex House was located a few doors down the Strand.

The changes Lucy encountered in London were not just those associated with settling in to a new home. She was now drawn into contact with the people Edward had known for years. Lucy was well educated and confident, but she was entering the close-knit group around the Earl of Essex, which included men and women who were much older and much more experienced than she in the ways of the world. There was Essex himself, soldier, explorer and, judging by the gossip concerning his romantic liaisons, something of a sexual adventurer. There was Essex's sister, Penelope Rich, cuckolding her husband with her lover, Lord Mountjoy. And then there was Southampton, stubbornly resisting calls for him to marry. The activities and the appearance of the Essex group were closely observed and, where possible, emulated by others. So Philip Gawdy wrote to his brother and told him that he had bought him 'a sadle w[ith] the furniture coryspondente no other then my L. of Essex, S[ir] Charles Blunt … and suche other cavilleros at this hower do vse'.[14] For Lucy life in London would have presented big challenges for there was no guarantee that she would be automatically integrated into this fashionable and glittering group.

One of Lucy's new neighbours on the Strand was Rowland Whyte, the agent for Sir Robert Sidney and a prolific letter writer. In early November 1595, Whyte penned a gossipy missive to Sidney, who was stationed abroad at the time. In the letter Whyte described the mood of dissension permeating the court at around the time Lucy moved to London. As so often in the mid-to-late 1590s, the source of that dissension lay in the tempestuous relationship between the Earl of Essex and the Queen. Writing, partially in cipher, Whyte began by telling Sidney that '1000' (his code for the Earl of Essex) had been in conference with '1500', Queen Elizabeth. The conference concerned a book, printed overseas and dedicated to Essex, which, according to Whyte, did 'hym harme'.[15] Whyte refused to name the book and claimed that possessing a copy of it was a treasonable offence. Although deeply nervous about writing of such matters to Sidney, he was at pains to keep his friend up to date with what was going on, telling him that 'To wryte of these Things are dangerous in so perillous a Tyme; but I hope yt wilbe no Offence to impart vnto you Thactions of this Place'.[16]

Whyte's reason for refusing to name the book is implicit in its title – *A Conference on the Next Succession to the Crown of England* – because even in writing the name of it he was referring to a matter that Elizabeth, in her every word and action, had declared to be taboo. Who should become sovereign after her death was a subject she steadfastly refused to discuss. Now she was suddenly being forced to confront it. The preface of the book claimed that it had been printed in Amsterdam, a Protestant city, but had been smuggled into England and had surfaced among Catholic spy circles in London, probably as part of a Catholic plot to stir up trouble. It seemed likely to cause Essex trouble, for not only was it dedicated to him, its author hinted that after Elizabeth's death the Earl might become king, or at the very least a king-maker. The book was clearly designed to play on Elizabeth's well-known fears: she had already reacted badly to Shakespeare's *Richard II*, after parallels were drawn between the usurping Bolingbroke as Essex and herself as the dethroned Richard.

On a less controversial note, Whyte went on to tell Sidney that 'My Lady of *Bedford* is in Town, and sayd to be with Child'.[17] Exactly how long Lucy had been living with Edward is not known, although it must have been time enough for her to have become pregnant and for gossip about her pregnancy to have become public knowledge. News of which ladies were 'breeding' or 'prettelie forward' with child, whose face had been marred by smallpox, who was suffering from gout, or was pregnant out of wedlock were the staple fare of letters of the time.[18] On occasion such social gossip could be wildly inaccurate – for some time it was believed that the Archbishop of York had died before it transpired that he was only suffering from a slight cold. What makes Rowland Whyte's news about Lucy reliable was that he was close to several members of the group with whom the Bedfords mixed.

Towards the end of 1595 life seemed promising. Lucy had established herself in London and was expecting her first child. Edward was about to take part in the Accession Day tilt, a prestigious social event held every year on 17 November to celebrate Elizabeth's accession to the throne. But, beneath the glittering surface, Edward and Lucy had a major problem. Like most of the people with whom they mixed, their finances were in a parlous state. Running Bedford House, maintaining country residences at Stepney and Chenies in Buckinghamshire and keeping up appearances at court all cost a great deal. Edward's participation in the Accession Day tilt meant spending yet more money on a showy costume, placing further strain on their finances.

Who took part and what happened at the tilt of 1595 is recorded in a poem written by George Peele called 'Anglorum Feriae'. Much of Peele's poem is devoted to flattering the Queen, to celebrating 'Elizaes Coorte, Astraeas earthlie heaven'.[19] But 'Anglorum Feriae' also provides an insight into how spectacular the event must have been. In the tiltyard at Whitehall, the Earl of Cumberland emerged on horseback clad in a suit of gilded armour to face his opponent, the Earl of Essex, who was dressed in 'innocent white & faire carnac[i]on'.[20] Peele's description of what the participants wore is much more than an attempt to make his poetry decorative; it describes an integral part of Elizabethan public relations: what a man, or woman, wore was a crucial means of transmitting messages. Cumberland's golden armour was exceedingly costly and in wearing it he was overtly drawing attention to his wealth and power. Essex's choice of the colour white saw him advertising that he was 'innocent' of all the disparaging claims being made against him concerning his meddling in the succession question. The tilt provided him with a prime opportunity to protest his innocence to the Queen, to the crowd gathered in the tiltyard and to the wider audience beyond its walls, who were eager to hear what the Earl was wearing and how he comported himself. Among the five knights fighting on Essex's side were Southampton and Bedford:

> Then Bedforde and South-Hapton [sic] made up five
> Five valea[n]t English Earles ...
> Valea[n]t in armes gentle & debonaire ...
> Lyke to himselfe & to his Ancestors,
> Ran Bedforde to express his redyness,
> His Loves to armes his Loyaltie to hir, ...
> Bravely ra[n] Bedforde ...[21]

After the tilt Edward and Lucy embarked on a journey north to Burley-on-the-hill to spend Christmas with the Harringtons. Travelling with the party was a Frenchman called Jacques Petit who went to Burley to assist in the education of the Harrington heir, the three-year-old John. John Harrington senior had informed a M. le Doux – an agent of the Earl of Essex who worked as a tutor in the Harrington household – that he wished to engage another French tutor. Harrington's request was dealt with by Essex's secretary, Anthony Bacon, who subsequently despatched Petit to Burley.

The first stopping place after leaving London was at lodgings in St Albans, and from there Petit wrote to Bacon describing the entertainments provided for Lucy and her ladies:

> ... my Lady ... [was] watching a tumbler do juggling tricks, and after many other clever tricks he threaded three threads in a needle of very fine quality, and unthreaded them – the ladies had provided them – turning and twisting quickly between two candles, to the sound of two violins.[22]

The entertainment was followed by dinner and according to Petit, 'when the meat was served, four trumpets sounded to call my Lord as it is done at the Court for the King'.[23]

In being summoned to dinner by the blast of a trumpet Lucy and Edward were observing normal household etiquette for an earl and his countess. Braithwait recommended at least one trumpeter but he did make it clear that the officers and servants considered necessary to the smooth running of the household could be 'added unto, or diminished, as pleaseth his Lordshipp'.[24] By engaging four trumpeters Edward and Lucy had clearly opted for quite conspicuous addition rather than diminishment.

Continuing their journey the following day, the party rested at Bedford and Edward was presented with gifts of apples and wine by the leading men of the town and the bells were rung in his honour. When they eventually reached Burley, Jacques was blunt in his description of John Harrington's house, which he swiftly condemned as 'short of order, and of money'.[25] An account of what took place at Burley over the Christmas period, and a telling insight into John's mounting financial worries, was contained in a letter Petit wrote to Bacon in mid-December:

> No day passes without hunting; both Madame the Countess and the Earl with their carriages drawn by four horses. The knight Mr Harrington alone pays the cost of all these pleasures, and pays dearly for the glory of the name of Countess for his daughter, and would like, from what I hear, that what is done were to be redone. He used to lease out all his lands without annual rent, being able to put in or eject whenever he pleased. Now he is forced to make a lease to this one, and a contract to that one for many years, and is bound to anyone who will provide him with ready money. Certainly he needs it, since more than 200 persons sleep and feed in the house, 30 or 40 horses, and as many couples of dogs; coming and going principally on Sundays.
>
> There is not an inn in London which covers so many tables as is done here. And there is much muddle and confusion this Christmas, making many useless expenditures on tragedies and games ...[26]

John Harrington may well have regretted paying for 'the name of Countess' for Lucy but there was now no turning back and the celebrations he had arranged at Burley were nothing short of 'magnificent':

> The orders were to receive and entertain 8 or 9 hundred neighbours who came every day to celebrate here. Twice a day there was a sermon in the church, morning and after dinner, and every day a new minister. Monsieur and Madame the Countess were mostly present. Monsieur the Count was served with all the honour and respect possible at dinner and supper, there was music, 30 or 40 gentleman servants, 2 or 3 cavaliers and their ladies, in addition to many gentlemen and demoiselles who were at table, then after the meal came the dance and amusing games to make us laugh and serve as recreation. Monsieur

Jean [John] dined in hall to receive his neighbours and principal farmers, entertaining these with an excessive choice of all kinds of dishes, and all kinds of wines. His maitre d'hotel took care to see that nothing was lacking, and in addition laid out 4 or 5 long tables of meat for 80 or 100 people at a time, who having finished made way for as many others, and took their leave. After it was over, the bread and wine in barrels were carried to the poor who were all satisfied, so that there were no left-overs. New Year's Day was demonstrated by the generosity of these people, and principally of Madame the Countess, for, from the greatest down to the smallest, she gave good evidence ... The comedians from London were come here to have their share. They were made to play the day of their arrival, and the next morning were sent on their way. We had a masquerade here written by Sir Edward Wingfield, and they all played the tragedy of Titus Andronicus, but the presentation was worth more than the subject matter.[27]

The festivities culminated with a 'masquerade' followed by a professional theatrical production. The masque was the work of Sir Edward Wingfield, who was married to John Harrington's sister Mary, and it was probably acted by members of the family and perhaps some of the assembled 'cavaliers and their ladies' along with servants of the household and workers from what was left of John's rapidly fragmenting estate. The combination of masters, servants, rustics and family friends coming together in order to present an amateur entertainment was not uncommon. Ben Jonson remarked upon similar entertainments that were held at Sir Robert Wroth's estate in Enfield:

> Thus *Pan*, and *Sylvane*, hauing had their rites,
>   *Comvs* puts in, for new delights;
> And fills thy open hall with mirth, and cheere,
>   As if in *Satvrnes* raigne it were;
> *Apollo's* harpe, and *Hermes* lyre resound,
>   Nor are the *Muses* strangers found:
> The rout of rurall folke come thronging in,
>   (Their rudenesse then is thought no sinne)
> Thy noblest spouse affords them welcome grace;
>   And the great *Heroes*, of her race,
> Sit mixt with losse of state, or reverence.[28]

The masque written for the evening's entertainment at Burley probably depicted the deeds of illustrious Harrington forebears. As he watched the scenes unfold before him John might feel that although his money was draining away his efforts on behalf of Lucy had at least enabled her to join the ranks of esteemed Harringtons whom he saw progressing across the stage. Around ten in the evening a professional acting company performed Shakespeare's tragedy, *Titus Andronicus*. It was not uncommon for members of London theatre companies to tour outside the capital 'either under the pressure of the plague, as they did in

1593, or during the slack summer months',[29] but for a company to travel away from London in the winter months when play performances were in full swing was unusual although not impossible. One of the London theatre companies made the long trip up to Burley, but exactly which one remains a mystery.

Petit's negative verdict on the 'subject matter' of the tragedy reflected his response to a rather shocking plot, which was based on the Ovidian myth of Tereus and revolved around rape, female mutilation and cannibalism. Yet there was much in the play that would have struck a chord with the assembled spectators, not least the references to hunting which some of the audience had been so busily engaged in themselves:

> The hunt is up, the morn is bright and grey,
> The fields are fragrant and the woods are green.
> Uncouple here and let us make a bay,[30]

So too Shakespeare's presentation of images of ambition would have resonated with the Harringtons as they surveyed their eldest daughter so successfully married. No doubt they also hoped that they, and their daughter, could ascend to such dizzy heights without fickle fortune striking them all down:

> Now climbeth Tamora Olympus' top,
> Safe out of fortune's shot, and sits aloft,
> Secure of thunder's crack or lightning flash,
> Advanc'd above pale envy's threat'ning reach.[31]

And even one of the most shocking scenes in the play, in which the character of Lavinia appears raped, her hands crudely amputated and her tongue cut from her mouth, would have been interpreted as rather more than theatrical shock tactics. Discovering his ravaged niece, Lavinia's uncle asks her:

> … what stern ungentle hands
> Hath lopp'd and hew'd and made thy body bare
> Of her two branches, …
> Alas, a crimson river of warm blood,
> Like to a bubbling fountain stirr'd with wind,
> Doth rise and fall between thy rosed lips,[32]

The profusely bleeding Lavinia did not make appetizing viewing, but Elizabethan audiences were far from squeamish and as they watched her some of them at least would have recognized that Lavinia's movements could be understood as a form of language in precisely the same way that dance was. Indeed, Shakespeare's description of the mutilated Lavinia relates to one given by John Davies in his poem about dancing where he attempted to emphasize the physicality of language:

> ... the Queene with her sweet lips divine
> Gently began to move the subtile ayre,
> ... which gladly yielding, did it selfe incline
> To take a shape betweene those rubies fayre[33]

By contrast, in *Titus Andronicus*, Shakespeare used Lavinia to underline that silence also possesses a physical aspect. Thomas Elyot discussed a claim that dance originated when the people ruled by the Sicilian tyrant Hiero were 'forbidden speech and instead evolved a system of bodily communication.'[34] A contemporary audience would have observed that although deprived of her tongue and hands Lavinia was capable of a form of speech through the movements of her body.

Petit's correspondence also reveals that during the mid-1590s the Harrington education project was proceeding apace and while the focus of that activity centred upon the Harrington heir, John, when Lucy visited her family she continued with her education alongside her eight-year-old sister, Frances. Jacques's stay in the Harrington household was brief. He left Burley in late January, apparently after quarrelling with another tutor in the household. M. le Doux also left the household at around the same time and was charged with carrying two letters written by a French tutoress in the household named Madame Valerienne du Vaulx. Madame du Vaulx was angered by Petit's usurping of her role as the teacher of Lucy and Frances. Mme's letter survives only because it was tampered with by Petit, who took it, hurriedly copied it, and then sent the copy to Anthony Bacon. Madame du Vaulx's letter makes it clear that Lucy was capable of corresponding in French and was writing to a woman named Mademoiselle Molet. Mlle Molet confidently predicted that in time Lucy would soon be 'le soleil dangleterre & sa soeur', Frances, 'la Lune'.[35] Mme du Vaulx, however, was far less charitable about Lucy. In madame's opinion Lucy conformed to all the worst excesses of her social class: she was consumed by a passion for hunting – something she shared with Edward – but which madamoiselle considered vulgar.

In the February of the following year, Rowland Whyte, at home on the Strand, wrote to Robert Sidney again to inform him of the arrangements which were being made for the forthcoming christening of Sidney's infant daughter. Sidney's friend, the Earl of Southampton, had been chosen to be godfather and the Countess of Sussex and the Countess of Bedford were to be invited to act as godmothers. A few days later, Whyte informed Sidney of how pleased Southampton was to assume the role of godfather – he 'did take it exceedingly kindly' – and Lady Sussex 'sware that she longed to be a Godmother, and is proud that she is chosen to be one'.[36]

But by the end of the month all was not well. The christening of the baby was due to take place the following day and Lucy Russell had just sent word to say that she could not attend. Worse still, she had failed to nominate a person to stand in her stead and this clearly caused Rowland endless difficulties with his wife because, as he confided to Sidney, 'it was my Fortune to name my Lady of Bedford at the first, and theirfore [sic] my Lady blames my Choice'.[37] As the harmony of the Whyte household was racked by squabbling over Rowland's poor choice of godmother, Bedford House, a few doors down the Strand, was a deeply unhappy place. For in the depths of the bitterly cold February of 1596, it appears that the fourteen-year-old Lucy miscarried her first child. Lucy seems to have recovered herself sufficiently to prevent her absence turning into a social gaffe. She sent her mother and father to attend the christening in her place, and excused her absence with 'deepest Protestations, that no other Cause, but her not being well, kept her away, which greued her more then her Sickness'.[38] But Lucy's 'Sickness' did not cause her to overlook her public duty to report any evidence of Catholic activity. A month later she sent a messenger to Cecil with a letter in which she claimed that 'This bearer my servant hath this morning apprehended a couple of very suspicious persons, whereof one hath already confessed himself a Jesuit, the other seems a desperate villain, denying he had any acquaintance with the said Jesuit, yet a great likelihood he came over with him'.[39]

Jesuits were only one of the sources of anxiety in the England of the 1590s. There was also the year upon year of poor harvests that led to widespread starvation, death and a deepening economic and social crisis as the 'great complaining of Want of Corn' caused 'the People [to] murmur'.[40] For the courtier, lingering day after day about the court waiting for news of a job or an appointment that might never materialize, there was a different kind of sadness altogether. Writing from the court, Whyte told Sidney of how 'Yt grieues my Sowle that this Day brings foorth no better Fruit of my Labor and Attendance'.[41] But for the courtier there were some compensations: when all else failed there was always the company of friends to cheer the spirit. A little over a year after the mishap with the christening, a lavish dinner party was held at Essex House. After the dinner, two plays were performed and the assembled guests finally made their way home around one o'clock in the morning. This glittering social event was hosted by Gelly Meyrick, a Welshman who had known Essex for years, and who had become his trusted steward. The dinner in question was attended by 'my Ladys *Lester*, *Northumberland*, *Bedford*, *Essex*, *Rich*; and my Lords of *Essex*, *Rutland*, *Monjoy*'.[42] Although no mention is made of him, Edward may well have been present, but the naming of Lucy as one of the guests is noteworthy because it indicates that she had been invited in her own right, without being specifically linked with Edward, so beginning a pattern her future life would take. Lucy was not the only member of the Harrington family in contact with the Earl of Essex. At the end of 1598 her father wrote to Essex asking a favour on behalf of his younger brother, James. Specifically, John Harrington informed the Earl that Sir James wished to serve the

Queen in Ireland. Furthermore, according to Harrington, his brother 'much the willinglier he offered himself understanding he is to serve under you, whom the family he and I are of do so much honour'.[43] Just how highly John Harrington respected Essex is attested to in his claim that 'if my son ... were able to bear arms, I vow he should adventure his life in your service'.[44] John could afford to make such grandiose claims on behalf of his son and heir who was far too young to take up arms, but that the Harrington 'family' honoured Essex was almost certainly a genuinely held sentiment. As events transpired, Henry Harrington's great desire to serve in Ireland ultimately proved disastrous, just as the Irish campaign proved disastrous for so many men, including its leader, Essex.

One of the many difficulties confronting Elizabeth in the latter part of her reign was the ongoing problem of rebellion in Ireland. Against her better judgement she allowed Essex to persuade her into letting him tackle the problems there, and in March 1599 he had set out for Ireland with the largest army ever raised during Elizabeth's reign. But almost from the very start the campaign was mired in difficulties, and Essex became increasingly distracted by fears that his political enemies – Robert Cecil, Principal Secretary to the Queen, and Lord Buckhurst, the new Lord Treasurer – were consolidating their power in his absence. In September, against Elizabeth's express orders, Essex abandoned his post and sailed home to England. On landing he rode across country for three days only to reach Westminster and find that the Queen had removed to Nonsuch in Surrey. Undeterred, Essex galloped on and arriving at Nonsuch; he 'staied not till he came to the Queens Bed Chamber, where he found the Queen newly up, the Hare about her Face; he kneeled vnto her, kissed her Hands, and had some priuat Speach with her'.[45]

Essex's behaviour was rash in the extreme. He had abandoned his post and returned without permission to England. He had then compounded matters by bursting in upon the Queen in her private bedchamber. The two people facing each other in the royal bedroom must have looked little short of bizarre. The elderly Queen was totally unprepared: what little hair she still possessed hung around her face, and she lacked the wig and the layers of make-up she habitually wore in public. The Earl of Essex faced his sovereign with the 'Dirt and Mire' thrown up by the hooves of his horse still stuck to his face.[46] The Queen's first reaction to her unexpected visitor was calm, but within hours her mood had changed dramatically. Her Council was hurriedly summoned to a conference and Essex was promptly charged with:

> ... contemtuous Disobedience of her Majesties Lettres and Will, in returning ... presumtuous Letters wrytten from Tyme to Tyme: His Proceedings in *Ireland*, contrary to the Points resolued vpon ere he went: His rash Manner of coming away from *Ireland*: His ouerbold going ... to her Majesties Presence to her Bedchamber.[47]

As the Earl was placed under house arrest at York House on the Strand the
optimistic hopes of a new golden age entertained by the group of men and
woman surrounding him lay in tatters. The deep sense of unease generated by
Essex's behaviour and the official response to it is palpable in a letter Rowland
Whyte wrote to Robert Sidney in the latter part of 1599:

> Yt is a World to be here, to see the Humors of the Tyme. Blessed are they that can be
> away, and liue contented ... I must beseach your Lordship to burn my Lettres, els shall
> I be affrayd to write, the Tyme is now so full of Danger. And be very carefull what
> you wryte here ... If you wryte by Post, take heed what you wryte, for now Lettres are
> intercepted.[48]

Whyte's letter indicates that the vigilant and highly efficient Elizabethan intelli-
gence network was busy monitoring what individuals were saying about the Essex
business in private and looking for signs of dissent over the Queen's treatment
of her former favourite.

The dark mood hanging over Essex was closely matched by the weather. In
November 1599, there was so much rain the Accession Day tilt was postponed
for two days. When the tilt was finally run, Lord Compton appeared mounted
on his horse dressed as a fisherman. But Compton's novel attire provided only a
temporary diversion. The people gathered before Elizabeth in the tiltyard knew
well that she and her Council had forcibly confined the star of past tilts to a
house just a short distance away along the Strand. Furthermore, Essex was ill
with a stone in the kidney and a bout of dysentery contracted in Ireland, as well
as being perturbed by what was happening to him. At court, the women closest
to him – his wife, Frances, and his sister Penelope – deployed all the means at
their disposal to encourage the Queen to look favourably upon him. Frances, who
was just as adept as her husband at manipulating her appearance, presented at
the court – as if in mourning – dressed from head to toe in cheap black fabric.
Frances's choice of black to make a visual statement was all the more dramatic
given that the women of the court favoured the colour white for their gowns. As
the Essex drama unfolded Lucy watched and learned: many years later, and for
very different reasons, she herself would attend the court dressed in a manner as
austere as Frances. Penelope Rich, in contrast, tried a different tactic altogether,
attempting to win Elizabeth to her brother by plying the Queen with gifts of
precious stones. Never one to refuse a gift, Elizabeth accepted the jewels but her
anger remained undiminished.

While Frances and Penelope tried to keep Essex's plight on the agenda, the
rest of the court, aware of Elizabeth's animosity toward him, barely mentioned
his name. But Essex still had friends other than his immediate relatives and the
actions of these friends began to infuriate the Queen's advisers. Essex had been
isolated in York House as a punishment. Now some of his associates gathered at

a window in the house next door to communicate with the disgraced Earl when he was well enough to walk in the garden of York House. Southampton was named as one of the well-wishers and Edward's friendship with Southampton and Essex, together with some cryptic remarks from his aunt about him behaving in a manner which will render him 'vnfitt for better company',[49] suggests that he was amongst the group greeting Essex from the window.

Edward and Lucy's association with the disgraced and marginalized Essex did not bode well, but it was not their only problem. There was also the perennial trouble with money. Both Edward's aunt and John Harrington were deeply concerned by the financial profligacy of the couple. Towards the end of 1599 Edward attended a humiliating conference with his aunt and signed a financial undertaking in which he promised to behave in a fiscally responsible manner. It was decided that the only sensible solution to the couple's deepening financial problems was for them to live within their means. They were forced to adopt the basic financial measure of 'conformeing expenses to certen revenue'.[50] For some years Edward had been prevented from selling any property without permission, but he had circumvented this by adopting the equally unstable course of collecting rent from his properties in advance and then promptly spending it. Now he was forbidden to undertake any financial dealings whatsoever without having them approved by an auditor appointed by Anne. Edward agreed to the conditions set by his aunt, but he was incapable of keeping his word, and by the middle of the following year it was apparent that Edward and Lucy had spectacularly failed to mend their ways. Edward had to endure yet another humiliating conference with the determined Anne, who this time took a very hard line with her nephew, telling him that if nobody stood up to him and pointed out the error of his ways everything would 'worke upon him to his vndoing'.[51] Edward took the meeting badly, complaining petulantly that he was being deprived of 'all matters of pleasure ... to take awaie his spirites'.[52] However, under pressure from his aunt, he dutifully listed the measures he would take to extract himself and Lucy from the financial mess they were in. Edward's priorities were curious: his first concern was to 'provide for [the] dogges', presumably the hounds which he used for hunting, and then he wished to furnish 'meat for men', 'pay [his] fines', and 'make money of ... tymber'.[53]

The thorny problem of the Bedford finances emerged again just as Edward and Lucy were about to attend the social event of the year. In June 1600, Edward's cousin, Anne Russell – a favourite maid of honour to Elizabeth – married William Herbert. The Queen attended the wedding, being met by the bride at the waterside at Blackfriars and then conveyed to the ceremony in a half litter carried by six knights. A large and sumptuous feast had been prepared and after the meal the entertainment took the form of a 'straunge Dawnce newly invented'.[54] The Bedfords went to London for the wedding and as Lucy watched the proceedings she may have been thinking of how much attending the celebration was costing them. Lucy and Edward could ill afford the new clothes of gold and silver lace and satin in which they were obliged to dress, nor the lavish wedding present they were expected to give. The gifts of plate and jewellery presented that day by the assembled wedding guests were valued at over £1000. But if Lucy gave any thought to her finances it was quickly displaced by her fascination with the dance. As the women dancers, each dressed in a skirt of silver cloth topped with a gold silk waistcoat, their loosely knotted hair flying about their shoulders, moved about the room, Lucy was watching and her observation paid dividends for as she grew older she became closely involved in similar courtly entertainments.

On 26 August 1600, Elizabeth heeded the advice of her ministers and set Essex at liberty. His release was conditional on his not going to the court or holding public office. He quickly announced that he intended to retire to the country. But Essex was not suited to a life of rural seclusion. At heart he was a politician, and although the limits placed on his activities caused him extreme frustration, he was incapable of turning his back on London. More urgently, he also needed money. One of the indirect causes of the uprising that has come to be known as the Essex Rebellion was, curiously enough, wine. One of Essex's main sources of income was his monopoly on the importation of sweet wines into England and this monopoly was due for renewal in October 1600. But the granting of the monopoly lay within the Queen's gift and, although Essex wrote and pleaded with Elizabeth, she refused to renew it in his favour, announcing that henceforth all the profits would be reserved to the crown. For Essex this represented a crippling blow, as he was deeply in debt with no means of paying his creditors. He faced financial ruin. The combination of intolerable financial pressures, lingering illness, and his feeling that at court Robert Cecil, Walter Raleigh and others were moving against him proved too much. Late in 1600 John Harrington of Kelston, who had fought with Essex in Ireland, paid the Earl a visit and found him raving.

Essex had become convinced that Cecil and Raleigh intended to kill him and were conspiring to place the Spanish Infanta on the English throne. He further believed that it was his mission to warn the Queen of these evil plots and so restore himself to her favour, but he could not do it alone. He set about assembling a group of men around him, in the main composed of old and loyal friends like the Earls of Southampton and Rutland, his secretary and former Latin tutor, Henry Cuffe, and his steward Gelly Meyrick. A series of secret meetings to discuss strategy began to take place at addresses on the Strand: first at Essex House, and later at Southampton's Drury House. One of the unifying forces in the group gathering about Essex was their chronic lack of money; these men had nothing financially to lose by overthrowing the existing power brokers and helping their friend Essex back to his former fortunes. And while there is no evidence to suggest that Edward was a key conspirator, his longstanding friendship with Southampton and Essex makes it more than likely that he was one of the young men plotting change. According to a contemporary source, around this time Essex received from:

> the Countess of *Warwick* (a Lady powerful in the Court, and indeed a virtuous user of her power) the best advice that … was ever given from either sex; That … he should closely take any out-lodging at *Greenwich*, and sometimes when the Queen went abroad in good humour, (whereof she would give him notice) he should come forth, and humble himself before her in the field.[55]

Perhaps Anne hoped to avert disaster and protect Essex and young men like Edward from themselves, but in any event her advice to the Earl on how to mollify the Queen and restore himself to her favour were not followed, for although:

> this Counsel sunk much into him, and for some days he resolved it: but in the mean time, through the intercession of the Earl of *Southampton*, whom *Cuffe* had gained, he was restored to my Lords ear … [and] spun out the final distruction of his master and himself.[56]

As the Essex conspiracy gathered momentum Lucy welcomed John Florio into her house to complete his translation of Michel Montaigne's essays. In 1598 Florio had dedicated an Italian English dictionary called *A Worlde of Wordes* to Lucy and the Earls of Southampton and Rutland, all three of whom had been his pupils at various times. As the dictionary was published Sir Edward Wotton urged Florio to begin a translation of Montaigne's essays. A number of attempts had already been made to translate Montaigne into English but none had proved successful. Florio dutifully began the work suggested by Wotton but after finishing the first chapter reported that he felt himself 'over-charged'[57] by the task. According to Florio, Lucy happened to read what he had translated and she then 'commaunded' him to continue.[58] The note of imperiousness implicit in the word 'commaunded' is consistent with what Florio described, rather floridly, as Lucy's pitilessness when he felt inadequate to the task confronting him. According to Florio, Lucy paid no heed to his 'failing … fainting … labouring … gasping for … breath'[59] as he struggled with the complexities of the translation, and while a large part of his dedication is undoubtedly mock-serious in tone, there is also a real sense of a determined woman driving the translator on in his undertaking. Perhaps closer to the real situation was Florio's report that as he passed Lucy within the house she would give him encouragement by calling out '*Coraggio*' and applauding him.[60]

Various parts of the translation were completed in the different houses in which Florio was employed as a tutor, and by 1600 some of the work was circulating in manuscript. The final work was completed at either Bedford House or Harrington House and by taking Florio into her household Lucy was continuing in the patronage tradition in which she had been raised. Throughout the dedication to Lucy, Florio writes of her as being without pity and then asks her: 'do I flatter you?'[61] The repeated questions sound like the continuation of a private game or debate – perhaps on the nature of literary flattery – that may have taken place between the writer and his patroness, echoes of which remain embedded in the work. That Lucy's role in connection with the translation also extended to establishing relationships between writers is clear as Florio recorded how, when he became troubled by difficult and impenetrable parts of the translation, she introduced him to Theodore Diodati and Matthew Gwinne. Diodati and Gwinne assisted Florio in various parts of the work and he went on to collaborate with them in other projects. Florio likened Diodati to a 'good Angel' in his endeavours and indicated that he was also involved in the education of Lucy's brother, John.[62] Florio was fulsome in his praise of Diodati who, so he told Lucy, 'in all good learning, and doeth with all industrious attention instruct, direct, adorne that noble, hopefull, and much-promising spirit of your beloved brother and house-heire Maister *Iohn Harrington*'.[63] The very high expectations the Harringtons had for their son are implicit in the phrase 'hopefull, and much-promising' to describe him and the reason why he was so important is contained in the reference to him as the 'house-heire'.

Florio's translation was licensed for the press in June 1600 but it was not published until 1603. When it finally appeared it was dedicated to six women: Lucy and her mother, Anne Harrington, Elizabeth Countess of Rutland and Penelope Rich, Lady Elizabeth Grey and Lady Mary Neville. Amongst the dedicatory material were two sonnets written by Matthew Gwinne which refered specifically to Lucy's role in the project. In a poem titled *A reply vpon Maister Florio's answere to the Lady of Bedfords invitation to this work*, dated 1599, Gwinne represented Lucy as Minerva and he encouraged Florio to 'Attend the vertue of *Minervas* writtes'.[64] Gwinne's poem was sprinkled with language and phrases related to horses and hunting which must have appealed to the hunting-mad Lucy. For Gwinne the management of translators was analogous with the management of horses where 'Colde sides are spurrd, hot mouthes held-in with bittes; ... / Who never shootes, the mark he never hitt's [sic]'.[65] The final line of the sonnet read, 'And who would ... rest, when *shee* bids rise?'[66] This rather stock idea, of a writer taking up his pen because a lady has ordered it, appears in many poems dedicated to Lucy but it assumes a new and rather different meaning when it is remembered how she bullied and badgered the faltering Florio to finish the work he had begun.

Florio's translation of Montaigne became one of the most influential works of its time and was read by men like Jonson, Shakespeare and Donne. Donne disliked Florio but the intellectually rigorous Ben Jonson knew and admired him. Indeed Jonson paid Florio a lavish compliment by inscribing a quarto of his own play *Volpone* to 'his louing Father, & worthy Freind Mr. John Florio: The ayde of his Muses. Ben: Jonson seales this testemony of Freindship, & Loue'.[67] In 1601 Jonson inscribed a printed copy of one of his plays as a gift for Lucy. The play, *Cynthias Revels*, had been performed before Elizabeth at court in January 1601, and on its publication Jonson sent a copy to Lucy with a short verse on the flyleaf instructing the book to:

Goe little Booke, Goe little Fable
vnto the bright and amiable
LVCY of BEDFORD ... / ...
Tell her, his Muse that did inuent thee
to CYNTHIAS fayrest Nymph hath sent thee,[68]

The gift of the book and the language used to address Lucy suggests that Jonson was established on terms of familiarity with her. Just how cordial the relationship between the two appears to have been can be gauged by comparing Jonson's dedication with one offered to Lucy by her relative, John Harrington of Kelston, at around the same time. Rather than Jonson's breezy salutations to the 'bright and amiable Lucy', her Harrington relative hailed her in much more formal language as 'my most honored good Ladie'.[69] John Harrington was offering Lucy copies of psalm translations by Mary Sidney and some of his own works, which he self-deprecatingly referred to as 'som shalowe meditations of myne owne'.[70] Harrington's uncertainty over Lucy's response to his unsolicited outpourings manifested itself in elaborate literary obsequiousness which culminated in:

But as your cleare-sighted judgement shall accept or praise them, I shall hereafter be embouldned [sic] to present more of them, and to entytle som of them to your Honorable name, unto which I vowe to rest a ever much devoted servant.[71]

It appears that Lucy did not avail herself of John Harrington's generous offer to send her more of his poetry.

John Florio was both a tutor and a translator, but his presence in Bedford House around 1600 may also have served a rather different purpose. On 10 August 1600, he received a letter from a man named Nicolo Molina. Precisely who Molina was remains unclear. There was an ambassador from the Venetian court with the surname Molina, but he was not present in England at the time when the letter to Florio was written. The Molina who wrote to Florio informed him that he had 'sent you last week the answers, as I do now by a post sent into Scotland, according to orders left me by the Queen's secretary. I should like to hear of their receipt'.[72] The meaning of the letter is obscure. What were Molina's 'answers' a reply to? Was Florio engaged in some kind of translation work? If so, who was were the translations for, and what precisely was he translating? One thing that is clear is that the letter in some way concerned Robert Cecil, the 'Queen's secretary'. This then begs the question of why Florio, who was close to key members of the Essex group like Southampton and Rutland, was also linked in some way with Essex's arch-enemy, Cecil? Florio was no novice in matters of espionage. In the early 1580s he had been employed at the French embassy in London, and during his time there he secretly passed information to Francis Walsingham, the Elizabethan spymaster general and a close ally of Robert Cecil's father, Lord Burghley.[73]

As Florio worked away on his translation inside Bedford House he may have been fulfilling a role similar to the one he had performed inside the French embassy: relaying snippets of overheard conversations and reporting to Cecil on the comings and goings of various members of the Essex group. Although it seems almost inconceivable that Florio should act in such an underhand manner in the household that had offered him such generosity, it may be that the Cecil camp did not consider Edward to be a prime mover within the Essex group, which meant that Florio could pass on information without feeling he was abusing the hospitality of his patrons.

By the beginning of 1601 Essex's plans had taken firm shape; a coup would take place in March. But then came a major blow. One of the Earl's friends, Sir Fernando Gorges, developed cold feet and revealed everything to Essex's arch-rival Raleigh, who promptly informed Elizabeth's Council. Essex's adversaries were clever men and they could scheme just as well as he. In early February Cecil began circulating a rumour that the Earl was to be arrested, then on 7 February a messenger arrived at Essex House demanding that he present himself before the Council. On the advice of his friends, Essex refused to respond to the summons, pleading that he had been playing tennis and was resting in bed. But his hand had been forced. On the following morning, Sunday, 8 February, he made his move.

The Earl's supporters were summoned to the yard which lay at the front of Essex House and the assembled crowd of friends, hangers-on and a company of two hundred soldiers made such a commotion that Elizabeth sent Lord Keeper Egerton, the Lord Chief Justice, Sir John Popham, the Earl of Worcester and Sir William Knollys to investigate. On their arrival at Essex House, the Earl ushered the Queen's representatives upstairs and promptly locked them in his library. Then, striking out on foot, and followed by his band of supporters, he began to make his way toward the City, shouting as he went that his life was in danger and that the crown of England was about to fall into the hands of a Spaniard. On reaching Ludgate the conspirators were met by soldiers armed with pikes, while at Charing Cross and at Westminster barriers were hastily erected to prevent them from reaching the court. Essex had counted on his actions sparking a popular uprising, but his hopes did not materialize. The people of London stayed indoors. By mid-afternoon, hopelessly outmanoeuvred by the Queen and her advisers, Essex realized that his great venture had failed. He fled briefly to Queenhithe with Southampton before taking a boat back up the river to Essex House. As he set about destroying incriminating evidence, the Queen's soldiers surrounded Essex House and threatened to blow it up. The Lord Admiral allegedly only decided not to carry out this dire threat because the ladies Essex and Rich were inside the house at the time. For Essex, however, there was now no way out. Shortly after ten in the evening, he surrendered. Within hours nearly a hundred of the men who had thrown their lot in with him were in custody.

Edward's account of his role in the Essex Rebellion was intended to convey the impression that he was an innocent man caught up in extraordinary events. In a letter addressed to the Privy Council, written while he was still in custody at Alderman Holliday's house, Edward describes how he 'did demean' himself 'on Sunday, the 8th of February'.[74] According to Edward:

> after 10 of the clock, prayer being ended and a sermon begun, the Lady Rich came into my house desiring to speak with me speedily: which I did in the next room to the place where the sermon was, her ladyship then telling me the Earl of Essex would speak with me. Whereupon I went presently with her in her coach, none of my family following me out of the sermon-room, and so departed with her unknown to my said family. About 11 of the clock I came to Essex House, where shortly after the Earl of Essex with others of his company drew themselves into a secret conference, whereto I was not called, nor made acquainted with anything, but only of some danger which the Earl of Essex said he was in by practice of some private enemies. Howbeit, I doubting that the course tended to some ill, and the rather suspecting it for that I saw not my uncle Sir William Russell there, and for that purpose withdrew myself so far that I neither heard anything of the Earl of Essex's consultation, nor yet of the speeches with the lords of the Council. From that time I endeavoured to come from the Earl of Essex as soon as I might with safety, and to that end severed myself from him at a cross street end, and taking water before I heard any proclamation came back to my house about one of the clock. Where I made no delay, but with all convenient speed put myself and followers in readiness, and with the best strength I could then presently make, being about the number of 20 horse, I went toward the Court for her Majesty's service.[75]

Edward's claim that, on arrival at Essex House, he was 'not called, nor made acquainted with anything' is highly suspect. In evidence given by two separate individuals who were present at Essex House on the morning of the rebellion, Edward's name appears prominently alongside those of the key conspirators. Ellis Jones testified that 'With the Earl of Essex were Earls of Rutland, Southampton, and Bedford',[76] while Sir John Davies told of how on 'Sunday morning [he] ... accompanied the Earl of Essex, the Earls of Rutland, Southampton, and Bedford, Lords Monteagle, Sandys, and Chandos'.[77]

Edward's story also varies somewhat from an account given by a certain Henry Woodrington, who confessed that on 8 February 1601 he and his uncle had gone to see the Earl of Rutland at Essex House and that, once there, being swept along by the throng of people, followed the company with the express purpose of withdrawing the Earl of Bedford, Woodrington's uncle, Ephraim, being one of Edward's servants. According to Henry Woodrington, as soon as he and his uncle could find a suitable opportunity without danger either to the Earl or to themselves, they removed him from the company and carried him away in a boat down the Thames to Bedford House.[78]

Did Edward know what was about to happen at Essex House when he went with Penelope Rich in her coach? Edward may well have been innocent of how events were unfolding, and Penelope may have lured him to her brother on a pretext, but he knew of the conspiracy and he would almost certainly have heard of the troubling visit Essex had received on the previous day. He must have heard the commotion taking place at Essex House. Most of Edward's statement is probably a tissue of lies manufactured by a man in fear of his life. All that does seem certain is that someone at Bedford House knew exactly where the Earl had gone and, realizing the seriousness of the situation, had sent Henry and Ephraim Woodrington on a rescue mission. Perhaps Lucy, enquiring from a servant why her lord was absent so long from prayers, and hearing of his departure with Lady Rich sent the servants after him. Once back at Bedford House she may have been one of the people who suggested that Edward raise horse and fly to the Queen in a last-ditch attempt to make the best of a rapidly deteriorating situation.

The one thing that is striking about Edward's declaration is the great lengths he went to in order to protect his family from blame, in his insistence that in following Lady Rich out of the sermon room he acted alone: 'none of my family following me' and going 'unknown to my said family'. Edward sought to protect Lucy, who, in the first confused hours and days after the rebellion may have been viewed with suspicion due to her close association with the other conspirators and their wives, a few of whom, including Penelope Rich, played a part in the uprising.

Elizabeth's retribution in the aftermath of the Essex rebellion was swift and decisive. Edward was fined £20,000, which in his straitened financial circumstances he was incapable of paying. But a fine was far preferable to the punishments meted out to other conspirators. Southampton was imprisoned in the Tower where he fell ill with a quartern fever and the muscles in his legs began to weaken and atrophy from lack of exercise. Essex was condemned to death. On 25 February 1601 he mounted a scaffold that had been specially erected in the courtyard of the Tower. Dressed somberly in a black velvet coat over a black satin suit, he knelt before the executioner's block. He sought pardon for his abortive rebellion, for what he called:

… this my last sin, this great, this bloody, this crying, and this infectious sin, whereby so many, for the love of me, have ventured their lives and souls, and have been drawn to offend God, to offend their Sovereign, and to offend the world.[79]

Even on the point of death, Essex still possessed an unerring sense of spectacle. Unfastening his cloak and doublet in order to place his head on the block, he revealed a scarlet waistcoat beneath: the colour a perfect match for the blood he was soon to shed. The executioner set about his work: the first blow fell on the Earl's shoulder, the second also missed its mark. Only on the third strike did the head become detached from the body. On 13 March 1601 Essex's loyal followers Sir Gelly Meyrick and Henry Cuffe were taken to Tyburn and hanged, drawn and quartered. Two days later Sir Christopher Blount and Sir Charles Danvers were beheaded in the Tower.

Essex was a popular figure among the common people and there were many who felt that his actions did not constitute treason. When, many years after the affair, John Donne delivered a sermon on the nature of virtue and vice he might easily have been thinking about the disgraced Earl:

… vertues and vices are contiguous, and borderers upon one another; and very often, we can hardly tell, to which action the name of *vice*, and to which the name of *vertue* appertains. Many times, that which comes within an inch of a noble action, fals [sic] under the infamy of an odious treason; At many executions, half the company will call a man an *Heretique*, and half, a *Martyr*. How often, an excesse, makes a naturall affection, an unnaturall disorder?[80]

After Essex's execution Elizabeth's ministers were aware that many men did feel that his actions had been noble in origin and considered the earl a 'martyr' and they made great efforts to suppress dissent about his fate. Bacon was charged with writing *The Declaration of the Treasons of the Earl of Essex*, which sought to justify the official response to Essex's behaviour. Yet, despite the best propaganda efforts of the Council, ballads sympathetic to the Earl began to circulate and in the streets people began singing songs entitled *Sweet England's Pride is Gone Well-a-Day, Well-a-Day and Essex's Last Good Night*. It was widely rumoured that the author of *Sweet England's Pride* was none other than Essex's ever-loyal sister, Penelope Rich. But ballads sympathetic to Essex were not the only kind of verse circulating at the time: there was also another, much more bitter piece of writing which commented on the events lately passed. One of the individuals referred to in this untitled poem was Edward. But he was no longer the brave 'valiant English Earle' celebrated by Peele in the poem written to mark the tilts of 1595:

> Bedford hee ranne awaie
> when ower men lost the daie
> so't is assigned

> except his dancing Dame
> do their hard hartes tame
> and swear it is a shame
>   fooles should bee fined.[81]

Edward was the only conspirator, or would-be conspirator, singled out for criticism in the poem. The verse in which he was mentioned took its place alongside others that were devoted to lambasting figures like Cecil and Raleigh who had succeeded in crushing the rebellion. Edward was publicly denounced as a coward and a fool, and it was only Lucy who mitigated the anger felt toward him. If Lucy still retained social credibility in some circles, she was losing it rapidly in others. She had been engaging in financial transactions on her own account and had borrowed money from the Earl of Lincoln that she could not fully repay. Lincoln was incensed by her shabby dealings:

> I should have received five hundred pounds of the Countess of Bedford (if she had dealt truly and honourably with me) ... she offers to put me off with two hundred pounds, and to arbitrate the rest, contrary to all reason, honour, or conscience.[82]

For Lucy, the matter of repaying a few hundred pounds to Lincoln was probably the very least of her concerns. In the aftermath of the Essex Rebellion Edward had not only incurred a massive fine; he had been forbidden to visit the court, and was confined to Bedford House. He continued to plead his innocence. He claimed that he had only made a 'pretence' of speaking with the Earl of Essex on the day of the rebellion and, although he eventually admitted that he had gone to an upper chamber at Essex House – presumably the one in which Essex had imprisoned the members of the Council – he said that once there he had 'heard nothing'.[83] Still under a dark cloud of official suspicion, his actions bordered on lunacy, as defying the express orders of the Council that he not leave Bedford House, he went out hunting on at least four separate occasions. When Cecil made it clear that he was aware of these unauthorized outings, it was claimed that the forays had been conducted with 'great moderation' and that in order to avoid 'further offence [he] had resolved forthwith to send his hounds awaie into the Countrey'.[84]

While Edward sat fretting about his lack of liberty, his aunt worked behind the scenes. Her agent approached Cecil 'att verie good leisure walking alone in Lord Burghley's gardeyne',[85] which adjoined Bedford House, and pleaded for the fine to be reduced, which it eventually was to a sum of £10,000. Lucy's father, John Harrington, wrote to Cecil on behalf of his son-in-law and attempted to raise capital to pay the fine. But Bedford House was unsettled and fraught with tension. There were reports that the house was 'disorder[ed]' and that Edward was as 'untractable as ever'[86] since having his liberty curbed. In mid-July he wrote a series of desperate letters to Cecil explaining how difficult it was for him to borrow the money required to pay his fine, and begging 'That he maye after so long restraint … retier himself to his howse in the countrie'.[87] Lucy also approached Cecil on behalf of Edward and he was not indifferent to her pleas. In March 1601 John Harrington wrote to Cecil thanking him for his intervention:

> I have been advertised by my daughter of Bedford of your noble usage of her in her suit to you concerning the enlargement of my Lord, her husband. If by any my merit [sic] I could testify my gratitude it would be no small happiness unto me.[88]

As with his earlier letter to Essex on behalf of his brother, Sir James Harrington, John Harrington expressed his gratitude by suggesting that, in time, his son would also come to 'love' Cecil: 'Did I think my son would not be alike obsequious of the love of you, it would much diminish my hope of him, but hitherto his few years have promised some discretion'.[89]

Lucy and Edward were eventually granted permission to go to their country house, Chenies, where they lived for months in a strange kind of limbo. But in early 1602 they suffered another terrible blow. On 19 January Lucy gave birth to a son, but her experience of motherhood was fleeting: the child named John lived only a month. As they buried their baby in the bleak February of 1602, Lucy and Edward must have wondered if their situation would ever improve. Would they ever be 'Safe out of fortune's shot'?

3

Courtier

Courts are Theaters, where some men play.

JOHN DONNE, *TO SIR HENRY WOTTON*

The men and women who had surrounded Essex were politically weakened in the aftermath of the failed rebellion, yet bound by strong ties of blood and friendship they still existed as a distinct group. In December 1602, John Harrington invited some of those who still remained at liberty to journey north into Rutland to celebrate Christmas with him at Exton. Commentators on this gathering reported that John and his guests celebrated a 'royall Christmas' and judging by the entertainment he had arranged in 1596, it is clear he was more than capable of organizing a house party that lived up to the richly evocative epithet of 'royall'.[1] Lucy and Edward were among a party that included the Earls of Pembroke and Rutland, Sir Robert Sidney and 'many moe gallants'.[2]

The Earl of Pembroke, William Herbert, was Lucy's first cousin. He had not participated in the Essex Rebellion, because when it took place he was banished from London by Elizabeth for his illicit relationship with the Queen's favourite maid of honour, Mary Fitton. Toward the end of 1600 the Pembroke–Fitton liaison had been the whispered gossip of the court. Mary Fitton was a beautiful, strong-willed woman completely infatuated with the handsome Pembroke. Determined to meet her lover undetected by the wiser souls who might have put a stop to such an ill-judged relationship, Mary took to tucking up her clothes, taking 'a large white cloake and marche[ing] as though she had bene a man to meete the ... Earle out of the Courte'.[3] However, by early 1601 Mary was pregnant and, unable to conceal her condition, the relationship was discovered by an irate Elizabeth. Great pressure was bought on Pembroke to marry Mary but he stubbornly refused and was sent to the Fleet prison to consider his position. But cooling his heels in the Fleet did nothing to change his mind and he continued to 'utterly renounceth ... marriage'.[4] Mary subsequently gave birth to a son who died within days, and Pembroke was eventually released from prison and ordered to return, in disgrace, to his estate at Wilton.

Pembroke was highly respected and admired by his friends, but those same friends sometimes felt that his 'natural vivacity and vigour of mind' were impaired by an 'excessive' appetite for women.[5] Furthermore, his attraction to women was not matched by a tendency to treat them well. By the time he embarked on the affair with Mary he was rumoured to have already turned down at least four prospective brides. His indifference to Mary's plight was symptomatic of a consistently negative attitude toward women that was often dismissive and frequently bordered on hostile. Edward, Earl of Clarendon, a contemporary historian and a man who may have known Pembroke personally, was of the view that he 'was not so much transported with beauty and outward allurements, as with those advantages of the mind, as manifested an extraordinary wit, and spirit, and knowledge, and administered great pleasure in the conversation'.[6] One of the few women with whom Pembroke maintained a strong and positive relationship was Lucy. The two cousins had known each other from childhood, but it is unlikely Pembroke would have bothered to maintain his friendship with Lucy if she had not met his exacting expectations of 'wit ... spirit, and knowledge'. But Lucy and her cousin had a great deal in common. It is possible that Pembroke had received tuition from John Florio, whose influence must inevitably have led to certain similarities of literary taste with Lucy, who was also one of Florio's students. Indeed the relationship between Pembroke and Florio was sufficiently strong for Florio to leave his library of Italian, French and Spanish books to Pembroke on his death. Around the early 1600s Pembroke and Lucy were active patrons of writers and dramatists, and one dramatist they both supported was Ben Jonson. Pembroke was a generous benefactor, something which Jonson readily acknowledged, telling his patron, 'You haue euer been free and Noble to mee'.[7] Pembroke gave Jonson a gift of twenty pounds a year to purchase books and he also paid for Inigo Jones to study in Italy. Pembroke and his brother, Philip Herbert, later created Earl of Montgomery, were the joint dedicatees of Shakespeare's First Folio in 1623. In later years Pembroke and Lucy shared a passion for designing and creating gardens. Pembroke's presence at a gathering of the remnants of the Essex faction was probably due both to his family connections with the Harringtons and Sidneys, but it also implies he was sympathetic to the political aspirations of the group.

At her father's house in the depths of the winter of 1602 Lucy and her cousin had plenty of opportunity to enjoy one another's company. The wintry days would have provided ample opportunities for hunting with John Harrington's renowned hounds while the long evenings were probably spent eating, drinking and talking. In the unlikely event of the conversation flagging, Pembroke had brought along his fool to enliven the proceedings. Perhaps, too, there was an opportunity for the group to reflect upon the miseries of recent years and to remember absent friends like Southampton, who still languished in prison. But beyond the problems of the present the gathering presented a natural opportunity for discussing the succession question which had so haunted Essex. Viewing

James VI of Scotland as the preferred successor to Elizabeth, Essex had initiated secret communications with him in the late 1590s. But the Earl was not alone in looking north of the border in anticipation of England's future monarch. After Essex's execution Robert Cecil wielded more power than ever and he sought to smooth the way for the succession of the new king, and protect his own claims to power, by initiating secret communications of his own with James at some point around 1601.

While the celebrations were taking place at Exton, the Queen was watching from afar. It is clear that Elizabeth was aware of the gathering in Rutland, and that she was highly displeased by it. In late December, Roland Whyte wrote an agitated letter to Robert Sidney at Exton, urging him to return to London for at least 'Part of the Christmas, lest the Queen take some Offence'.[8] According to Whyte he had been prompted to write to Sir Robert because an unnamed 'great Cownsailor'[9] who had just come from a conference with the Queen decided that notice of how matters stood in London should be sent to Sidney. Somewhat cryptically, Whyte wrote of how the 'Storme continues now and then, but all depends upon my Lady Riches being, or not being amongst you'.[10] The reference to a 'storme' is unclear and was perhaps a euphemism for Elizabeth's anger. Penelope Rich was not named as a member of the Exton party, but that does not mean that she was not present at a gathering that clearly included many whose names were not recorded. The relevance of Penelope 'being, or not being' in Rutland is also unclear. Elizabeth was certainly hostile to Penelope and she may have resented the fact that those whom she had sought to punish were enjoying themselves. Wherever the truth lies, the fact that Whyte considered that Penelope might be one of the party gathered at Exton further indicates how close members of the Essex group still were.

As the Queen watched displays of dancing and the party in Rutland pondered the wit of Pembroke's fool, no one could have guessed that in just over a year Elizabeth would be dead. The Queen was elderly but her health was reasonably good. However, from the beginning of 1603 she began to fail. She was deeply affected by the death in February of her close friend and cousin the Countess of Nottingham, and her grief caused her to spend days on end shut up in mourning. By the end of February she had developed swellings in her throat and, soon after, a fever. The French ambassador to London, Beaumont, reported to the French ambassador in Spain that in the opinion of her doctors Elizabeth's final illness was due to a 'profound sorrow which had fallen on her secretly a few days before she succumbed to it'.[11] Beaumont was convinced that Elizabeth's 'sorrow' was caused by 'the death of the Earl of Essex' which led 'her to desire and seek her own demise'.[12] It is possible that Beaumont assigned the grief Elizabeth felt over the loss of the Countess of Nottingham to Essex in order to conform to his own notions of the relationship between the Earl and the Queen. But if Elizabeth felt any sadness over her treatment of her former favourite, she took it with her to the grave. For the great monarch who had ruled for an astonishing 45 years finally died, peacefully, in the early hours of 24 March 1603. Within a short time proclamations were made in Whitehall and in Cheapside, announcing what so many of her subjects had already guessed or deduced: James VI of Scotland was to become King James I of England.

James lost no time in claiming his new kingdom. Leaving Scotland twelve days after Elizabeth's death he began to journey south intending to arrive in London around early May. As James travelled south he stopped at various houses to be welcomed and entertained by those of the aristocracy eager to make contact with their new monarch. James visited Belvoir Castle where he was entertained by the Earl of Rutland, and on Saturday 23 April he dined with Sir John Harrington at Burley-on-the-Hill. Determined to make an impression on the new king, John had arranged for James to engage in his favourite sport, hunting. Making his way across Empingham Heath towards Stamford, James was met by men carrying hares in baskets which were then released so that the king could pursue them with Harrington's best hounds. But John Harrington's efforts to entertain the king were not confined to outdoor pursuits; he had also engaged Samuel Daniel to write an address of welcome for James, known as the 'Panegyrike Congratulatory'. In the address Daniel struck a hugely optimistic note, which, given the low reputation James's court eventually came to acquire, was wildly misplaced:

> We finde that Good shal dwell within thy Court;
> Plaine zeale and truth free from base flatterings,
> Shall there be entertain'd and have resorte: ... /
> ... there is no accesse
> By grosse corruption, bribes cannot effect
> ... Nor shall we now have use of flattery,[13]

James spent Easter Sunday at Burley, and the following day resolved to return for more sport but in this he was prevented: his horse fell and he bruised his arm severely. He spent the night at Burley and left by coach the following day.

England's new queen, Anna, departed for England a little later than James. She travelled with two of her children: the heir apparent, the nine-year-old Prince Henry, and his seven-year-old sister, Princess Elizabeth. Etiquette dictated that Anna could not cross into England without the company of aristocratic Englishwomen as an escort, but many of the women who might perform this duty were still in London awaiting the funeral of their dead queen.

It was not until the middle of May, with Elizabeth's funeral over and a proper period of mourning observed, that the Privy Council sent an official party of 'Six great ladies' of the court, accompanied by 200 horsemen, to meet Anna who waited on the border at Berwick-on-Tweed.[14] The women chosen for this important journey were primarily those who had formed Elizabeth's inner circle of ladies-in-waiting. Because the elderly queen had surrounded herself with women near her own age, so the ladies sent to meet Anna tended either to be older or linked in some way to the ruling circle in London. A rather unexpected member of the party, perhaps invited at the request of James, was Penelope Rich. James was sympathetic to those who had supported the ill-fated Earl of Essex. Soon after his arrival in England he made a point of publicly acknowledging Essex's son, Robert Devereux, by taking the twelve-year-old boy in his arms and kissing him before 'openly and loudly declaring him the son of the most noble knight that English land has ever begotten'.[15] He subsequently appointed the boy to bear the sword before him on his entry into London and designated him to be the lifelong companion of his own son, Prince Henry. Reporting to the Doge and Senate, Scaramelli, who witnessed the scene, shrewdly observed that James's actions demonstrated 'not merely that change of Kings means change in kingdoms, but also that what is impossible at one period becomes easy at another'.[16] Scaramelli was not alone in detecting a shift in the political climate. James's actions, acknowledging Essex's son, appointing formerly disgraced men back into positions of power, and releasing others like Southampton from prison, meant that Lucy and Edward might at last be able to achieve what had been denied them under Elizabeth: complete social rehabilitation.

When the ladies sent by the Privy Council eventually met their new queen, they discovered that another group of English noblewomen were already firmly established around her and that the pre-eminent lady in this alternative party was Lucy Russell. Lucy had not lingered in London to attend the funeral of the old queen who had banished her and Edward from the court. Instead, accompanied by her mother, she stole a march on the officially sanctioned welcoming party and headed for Scotland. Lucy and Anne's journey was a very practical expression of Francis Bacon's view that 'the mould of a Mans fortune is in himselfe'[17], because in going to meet their new queen the women decided not to wait and see how events unfolded. Rather, they attempted to control notoriously fickle fortune in the hope of securing promising futures for themselves in the new reign. Lucy probably embarked on the journey with a mixture of feelings. She almost certainly felt a sincere desire to offer her services to the new queen, for she possessed a strong sense of duty. But equally, she would have seen the attempt to make contact with Anna pragmatically as a piece of 'busnes',[18] a matter that needed to be attended to, albeit a highly important one. Having decided to travel to Scotland, she was single-minded in her efforts to make the best possible impression on Anna for once she set her mind to something she was extremely determined. This aspect of her character was sometimes all too obvious to her contemporaries for, as an exasperated Robert Cecil remarked, Lucy was in every respect a typical woman insofar as she 'resembled her sex in loving her own will'.[19] Furthermore, the intensely competitive atmosphere – which saw nobles literally riding their horses to death in their haste to introduce themselves to the new King and Queen – would have provided an added impetus for Lucy, who thrived on competition, even if it did not always bring out the best in her behaviour. Years later she made frantic attempts to buy a number of Holbein paintings before her arch-rival, the great art collector Thomas Howard, 2nd Earl of Arundel, acquired them, while showing no concern whatsoever that the owner of the paintings lay on his death bed and that her actions might be construed as tactless, if not tasteless.

By contrast, Edward made little more than a token effort to catch the eye of either James or Anna. Shortly after Elizabeth's death, Edward, along with the Earl of Kent, Sir Edward Ratcliffe, Sir William Russell and Lord Oliver St John of Blestsoe, sent a messenger to James at Berwick with letters conveying their congratulations on his accession. James responded with a polite if somewhat cautious reply. But more importantly, James relieved Edward of £3000 of the fine he still owed for his part in the Essex uprising. The debt was considerable and the release from paying it was of enormous help to the Bedfords, who spent most of their time teetering from one financial crisis to the next. Yet Edward did not appear to make any strenuous efforts to make a good impression on the new royals. Indeed, he declined an invitation to be created a Knight of the Bath in mid-1603, possibly because the honour involved paying for the privilege, a strategy James had been using as a means of revenue raising. Edward's decision to stay away from what his wife and her parents planned perhaps stemmed from his own troubled family history. His father, Francis Russell, had been murdered on the Scottish borders, and one of those suspected of involvement in Russell's death was the Scottish noble, Lord Arran, who was a personal friend of James. When an enraged Elizabeth had demanded that the Scots hand over Russell's murderer, James agreed to comply, but only if it could be clearly established who the guilty party was. James eventually placed Arran under house arrest, but within a short space of time he was free to come and go as he pleased. Although Edward had supported Essex, and presumably shared the Earl's wish to see James as the successor to Elizabeth, when James did in fact take the throne Edward may have felt less than enthusiastic toward his new ruler, who had allowed the man suspected of murdering his father to go virtually unpunished.

While Edward resisted taking to his horse and rushing to meet James, the great gamble undertaken by Lucy and her mother paid off handsomely. The meeting between Lucy and Anna gave rise to a relationship founded on shared interests and sympathies, which lasted until the Queen's death in 1619. At 28, Lucy was a year younger than Anna and she was both beautiful and cultured. Lucy's patronage of writers, and her links with other prominent literary patrons such as Pembroke and his brother Philip, meant that she had access to, and a knowledge of, the most current ideas and trends in literary writing. Lucy's interests coincided closely with Anna's ambitious plans to create a dazzling new court in England, a project most clearly manifested in the changes the new queen brought about in the masque. A further, less obvious reason for the early, close friendship between the two women may have been the shared experience of miscarriage. Immediately prior to her departure from Scotland, Anna had been expecting a baby, but the pregnancy ended in still birth. There was some suggestion that Anna herself brought about the loss of the baby by violently striking her belly during a particularly acrimonious argument with James. Ironically the alleged argument concerned the custody of Anna and James's eldest child, the heir apparent Prince Henry, a post traditionally assigned to a Scottish noble, but an arrangement to which Anna had been mounting a campaign of dogged resistance. Anna had refused to leave Scotland unless she was given custody of Henry, whom she had barely seen in the preceding five years, and although ultimately successful in claiming her son it appears she lost another child in the process. When Lucy met her new queen in 1603, she had herself suffered both miscarriage and the death of a baby. She was therefore well placed to understand the feelings of her new mistress, who was still suffering the effects of miscarriage. Lucy was certainly sensitive to the physical and emotional difficulties associated with pregnancy and childbirth. In later years she wrote to her friend Lady Jane Bacon, who was experiencing a difficult pregnancy and anxious about her impending confinement. She urged Jane not to 'sincke vnder that melancoly ... [which] ... hath already rought so ill effects vpon yo[u]r health, & so strong aprehencions in yo[u]r minde ... I trust owr good God will with a safe deliverance of a happy bearth restore yow'.[20] When, in 1611, Lucy suffered yet another miscarriage she was reported as being 'the queen's only favourite'.[21] Perhaps, as her friend lost 'the child there was so much hope of',[22] Anna remembered the sympathy and support Lucy had extended to her as she waited on the border of Scotland and England in 1603 and treated her with special kindness.

On 1 June 1603, Anna crossed into England with Prince Henry and an entourage of attendants. Princess Elizabeth had fallen ill and it was decided that she should follow on a little later. Some two weeks after Anna arrived in England, Sir Thomas Edmonds wrote to the Earl of Shrewsbury informing him that Anna had 'refused to admit my Ladye of Kildare and the Lady Walsingham, to be of her Privye-chamber'.[23] Any ideas the Privy Council might have had of discreetly manipulating the power within the new Queen's Bedchamber by placing loyal and reliable ladies of their own choosing within it were dashed. Anna was an independent-minded woman who would select her own companions and who clearly did not want to be surrounded by the women the Council considered suitable companions. Edmonds confirmed that the only woman Anna had sworn into her privy chamber was Lucy. Anna's choice of Lucy as an intimate companion had the effect of immediately increasing her status among her peers. As Lady Jane Clifford noted, 'my Lady of Bedford who was so great a Woman with the Queen as everybody much respected her'.[24]

In addition to attempting to keep an eye on the composition of the new Queen's Bedchamber one of the many tasks facing the Privy Council was ensuring the safety of the royal family. The Council became increasingly concerned that the large numbers of people keen to glimpse a sight of their new rulers might overwhelm or crush the royal family, and accordingly they passed laws to prevent the population from travelling. Predictably the laws proved totally ineffective. Along narrow dusty roads in the burning heat of one of the hottest summers on record, large numbers of horses and people were on the move. But if the new king's subjects were keen to meet and greet him, the feeling was not always mutual. James found large groups of people frightening and avoided such situations wherever possible. His attitude was in stark contrast to his predecessor Elizabeth, who had been a confident and accomplished communicator and who had understood very clearly the benefits to be gained from engaging directly with her subjects. The new king's reluctance to make contact with his people was perceived by some as evidence of a cold and uncaring attitude and gave rise to whispers of discontent. As a result of his reticence James became the recipient of unsolicited advice to take notice 'of the generall murmurings and complaints ... that you grace not your people, you speake not to them, you looke not at them, you blesse them not; and therefore (say they) you love them not'.[25]

In late June the entourage that travelled with Anna halted at Sir Robert Spencer's household at Althorp in Northamptonshire where an 'infinite number of Lords & Ladys'[26] had gathered and the assembled party was treated to an outdoor entertainment written by Ben Jonson which has become known as *The Entertainment at Althorp*. As the King and Queen made their way further south the crowds increased and the numbers involved were little short of staggering. When Anna moved on to Windsor she was accompanied by 250 carriages and somewhere in the region of 5000 horses. On finally reaching Hampton Court many in the vast retinue were lodged within the palace, but others stayed in tents that had been specially erected in the grounds. But in the midst of the heat and the great throng of people a deadly menace lurked. Large numbers of people in close contact created the perfect breeding ground for plague.

The plague had begun its progress in late May, and while there was anxiety about the spread of the disease, no practical steps had been taken against it beyond killing dogs, who it was believed carried the disease, and marking the doors of houses of those unfortunate enough to be infected. London was a city in distress with its inhabitants 'dying by the thousand every week'[27] and while some city dwellers physically removed themselves from the risk of infection others were in no position to make any kind of escape. Catholic prisoners in the Fleet who were in 'great danger of the syckness'[28] hoped anxiously that James would honour a promise he had made to release them as they saw common prisoners in the wing adjacent to theirs fall ill and die of the plague.

The presence of plague also prompted endless discussions about how best to proceed with the forthcoming coronation of James and Anna. Should it go ahead or should it be delayed? In the event, the coronation took place on 25 July 1603 but the celebration was not the grand event it should have been and London was in many respects a closed city. Tickets for the coronation were issued to individuals attached to the court, but strict orders were enforced to prevent ordinary Londoners from coming anywhere near the participants in the ceremony. On the morning of the 25th James and Anna boarded a boat at Whitehall steps, and so great was the fear of plague that while the king was on the water 'it was the penalty of death to bring people in boats from the City' to view the sight.[29] After travelling a short distance down the Thames, the royal party landed at the Palace of Westminster from where they walked to the Abbey on foot while curious onlookers were kept well away by guards. Anna walked to her coronation dressed 'in a robe of crimson velvet with her seemly hair down hanging on her princely shoulders and on her head a coronet of plain gold, followed by the ladies of her household in their crimson velvet robes'.[30] Despite the pouring rain which threatened to mar an already less than auspicious occasion, walking in the procession to Westminster Abbey as one of the Queen's most favoured ladies must have been a moment of profound satisfaction for Lucy as the bitter memories of the past were finally erased and a promising new future beckoned. But in the same month that saw Lucy ascending to high royal favour by taking a role in the coronation and an active part in the initial shaping of Anna's court, the risks of the plague sweeping London became a reality for her. She fell ill of a 'pestilent hott feuer' severe enough to cause her to be carried from the court and for her illness to be 'vehemently suspected of plage',[31] a theory made more credible by the news that one of Edward's servants had recently died of the disease. It was a cruel irony that as Lucy was finally achieving what she and her family had spent their lives striving for, she was suddenly struck down by a killer disease. Taken from the court she was attended by physicians who searched for further tell-tale symptoms. In addition to a high fever, plague caused excruciatingly painful swellings of the lymph nodes, known as buboes, vomiting, dizziness and slurred speech, all of which caused terrible suffering and foretold almost certain death. Yet whatever the illness that caused Lucy to collapse so dramatically it was not plague. No further reference was made to her sickness and she made a full recovery. Fortune had smiled on her.

Although Lucy occupied a high place in Anna's favour, that favour was a precarious gift liable to be withdrawn at any time if the Queen believed she had been crossed or slighted. Anna could be stubborn and petty. After the coronation the court returned to Hampton Court and the balance of power within the Bedchamber changed, as, according to Anne Clifford, 'Now was my Lady Rich grown great with the Queen, in so much as my Lady of Bedford was something out with her, and when she came to Hampton Court was entertained but even indifferently, and yet continued to be of the Bed Chamber'.[32] Penelope Rich represented a formidable competitor for the Queen's favour. She was a highly experienced courtier and she was the woman whose brother, the Earl of Essex, had in his confession claimed to be strong-willed. Anne Clifford's view that Lucy was 'something out' with Penelope points to antagonisms that were not politely concealed under courtly behaviour, but clearly visible to onlookers. What exactly Anna's 'indifferent' treatment of Lucy amounted to is unknown. Perhaps it was a less than effusive greeting, maybe a barbed remark, perhaps no greeting at all. Whatever the real story, the anecdote hints at the personal slights Lucy endured in order to cling to power. Yet despite such difficulties Lucy's influence with Anna was not permanently affected, because a short time later Anne Clifford's mother, the Countess of Cumberland, was seeking royal assistance in property disputes with her husband and to that end writing letters to 'the Q. by my Lady of Bedford'.[33]

Lucy used her position with Anna to promote the interests of people close to her, be they relatives or friends. In August 1603 rumours began to circulate that Sir Robert Sidney was to be appointed as Anna's Lord High Chamberlain, an introduction between Sidney and Anna which was almost certainly engineered by Lucy. Sidney was on good terms with his Harrington relatives and the links between the two families had been forged and nurtured over the years. Anna had initially appointed a Mr Kennedy as her Lord Chamberlain, an act which incensed James who wanted the honour to go to Sir George Carew. But when the Queen decided to dispense with Kennedy's services she did not opt for James's preferred candidate, Carew; instead she chose Sidney. As Lord Chamberlain, Sidney was responsible for granting access to the Queen and for overseeing her comfort. With Lucy as a prominent lady of the Queen's Bedchamber and Robert Sidney as her Lord Chamberlain, the two became formidable gatekeepers to Anna's royal influence. The appointment of Sidney as Lord Chamberlain not only enabled Lucy and her family to maintain a position of power within Anna's court; it was also an introduction that proved crucial in shaping the artistic and cultural tendencies of that court. Robert Sidney followed in the Sidney family tradition by penning poetry himself, and he was a keen supporter of the arts. Like Lucy, Robert Sidney could introduce Anna to a thriving and well-established network of writers, poets and playwrights. Some of those writers were appointed to positions in Anna's new court, so John Florio became Anna's Italian tutor and Samuel Daniel and Ben Jonson were commissioned to write masques for the Queen.

But Lucy was not the only Harrington to benefit from associations with the new royal family. The impression that Lucy and her parents had made on Anna and James were key factors in the royal couple's decision to appoint the Harringtons as the guardians of Princess Elizabeth. Elizabeth was initially entrusted to the care of the Countess of Kildare, the daughter of the Earl of Nottingham, the Lord Admiral and the wife of Baron Cobham who was warden of the Cinque Portes. Lady Kildare had been refused a post in Anna's Bedchamber, but she was rewarded with the task of escorting Elizabeth on her journey out of Scotland, and the two had stayed briefly with the Harringtons at Combe Abbey as they made their way south on two occasions in June. Yet the Countess of Kildare did not remain sole governess of Elizabeth for long. By July 1603 Anne Clifford reported that the honour was being shared between Kildare and Anne Harrington. But even Lady Kildare's shared guardianship of Elizabeth proved brief. Kildare's husband became implicated in the so-called 'Main' plot which, so it was claimed, was intended to kill James and his children and place Arbella Stuart on the throne. Her husband's disgrace and imprisonment meant that Lady Kildare was automatically an unsuitable person to wait on the young princess, and Elizabeth became the sole responsibility of John and Anne Harrington. For John Harrington, Elizabeth was an 'honourable charge, entrusted to us by the King's Majesty' and he was determined that he and his wife would do the little girl 'such service as is due to her princely endowments and natural abilities; both which appear the sweet dawning of future comfort to her royal father'.[34] The Harrington property at Combe Abbey underwent alterations to make it fit for its new inhabitant and the 'godly' Anne, and John again embarked on the very careful education of a young girl. Elizabeth's entourage at Combe included, amongst others, 'her nurse, three chamberwomen, a French dresser and her tutors, a physician, two Scots footmen dressed in the royal livery, grooms of the presence-chamber, and grooms of the bedchamber. Her household further included a sempstress, a laundress, grooms of the stable, yeomen of the horse, yeomen of the cellar and sumptermen'.[35] Not only did Combe become home to the small army of retainers around Elizabeth, it also played host to a menagerie of exotic creatures – including parrots and monkeys – which were kept for the amusement of the young princess. John and Anne Harrington's association with the princess ultimately proved financially crippling to them as they were poorly and erratically reimbursed for the expenses they incurred in caring for Elizabeth, but a genuine and enduring affection developed between them and their charge. The care of Elizabeth also brought John Harrington into frequent contact with Prince Henry and his circle as Harrington was required to escort Elizabeth when she met up with her brother.

Lucy too grew to know the young princess well, a relationship between the two women which was given an opportunity to develop when Lucy visited her parents or when the Harringtons accompanied Elizabeth to events at court.

When Samuel Daniel delivered his *Panegyrike Congratulatory* to James at Burley he referred to the unification of Scotland and England:

> Now thou art all great *Brittaine*, and no more,
> No Scot, no English now, nor no debate:
> No Borders but the Ocean, and the Shore,
> No wall of Adrian serves to separate
> Our mutuall love, nor our obedience,
> All Subiects now to one imperiall Prince.[36]

In time James did bring about the union of the two countries, but in the early years of the new reign many within the English court deeply resented the Scottish newcomers. The presence of yet more nobles meant increased competition for royal favour and the arrivals from over the border were perceived as a group of grasping hangers-on who would deprive the English of opportunities they considered rightfully theirs. The reality was far more complex. Many of the Scots who followed James into England were administrators, still deeply involved in running Scottish affairs; others came to England for a brief time before returning to Scotland. Yet some did stay. Unlike some of the English aristocracy who carped and complained about the arrival of the Scots, Lucy understood very clearly that there was nothing whatever to be gained from distancing herself from the new arrivals from north of the border. Moreover, she had a kind of automatic entrée in that she was distantly related to the Bruces. Three Scots with whom Lucy formed lasting friendships were James Hay, Earl of Carlisle, Viscount Doncaster, Ludovick Stuart, Earl of Lennox and Duke of Richmond, and James, Marquis of Hamilton.

James Hay arrived in England at some point around the end of 1603. Hay was a man of modest birth who had spent some years living in France. On his return to Scotland he was appointed a gentleman of the Scottish Privy Chamber and subsequently, at the request of Anna, achieved promotion to the Bedchamber. Despite this position Hay did not really begin to enjoy the benefits of James's favour until he arrived in England and was granted a lucrative five-year licence to export broadcloths, a privilege he shared with Philip Herbert. Although Hay never became one of James's especial favourites in the way that Robert Carr, Earl of Somerset or George Villiers, Duke of Buckingham, did, he nevertheless enjoyed a particularly close relationship with the king who employed him at home and abroad as an ambassador and a mediator. Hay was a charming, expansive and profligate man whose capacity to spend his own and other people's money was nothing short of legendary in an age when such behaviour was so commonplace it usually passed without comment. Hay's extravagance was evident early in the reign when in March 1604 James sent him on a special diplomatic mission to Henri IV, allegedly in order to pay compliment to the French king. Hay was provided with the large sum of £300 for his trip; however, the actual cost of the visit came closer to a staggering £6000. Hay frequently took part in the masques performed at court and he suffered physically in order that his appearance conformed to the prevailing fashion. He reported that when he was a masquer it was the fashion 'to appeare very small in the wast, I remember I was drawne up from the ground by both hands whilst the tayler with all his strength buttoned on my doublet'.[37] Hay was keen not just to participate in masques but also to organize them. When in 1607 he married Honora Denny, the only daughter of Lord Edward Denny, he engaged Thomas Campion to write a masque for his wedding. Hay loved spectacle and artistic presentation and although he could not compete financially with the organizers like Anna of fabulously expensive masques, he indulged his love of sumptuous display by giving banquets. These banquets were ostentatious affairs designed to impress an audience that was not easily impressed. Course after course of food was presented in a gastronomic orgy of excess that saw the food frequently destroyed before it could be consumed. Yet for all his love of entertaining Hay gradually came to assume the role of an important courtier, and was close both to James and Robert Cecil, links that made him a powerful friend and ally to Lucy.

But Hay was not Lucy's only friend among the Scots surrounding James. She was also close to Ludovick Stuart, Earl of Lennox, and the Marquis of Hamilton. After his accession, James I appointed Lennox to the Privy Council, which he attempted to keep balanced between Scottish and English members. Lennox also had a much more personal involvement with James in his role as Steward of the Household. During the reign of Elizabeth the Privy Chamber had been the centre of political power, but when James I came to the throne that power shifted to the men who made up the King's Bedchamber. All the members of James's Bedchamber were Scots, the sole exception being Sir Philip Herbert. The men who formed the Bedchamber had direct access to the physical person of the king, just as Lucy in her capacity as a lady of the Queen's Bedchamber had direct access to Anna. Lucy was therefore intimately connected to the power bases within both Anna and James's innermost circles: she was the friend and relative to the Queen's Lord Chamberlain, Robert Sidney, and in James's court she was close to Pembroke and his brother Philip Herbert, Earl of Montgomery, as well as Hay, Lennox and Hamilton. All these men were to prove invaluable friends to Lucy, and her connections with them meant that her personal power and influence extended far beyond her role as a member of the Queen's court.

Lucy's duties to the Queen meant that she spent a quarter of the year waiting on Anna, and it appears that her 'quarter' ran from October to December. So in early December 1603 Lucy was waiting on the Queen when the Spanish ambassador invited the French ambassador's wife, Madame Beaumont, to dinner and urged her to bring some English ladies along with her. Madame Beaumont was obviously close to the women of the former Essex faction, for she 'brought my Lady Bedford, Lady Rich, Lady Susan, Lady Dorothe with hir and great cheere they had'.[38] Lucy's social life was clearly in full swing; she had an opportunity to demonstrate her accomplishment in languages and create an international profile as her appearance, talk and manners would be relayed straight back to the Spanish and French courts.

During the Christmas of 1603–1604 the court lay at Hampton Court in order to escape the plague which continued its relentless progress across London. For those gathered at the palace the Christmas festivities were eagerly awaited; Carleton wrote to Chamberlain telling him that there would be 'a merry Christmas at Hampton Court, for both male and female maskes are all ready bespoken, whereof the Duke [of Lennox] is *rector chori* of th' one side and the La: Bedford of the other'.[39] Masques had been performed in the time of Elizabeth, but under James and Anna they began to evolve in new and different ways. The masque form originally developed out of 'earlier entertainments, mummings, and disguisings' but it came to the centre 'on the arrival of aristocratic masquers, elaborately costumed, to perform their specially choreographed dances'.[40] Masques were performed at Christmas and often to celebrate specific events, particularly marriages. While at heart 'masques were always an elaborate frame for nothing more nor less than an aristocratic knees-up'[41] they were nonetheless important vehicles for conveying social, cultural and political messages. The masque was a highly privileged dramatic form which provided an opportunity for its aristocratic participants to, as it were, observe one another. The masque evolved to combine professional performers who presented an anti-masque prior to the arrival of the court masquers, who danced but did not speak. When a masque ended the courtiers who had participated in it approached the audience and chose partners with whom to dance in the revels. The very specific combination of social inwardness, exclusivity and political posturing inherent in the masque meant that attendance at them was much sought after, both by the local aristocracy and by foreign diplomats and ambassadors to England. As Anna began to exert her influence on the masque, so too a role in a masque became highly sought after by the ladies of the court.

At Christmas 1603, the 'female' masque, that is, the masque to be given by Anna and danced by her court ladies, was the *Vision of the Twelve Goddesses* written by Samuel Daniel. Daniel had a longstanding connection to Lucy through his links with John Florio, but he was also associated with Mary Sidney, Countess of Pembroke, and had formed part of the circle of writers she had assembled at Wilton. Daniel had also served as a tutor to Anne Clifford, daughter of the Countess of Cumberland, who was Lucy's relative by marriage. Lucy's role in commissioning Daniel for the work and in taking the lead role in organizing the event was significant. When Daniel published the text of the masque he made it clear that it was Lucy who had obtained the commission for him. Dedicating his work to Lucy, he explained what the masque was about and told her that he hoped this 'might clear the reckoning of any imputation that might be laid upon your judgment for preferring such a one to her Majesty in this employment as could give no reason for what was done'.[42]

Anna obviously had great confidence in, and respect for, Lucy's judgement in order for her to accept the recommendation of Daniel as the author of the first masque she would present as Queen of England. She had confidence, too, in Lucy's ability to organize the event and assume the role as leader of the masque, the *rector chori*. It is more than likely that Lucy conferred with or consulted Pembroke in arranging the masque, because one of Pembroke's tutors, Hugh Sanford, is named as playing an important role in arranging the production: 'Both the King's and Queen's Majesty have a humour to have some masques this Christmas time … special choice is made of Mr. Sanford to direct the order and course for the ladies'.[43]

Daniel's masque depicted twelve goddesses who were played by the Queen and eleven of her ladies and permission was given for the costumes of the masquers to be taken from the wardrobes of the dead Queen Elizabeth. Lady Suffolk and Lady Walshingham, two of the participants in the masque, were charged with sifting through the former queen's clothing and taking what they considered suitable for costumes. Lucy took the role of Vesta in the masque, and she wore 'a white mantle embroidered with gold-flames, with a dressing like a nun, presented a burning lamp in one hand, and a book in the other'.[44] It is impossible to say whether Lucy's costume was fashioned from any of Elizabeth's clothing, but if it was then wearing the 'mantle' must have been a strange experience indeed. Slipping on a garment that had clothed the body of the former queen was very tangible evidence that times had changed and that Lucy was moving on from an unhappy past. Even if Lucy's costume was not fashioned from the robes once worn by Elizabeth one thing she definitely did appropriate from the dead queen was the role of Vesta. Elizabeth had used the figure of Vesta – the wise and pious virgin – in constructing her own iconography. Lucy was wise but she was no virgin, and Daniel reshaped the role for her: her carrying of a book signalled her devotion to religion and the lamp became another manifestation of the light imagery habitually associated with her. Lucy entered the masquing stage as:

> … holy Vesta with her flames of zeal
> … clad in white purity:
> Whose book the soul's sweet comfort doth reveal
> By the ever-burning lamp of piety.[45]

Dudley Carleton attended the performance and was greatly taken with Anna's costume. Appearing in the role of Pallas, which she had expressly chosen to represent, the Queen 'had a trick by herself for her clothes were not so much below the knee, but that we might see a woman had both feete and legs which I never knew before'.[46] Carleton further noted that at the end of the masque, when the ladies chose partners from the audience to dance the revels, the young Prince Henry was taken out by the ladies and 'tossed from hand to hand like a tennis ball'.[47] But not everybody was charmed by the masque. Ben Jonson and his friend Sir John Roe attended the evening but were asked to leave the performance, being ushered from the great hall at Hampton Court by the Earl of Suffolk, the Lord Chamberlain. What precisely Jonson and Roe did to deserve expulsion is unclear, but it must have been sufficiently disrespectful or disruptive to have warranted such an undignified exit. The misbehaviour may have originated in Jonson's profound disagreement with Daniel over the significance of the masque form. Jonson believed that the masque had both '*bodies*' and '*soules*'.[48] Daniel believed the complete opposite. For him it was wrong to give too much weight to a masque because 'whosoever strives to show most wit about these punctilios of dreams and shows are sure sick of a disease they cannot hide and would fain have the world to think them very deeply learned in all mysteries whatsoever'.[49]

By 1604, Lucy still retained her privileged position within Anna's Bedchamber, but the atmosphere within that chamber was often fractious. In mid-February Philip Gawdy wrote a letter to his brother with some fresh court gossip, namely that 'the Queen hath fallen out greatly with my Lady Riche the cause you shall know hereafter'.[50] But Gawdy's promise to his brother to give the 'cause' of Penelope's falling out with Anna was never fulfilled. What exactly Penelope had done, or not done, to invite the displeasure of Anna was never mentioned again. What Gawdy's comments make clear is how precarious the Queen's favour could be. Inner court circles were notorious for the backbiting and jealousy between those vying for the rewards of influence and power, and this appears to have been true of Anna's household. In early 1604 the Earl of Worcester listed the names of the women surrounding Anna and he 'wrote of ladies belonging to the Bed Chamber, the Drawing Chamber, the Private Chamber, and "Maids of Honor" as if in descending degrees of status'.[51] Worcester's list was arranged into four distinct sections:

Bed Chamber:	The countess of Bedford
	The countess of Hertford
Drawing Chamber:	The countess of Derby
	The countess of Suffolk
	Penelope Lady Rich
	The countess of Nottingham
	Susan de Vere
	[Audrey] Lady Walsingham
	[Elizabeth] Lady Southwell

Private Chamber:	'All the rest.'
Maids of Honour:	Cary
	Middlemore
	Woodhouse
	Gargrave
	Roper[52]

The desire of women from the outer chambers to move into Anna's innermost circle must have been strong and would have presented a challenge to the women immediately surrounding the Queen. But Lucy was an extremely tenacious woman and she was reported as holding 'fast to the bed chamber'[53] and by extension to the Queen's affections. It is impossible to know how many toes Lucy trod on or how many enemies she made among the other women in order to keep her place, but limpet-like she was not about to let all her hard work and her big opportunity slip through her fingers. Maintaining her place must have required some doing for there were ominous reports of doors within the Queen's Bedchamber complex being locked against other household women and an atmosphere of poisonous acrimony prevailing between some of the women waiting upon Anna. According to Worcester, amongst the Queen's ladies 'the plotting and mallice' was so great that he thought 'Envy hath teyd an invisible snake abowt most of ther neks to sting on another to deathe'.[54]

In addition to watching her back for any attempt to displace her in the Queen's favour, Lucy was required to negotiate with members of James's household in matters which involved Anna. In itself this did not prove an insurmountable problem, because James's Bedchamber contained people related to Lucy such as Pembroke and his brother Philip Herbert, and men like James Hay, Hamilton and Lennox whom she came to know as friends. One of the chief problems confronting Lucy in her service to Anna was trying to navigate the delicate territory of a frequently squabbling husband and wife, a task requiring the utmost diplomacy and skill, particularly when the King and Queen were on especially poor terms with one another. A surviving letter which Lucy wrote to Robert Sidney provides an insight into what appears to have been an ongoing war of nerves between James and his Queen. Lucy told Sidney that she had sent a messenger to him:

... who can bring yow from me no newse of any alteration in the Queens purposes, for she holds her resolution to see the Embasador of Venice tomorrow, & continues unsertaine of her remove to London, by reason the K[ing] hath not directly sent to her to ... but only by S[ir] Edmond Dawse sent a message of his desire shee should doe so, w[hich] I find shee will not take notis of, nor bee att Whighthalle ... if an expresse messenger bee not sent heather tomorrow ...[55]

Anna was determined to assert herself and when necessary stand her ground with James, and she refused to do his bidding unless asked to do so in a manner she considered appropriate. When these situations arose it was up to courtiers like Lucy and Robert Sidney to attempt tactful negotiation as best they could.

But as Lucy settled into her role at court the Bedford finances showed no signs of improving. Conspicuous consumption was the order of the day and debt was its inevitable outcome. Thomas Howard, Earl of Suffolk, warned John Harrington of Kelston that the King was attracted by a well-dressed courtier. James 'doth admire good fashion in clothes' and Howard advised Harrington to 'give good heed hereunto' how he dressed:

> I would wish you to be well trimmed; get a new jerkin ... be sure it be ... diversely coloured, the collar falling somewhat down, and your ruff well stiffened ... We have had lately many gallants who failed in their suits for want of due observance of these matters. The king is nicely heedful of such points, and dwelleth on good looks and handsome accoutrements.[56]

Dressing the part was not just a question of aesthetics; it was crucial for social success and it cost vast amounts of money. When Robert Sidney met James at Combe Abbey shortly after the accession he attired himself in a suit of satin overlaid with silver lace, with a cloth of silver doublet and a velvet-lined cloak, his appearance topped off by a silver-laced saddle to match, all of which cost him well over £100. Furthermore, participation in masques was an expensive business, because courtiers were frequently required to provide their own costumes which were always sumptuous and often decorated with jewels. Lucy solved her financial problems by borrowing money which she was often slow or negligent in repaying. With some friends this fiscal tardiness did not cause problems, so she borrowed from her friend Jane Bacon and apologized profusely for her delay in making the repayment:

> ... the only cause yow have binne so long without hearing from mee was that I was ashamed to send till I could retorne yow that part of yo[u]r wealth yow have so long binne pleased to trust me with ... now if yow bee so crewel, as yow cannot forgive mee this fault please yo[u]r selfe in imposing any punishment on mee yow thinke my offence deserves & I shall willingly vndergo itt so itt may purchas my pardon ...[57]

But others from whom Lucy borrowed were much less accommodating than Jane about her failure to pay her debts promptly. Lucy's manner of dealing with her financial difficulties earned her an unhappy reputation as the 'court cormorant'.[58] Contemporary imagery concerning cormorants depicted them as voracious birds and therefore applying the epithet 'cormorant' to Lucy was derogatory. What made the name-calling worse was the fact that there was a constant visual reminder of these birds, because James had taken to keeping them at court and using them for fishing:

His Majesty constantly has a pair of them [cormorants] hooded at ... Court. This very day he was to fish with them in the Thames from a boat. They ... dive in the ponds or streams, and after remaining some while under water, come to the surface with the prey in their mouth, or even in their craw, as they are unable to swallow because their throat is bound with a lacet.[59]

Negative images of cormorants also appeared in a satire of a masque in which the masquers were described as holding whips in their left hands while in their headdresses rather than the more usual decoration of heron feathers: 'they wore Anticke crownes of Feathers plucked from Rauens wings, Kites and Cormorants (beeing all Birds of Rapine and Catching:)'.[60]

As 1604 drew to a close the social activity about the court grew frantic. Anna was in the midst of preparations for a sumptuous masque to be performed on Twelfth Night. Roles in this masque were highly sought after and the consequences of a lady being denied a part were felt well beyond the walls of the court. Lady Hatton was desperate for a part in the masque, but was not offered one. Her response to this situation was to leave the court and go to her own house where her husband bore the brunt of her disappointment as she refused to allow him to 'lye either with her, or within her Chamber'.[61] But as the Hatton marriage experienced strains and before Anna's masque was performed there was a marriage to be celebrated. One of James's great favourites, Sir Philip Herbert, married Lady Susan Vere. Philip was the younger brother of the Earl of Pembroke and was immensely popular with James. Just how high he stood in the King's esteem was indicated by his bride being led to the church by Prince Henry and Anna's brother, the Duke of Holstein, who was visiting England at the time. As James gave the bride away he indulged in some uncharacteristically flattering comments about the lady, claiming that 'if he were unmarried he would not give her, but keep her himself'.[62] After the ceremony the newly married couple and their friends celebrated with a special marriage dinner, and afterwards a masque was performed by gentlemen of the court. The couple spent their first night in the Council Chamber and were greeted the following morning by the King in his night gown who 'spent a good time in or upon the Bed'[63] of the newlyweds.

Twelfth day was a momentous occasion for many at court. For the four-year-old Prince Charles it was the day on which he was carried by nine earls to be created Duke of York. For the Harringtons there was a twofold honour. During the course of the day, John Harrington was made a Knight of the Bath. All the social ambitions, all the desperate striving, and all the money spent on furthering those aims was finally coming to fruition. In the evening, Lucy's closeness to the Queen was publicly displayed as she appeared on stage next to Anna in the eagerly anticipated masque. *The Masque of Blackness*, written by Ben Jonson with a set designed by Inigo Jones, was performed at the old Banqueting House at Whitehall and the sight that greeted the ladies, gentlemen and ambassadors who had had the good fortune to secure an invitation was highly dramatic. At one end of the vast room a moving display featured images of sea horses and terrifying fish ridden by Moors, while at the opposite end there was a huge scallop-shaped shell of mother of pearl in which were placed four seats. On the lowest of these seats sat the Queen and Lucy Russell. The other ladies seated on ascending tiers were Anne Herbert, sister of Pembroke and Montgomery; the Countess of Derby; Lady Penelope Rich, the Countess of Suffolk; Frances Bevill; Anne Effingham; Elizabeth Howard; Lady Herbert; Mary Wroth and Lady Walsingham. It is extremely unlikely that Jonson had any say in which ladies sat where, for that decision almost certainly rested with Anna and she used it quite deliberately as a means of publicly signalling which ladies were in her favour. Lucy's pre-eminent place next to Anna on the first tier was an honour made all the more impressive by the vagaries of fortune because it is more than likely that if the Countess of Hertford, who shared the position of lady of the innermost Bedchamber with Lucy, had not been ill with measles the two women would both have appeared on the first tier next to their Queen. Hertford's absence allowed Lucy an opportunity to shine, her presence undimmed by sharing the place with another of Anna's ladies. For a court insider able to read the symbolism of the seating plan, it would have been obvious who possessed real power and influence with the Queen and who had been invited to take part in the masque as a mark of special favour. If one wanted to seek a favour of Anna it would be pointless to approach the young Anne Herbert who was present as a favour to her more illustrious brothers, William and Philip, and her mother the Countess of Pembroke. It would, however, be worth approaching a woman like Penelope Rich who formed one of the core of regular participants in Anna's masques and was, of course, a powerful favourite like Lucy.

The lady masquers represented Ethiopian nymphs who had journeyed from their homeland to England in the hope of becoming white skinned. As Anna and her ladies took the stage the assembled audience saw a highly unusual sight. They watched as the Queen, who was six months pregnant, led out her women, all of whom were painted black on their faces and from their elbows to their hands. The nymphs were arranged in pairs and each pair carried a fan on which was represented a 'Hieroglyphick'[64] while the other nymph carried a fan with names inscribed on it. The names were intended to convey what each of the nymphs represented. Anna and Lucy represented Euphoris and Aglaia respectively and the painting on their fan was of 'A golden tree, laden with fruit'.[65] In her advanced state of pregnancy, Anna was in fact a highly visible representative of royal fertility and the name she assumed in the masque – Euphoris – which derives from the Greek for fertile, was therefore entirely appropriate. Lucy took the role of Aglaia, the first of the three Graces and, like Euphoris, she was associated with fertility and productiveness. In Neoplatonic thought Aglaia was associated with splendour or spiritual beauty and she and Anna may have been intended to represent 'royal and spiritual beauty fertilizing the earth'.[66]

Contemporary responses to the masque were mixed. A shocked Dudley Carleton felt that although the dress of the masquers was rich it was:

> too light and courtesanlike. Their black faces and hands, which were painted and bare up the elbows, was a very loathsome sight and I am sorry that strangers should see our court so strangely disguised.[67]

But Carleton's views should be taken with some caution. Molin, the Venetian ambassador who also attended, pronounced it 'very beautiful and sumptuous'.[68] The evening was rounded off with a magnificent banquet and the assembled company must have been ravenous because the food was so 'furiously assaulted' that the tables and trestles on which it was arranged collapsed before anything could be eaten.[69] But the appetites of some of the masque goers were not confined to food. Carleton further reported that a lady had been discovered 'surprised at her business',[70] that is, in a sexually compromising position on the terrace of the Banqueting House. The reputation for masques as occasions for a decline in moral standards was thoroughly confirmed.

Toward the end of 1605, Jonson appealed to Lucy to intercede on his behalf in a highly problematic matter which concerned a play he had collaborated in writing with John Marston and George Chapman. The play in question was called *Eastward Hoe!*, a comedy which depicted city life in London and brought all three of its writers into conflict with the authorities. The problem was chiefly that two passages in the play were perceived to espouse anti-Scottish sentiments. The first of these passages referred to a knight who had 'stolen' his knighthood, thus making an unwelcome reference to the selling of honours which James had been indulging in as a means of propping up his ailing finances. This perceived slur was compounded by the line – 'I ken the man weel, hee's one of my thirty pound knights'[71] – which committed the double offence of mocking the King's accent and his finance-raising measures. The second offensive passage alluded to the presence of Scots in Virginia, which was populated 'by onely a few industrious Scots' who are useful to England only 'when they are out an't'.[72]

Performed and then printed, the threat of heavy punishment for those involved in *Eastward Hoe!* was real. It was suggested that the culprits should have their ears and noses cut, a painful mutilation seen as fitting punishment for those who dared attack the King. Imprisoned for his part in the play, Jonson wrote to every influential friend he could think of including Pembroke, D'Aubigny, Montgomery and Cecil among others. He also wrote to one unnamed woman, almost certainly Lucy, who moved in the same circle as Pembroke and Montgomery and whose friendship and patronage Jonson enjoyed. Although Jonson apologized for dirtying Lucy's hands with 'prison polluted Paper' his anger at what had happened to himself and Chapman was tangible, as he claimed, 'our offence a Play, so mistaken, so misconstrued, so misapplied, as I do wonder whether their Ignorance, or Impudence be most, who are our aduersaries'.[73] Jonson was well aware that not every member of an audience was capable of fully understanding what he presented. Commenting on the 'devices' he had contributed to the arch raised at Fenchurch for James's coronation he was aware that different spectators would see and understand different things:

> ... vpon the view, they might, without cloud, or obscuritie, declare themselues to the sharpe and learned: And for the multitude, no doubt but that their grounded iudgements did gaze, said it was fine, and were satisfied.[74]

Jonson was satisfied that people saw different things but for spectators wilfully to misconstrue what had been written in a play incensed him. That Jonson asked Lucy to intercede on his behalf indicates that he recognized how powerful she was and it was the combined influence of all whose help he enlisted and his consistent and continued pleas of innocence that eventually saw both he and Chapman released with their ears and noses intact.

The furore over the play had barely settled down when two months later an audacious and sinister plot to kill James was brought to light. A group of men had been discovered with barrels of gunpowder under the Houses of Parliament in Westminster. Robert Catesby, Thomas Percy, Thomas Winter, John Wright and Guy Fawkes had planned to blow the King and his Parliament to pieces. Terrifying and deeply shocking, the plot shook London and it touched the Harringtons closely, for the plans of the conspirators were not confined to the capital. They had also decided to snatch Princess Elizabeth and place her on the throne to rule in stead of her father. In early November 1605 John Harrington received a message from one of his neighbours that some horses had been stolen in the night by a group of men believed to be papists. Alarmed, Harrington sent frantic letters to London but received no reply and in the end had the presence of mind to take his young charge away from Combe and lodge her safely with a merchant in Coventry. Despite the fortuitous outcome, the event profoundly shocked Harrington and caused him to fall victim to a fever from which he was slow to recover. He saw clear historical parallels in the plan to kidnap Elizabeth, for in his view the plot was one which would 'shameth Caligula, Erostratus, Nero, and Domitian, who were but each of them fly-killers to these wretches'.[75] And he saw too that the men involved in such a heinous plan exhibited the physical signs of their malevolent intent, for as he told John Harrington of Kelston, 'I have seen some of the chief, and think they bear an evil mark in their foreheads, for more terrible countenances were never looked upon'.[76]

As John Harrington nursed his fever up at Combe, down in London there was a wedding to be celebrated. On 5 January 1606 the Earl of Essex's son,

Robert, married Frances Howard, daughter of the Earl of Suffolk. The wedding was marked by the performance of a double masque called *Hymenaei* written by Ben Jonson and designed by Inigo Jones, and it seems to have been arranged by friends of the couple. Lucy's participation in the masque stemmed from her elevated place at court and her longstanding friendship with members of the Essex family. More recently, however, her brother, John, had been waiting on Prince Henry in the company of the prospective bridegroom, Essex. The Harringtons had no strong links with the Howard family, whom they perceived as political competitors; indeed the marriage between a Howard and a member of the Essex family was intended to create a bond between the two rival factions. Lucy was one of eight female masquers who represented the nuptial powers of Juno, and each woman was dressed in white. A spectator of the masque reported that the lady dancers had 'a white plume of the richest herons fethers [sic], and were so rich in jewels vpon their heades as was most glorious. I think they hired and borrowed all the principal jewels and ropes of perle both in court and citty'.[77] As the newly married couple watched the masques given in their honour there was no inkling that the marriage of Essex and Frances would end in murder and a sordid trial in which the sexual adequacy of the bridegroom would become a matter of public discussion. Such matters lay well in the future, but the presence of Lucy as a masquer celebrating the marriage of Essex would have repercussions later in her relationship with John Donne.

As a supporter of writers, Lucy was the recipient of much complimentary verse, but the relationship between a patroness and a writer could also deteriorate. In 1606 Michael Drayton issued *Idea The Shepheards Garland*, a revision of a set of eclogues which had first appeared in 1593. In the eighth eclogue he concealed himself under the pseudonym Rowland, a faithful shepherd who pipes or writes poetry for a woman called Selena, that is, Lucy. According to Drayton's verse Lucy has ignored him in order to attach herself to 'deceitefull *Cerberon*', who is a:

> ... beastly clowne to [sic] vile of to be spoken,
> and that good shepheard [Rowland] wilfully she leaves
> and falsly al her promises hath broken,[78]

Cerberon is usually taken to refer to Ben Jonson with whom Drayton had a difficult relationship, but what is astonishing about the verse is the deeply personal attack Drayton aimed at Lucy. Her desertion of him earned her what amounted to a curse:

> Let age sit soone and ugly on her brow,
> no sheepheards praises living let her have
> to her last end noe creature pay one vow
> nor flower be strew'd on her forgotten grave.

> And to her last of all devouring tyme
> nere be her name remembred more in rime.[79]

Yet an aggrieved Michael Drayton was only one of the problems Lucy seems to have had to deal with in 1606. Two puzzling letters hint at bigger difficulties for her. On 8 August 1606 Tobie Matthew wrote to Dudley Carleton asking him: 'What was the reason that drove La: of Bedford thence [sc. from Court] and particularly how thrives shee, whom they needes persuade me I was in love withal?'[80] One of Dudley Carleton's letters to John Chamberlain, also written in 1606, refers to the disorderly festivities during a visit to the English court of Anna's brother, King Christian of Denmark, and also seems to allude to a flirtation or affair that Lucy had had with another of Anna's brothers, Ulric, Duke of Holstein:

> My Lady of Bedford had the grace to be sent for one day to the court; and she had not the grace but to come, where she was openly laughed at by the queen as she began to dance, and all she said to her (not having seen her since her discourting) was that her brother of Denmark was as handsome a man as the duke of Holstein.[81]

The festivities which Carleton referred to occurred in late July 1606 when the court decamped to Theobalds, Robert Cecil's country residence, to entertain Anna's brother, King Christian of Denmark, with 'carousal and sports of all kinds'.[82] The gathering was a sumptuous affair and inside the house there were women and copious amounts of wine. On one day a great feast and a short dramatic performance depicting Solomon and the Queen of Sheba were organized, but the best-laid plans went very much awry after the assembled party drank to excess. When the Danish king attempted to rise and dance, he was so inebriated that he fell over and had to be removed to an inner chamber to recover on the royal bed still smothered in the wine, cream, jelly, cakes and spices which had been spilled upon his person. Undeterred by the loss of the guest of honour, the planned entertainment went ahead, despite the fact that the performers were overcome by the heady effects of wine and were largely incapable of standing up. Of the ladies taking the roles of Faith, Hope and Charity, only Charity managed to perform her part. Faith and Hope made abrupt departures to the lower hall in order to vomit. An account of the proceedings was given by John Harrington of Kelston, but his words need to be treated with caution. Although Harrington's description of events is both vivid and compelling, it has been pointed out that 'alcoholism was Christian IV's trait, not James's', although as early as 1604 Anna had sarcastically confided to Beaumont, the French ambassador, that 'the king drinks so much, and conducts himself so ill in every respect, that I expect an early and evil result'.[83] A far stronger reason for treating Harrington's account with caution is that by 1606, after not having benefited as he had hoped under James, he was a 'disappointed and resentful man'.[84] Yet even if Harrington gave an unbalanced version of proceedings, his view was circulated and it must have played some part in shaping contemporary opinions about what happened at court. Apart from the two kings, Harrington did not name any of the participants, although it seems that Anna was not present, and with her royal mistress absent it is unlikely that Lucy attended either. Yet for many it would not matter who was or was not in attendance; all that was clear was that courtiers spent their time engaged in wickedness.

Anna's comparison of her two brothers – Christian and Ulric – to Lucy may have some link with Tobie Matthew's enquiry as to why Lucy left the court. In fact, Matthew's use of the word 'drove' suggests that she was chased from the court. Written in 1606, Matthew's letter refers to Lucy's attendance on Anna toward the end of 1605, and it is possible that the matter was linked to the Duke of Holstein's sojourn in England.

Ulric, Duke of Holstein, first visited England in 1604, hoping to raise an army of men to serve in Hungary. The Venetian ambassador Nicolo Molin described him as 'a young Prince of twenty-four without much knowledge of the world, who speaks and acts with great freedom'.[85] From the moment he set foot in England Ulric caused problems with the French and Spanish ambassadors. Primarily these difficulties arose from Ulric's complete failure to observe diplomatic etiquette and his innate rudeness. Yet despite raising the hackles of the French and the Spanish, he was active at court, taking part in the celebrations for the marriage of Philip Herbert, and in 1605 conducting a magnificent tournament. Ulric lived a 'life of pleasure', a life which may well have included an affair with Lucy.[86] It is possible that a relationship with Ulric was what 'drove' Lucy from the court and led to Anna taunting her that 'her brother of Denmark was as handsome a man as the duke of Holstein'. Lucy was a married woman, but she spent long periods apart from Edward who was content to stay at his country estates. Moreover, at the time there was a widely held perception that marriage was a convenient and discreet front for sexual licence. Such views certainly permeated the drama of the time:

> *Beaumelle:* I prithee tell me, *Florimell*, why do women marry?
> *Florimell:* Why truly Madam, I thinke, to lye with their husbands.
> *Bellapert:* You are a foole ... women marry husbands. To lye with other men.[87]

Lucy was both attractive and flirtatious. Mary Wroth alluded to her flirting with Pembroke, and Lucy may have engaged in similar behaviour with Holstein and then became tempted into a relationship with the handsome young prince. Perhaps Mary was remembering Lucy's flirtations when in her great prose work, *The First Part of the Countess of Montgomery's Urania*, she cast her as 'Lucenia', a woman who for her 'noble behauiour, courtesie, wit, and greatnesse of understanding' was 'loved, and admired of all such as could bee honord with her conuersation'.[88] But when the married Lucenia set her eyes on an unnamed prince 'shee who before had knowne love rather by name then subjection, now ... finds her selfe loves Prisoner ... now she finds it expedient to know that delightfull cruell, who had with so pleasing a dart, wounded, and ceazed her ... heart'.[89]

If Lucy did have an affair with Holstein, Anna and James would not have been greatly concerned by the morality of such an undertaking provided her marriage remained intact. The most infamous court lovers at the time were Penelope Rich and Lord Mountjoy who had been conducting an adulterous relationship for years. This state of affairs received no comment from James or Anna until Penelope obtained a divorce, and she and Mountjoy decided to marry. On his accession James had reinstated laws pertaining to divorce, and in 1604 bigamy became a felony punishable by death. James could turn a blind eye to lovers in his court, but the public flouting of his marriage laws was a step too far. As a consequence of their marrying, Penelope and Mountjoy did not receive the death penalty, but they did lose their privileged places at court.

When Ulric first arrived in England he was widely welcomed and his diplomatic gaffes were tolerated, but as his stay continued his relationship with Anna soured. According to the Venetian ambassador Nicolo Molin, the falling out between brother and sister was because:

> the Duke claimed to go into the Queen's rooms whenever he chose; she did not like this. He would not take the hint, and the Queen gave orders that he was not to be admitted without being announced. One day he went as usual, but when he was informed of these orders he broke out into impertinences. Whereupon the Queen declined to see him again, and he fell into disgrace with the King and Court.[90]

Ulric eventually left England 'very unwillingly'[91] in June 1605 and Lucy may have become the subject of Anna's derision for her involvement with a brother the Queen had grown to detest. For Anna, it would be far better for one of her ladies to choose the alcoholic Christian than the boorish Ulric. As Lucy grew older she wisely exchanged affairs of the heart for the much safer passion of gardening, telling Jane, 'I am so much in love with [the garden] as if I wear so fond of any man I wear in hard case'.[92]

4

Hermaphroditical Authority

The commonweal … in Twicknam is.

JOHN DONNE, 'TO THE COUNTESS OF BEDFORD'

It is fairly certain that Lucy Russell and John Donne knew of each other long before any friendship developed between them. Resident in London during the late 1590s, Donne could not help but be aware of Essex and the men and women surrounding him. One of the Earl's secretaries, Henry Wotton, was a friend of Donne's, and it may have been through the agency of Wotton that in 1596 John Donne joined the Cadiz expedition led jointly by Essex and Lord Howard of Effingham. On his return from Cadiz, Donne volunteered for another of Essex's ventures: an expedition to the Azores, which set sail in late October 1597. However, by November Donne was back in London and had secured employment as a secretary to the Lord Keeper, Sir Thomas Egerton, who lived at York House on the Strand.

It was at York House that Essex was imprisoned in 1599 after his ignominious return from Ireland and, going about his duties for the Lord Keeper, Donne saw the disgraced Earl and perhaps glimpsed Edward Russell among the Earl's supporters saluting their friend from the adjoining garden. At Christmas 1599 Donne wrote to a friend describing the various activities taking place about the court, adding 'My lorde of Essex and his trayne are no more mist here then the Aungells which were cast downe from heaven'.[1] Given that Lucy and Edward were a part of Essex's 'trayne' of fallen angels, and taking into account the close-knit world of Elizabethan London, Lucy Russell and John Donne would at the very least have known each other by sight. However, although their paths may sometimes have crossed they probably held little or no interest for one another. Toward the end of the 1590s Donne was busy with his work and secretly wooing his bride to be, Ann More, while Lucy was fully immersed in her life in London.

By 1602, however, Donne was definitely aware of events concerning Lucy and Edward, because in February of that year he wrote to a friend, 'I hope somebody else hath had the ill luck to tell you first, that the young Bedford is dead'.[2] The 'young Bedford' was Lucy and Edward's son who died while they were banished from the court and living at Chenies. By a strange coincidence, just as the Bedfords were limited in their movements at the time, so too was Donne. He wrote the letter while restricted to his London lodgings as a punishment for his marriage to Ann without the permission of her father, Sir George More. The recipient of the letter was Henry Goodyer, a close friend of both Donne and the Harringtons. Goodyer owned the estate of Polesworth in Warwickshire, which he had inherited on the death of his father-in-law and uncle, also named Henry Goodyer. The Goodyers were well known to their Warwickshire neighbours, the Harringtons, and the ties between the two families were sufficiently close for John Harrington to be one of the men chosen to oversee the will of the elder Sir Henry.

When the younger Sir Henry inherited Polesworth he encountered an estate saddled with debts, and his financial woes were further exacerbated by his tendency to overspend, particularly on hunting and hawking, of which he was especially fond. Henry Goodyer was a hospitable man 'ever pleasant and kind'[3] and many men enjoyed the benefits of his generosity. Under the tutelage of Goodyer, Ben Jonson learned to appreciate the finer points of hawking:

> Goodyere, I'am glad, and gratefull to report,
>   My selfe a witnesse of thy few dayes sport:
> Where I both learn'd, why wise-men hawking follow,
>   And why that bird was sacred to APOLLO,
> Shee doth instruct men by her gallant flight,
>   That they to knowledge so should toure vpright,
> And neuer stoupe, but to strike ignorance ...[4]

Henry Goodyer also lent support to Michael Drayton when he first sought the patronage of Lucy and the Harringtons. When Drayton dedicated *Matilda* to Lucy in 1594, the prefatory material contained within it a sonnet bearing the initials 'H.G.', that is, Henry Goodyer. By disguising his identity with initials Goodyer was following a well-established practice. Using initials rather than the full name enabled both disclosure and discretion. Men and women who knew, or knew of, Goodyer could identify him through the initials, but those who had no idea who was represented by 'H.G.' remained excluded. The initials created a privileged readership for a printed, and therefore publicly available, book. It also clearly signalled Goodyer's support of Drayton to the Harringtons.[5]

Sir Henry's talents did not lie in poetry, something he himself was aware of. In later years he was given to borrowing verses from the works of his more talented friend, Donne, in order to boost his own literary efforts. But Goodyer's lines in praise of the virginal Matilda were not intended to be of great literary merit; they were penned to help Drayton in his quest for patronage:

> Me thought I saw upon *Matildas* Tombe,
> Her wofull ghost, which Fame did now awake, / ...

> To view this Legend, written for her sake; / ...
> Glory shee might, that his [Drayton's] admired Muse,
> Had with such method fram'd her just complaint:[6]

Donne's knowledge of Goodyer's link with the Harrington and Bedford families was probably the reason why he mentioned the death of Lucy and Edward's son in his letter. The fact that he referred to the death of the baby at all indicates that he was observing events affecting Lucy and Edward, just as he would later confess to studying every aspect of Lucy's life, from the people she chose as her friends to what she decided to read and write:

> ... I study you first in your Saints,
> Those friends, whom your election glorifies,
> Then in your deeds, accesses, and restraints,
> And what you reade, and what your selfe devize.[7]

As Elizabeth's reign ended and James came to the throne, John Donne must have watched the dramatic upturn in the Bedford fortunes with interest. For news and gossip about what was happening within the Harrington and Bedford families he could rely on Goodyer, with whom he corresponded on a weekly basis. By mid-1605 Henry was actively involved in helping Lucy broker a marriage between her brother, John, and Robert Cecil's daughter. Marrying a Harrington to a member of the Cecil family was another attempt by Lucy and her family to manipulate fortune. Edward's reluctance or inability to become actively involved in the politics of the new court was a disadvantage, but a high-profile marriage to a member of the Cecil family would enable the Harringtons to gain a valuable political foothold and further increase their social status.

Lucy's brother was an eminently suitable groom and it was this that Cecil seized upon as he attempted to extricate his daughter, and himself, from the proposed marriage. According to Cecil, the younger Harrington, being 'heir to his father's honour and fortune' and 'in himself extraordinarily qualified', was much too good for his daughter who, so he claimed, promised 'little worthy affection'.[8] Cecil's view of the merits of the young John Harrington was not exaggerated. Carefully educated by his parents, John was a serious and religious young man who had formed an extremely close relationship with the future king, Prince Henry.

It is clear from a letter written by Cecil that it was Lucy who attempted to arrange a Cecil–Harrington match by taking the lead as the 'principal person' in bringing the two parties together.[9] But Cecil had no intention of marrying his daughter to a Harrington. He wrote to John Harrington senior, tactfully disengaging himself from any such plan and at the same time revealing the tenaciousness with which Lucy pursued the scheme. Cecil recorded that he found Lucy 'so absolutely fixed upon a resolution to allow of no reason'[10] and, curiously, totally compliant in furthering the aims and ambitions of her immediate family. Cecil obviously found Lucy's commitment to the Harringtons' plans for their son and heir somewhat unusual, claiming that her 'obedience to your [her father's] commands ... is more ... than is usual in this age towards parents'.[11] Cecil claimed that he wrote to John Harrington senior to inform him that the marriage would not proceed rather than 'press her [Lucy] to write that which she does not approve'.[12] It is, however, more likely that Cecil wrote not in order to spare Lucy being the bearer of bad news but so that John Harrington could be in no doubt of how he felt and that Lucy might not be tempted to meddle further in the matter. Cecil informed Lucy of his decision by letter, as well as verbally via Henry Goodyer, who acted as a go-between in the negotiations. Lucy robustly defended her behaviour in regard to the marriage. Writing to Cecil she claimed: 'I am not so void of discretion as not to know that if my desires be unreasonable I ought to rest satisfied with such an answer as proceeds from more judgement'.[13] She deferred, tactfully, to Cecil's 'more judgement', but having the proposed marriage thwarted did not please her. Lucy's plans for John were her first attempt at matchmaking, an activity which continued to occupy her throughout her life and in which she always took defeat badly. Whether it was the 'scurvie dealing' of a father who wanted his daughter to marry someone other than whom Lucy had chosen, or when the prospective bride died before the marriage could take place, Lucy never accepted her failures at matchmaking willingly.[14]

Lucy's attempt to marry her brother into the Cecil family was motivated by the social and political ambitions of her family. The same attention to the interests of family members that had ensured an excellent marriage for her naturally extended to her brother. John was, after all, the Harrington 'house-heire' and on his shoulders rested the very high hopes of the family. But beyond the interests of family, Lucy had a deep and abiding affection for her brother, and it was John who occasioned what was probably the first direct contact between Donne and Lucy. In an undated letter, perhaps written shortly after he returned from a journey on the continent with Henry Chute in April 1606, Donne relied heavily on Lucy's affection for John in order to capture her attention:

> Amongst many other dignities which this letter hath by being received and seen by you, it is not the least that it was prophesied of before it was born, for your brother told you in his letter, that I had written; he did me much honour both in advancing my truth so farre as to call a promise an act already done, and to provide me a means of doing him a service in this act, which is but doing right to myself; for by this performance of mine own word I have also justified that part of his letter which concerned me, and it had been a double guiltiness in me, to have made him guilty towards you.[15]

The opening of the letter had something of 'th'entangling laborinths' about it as Donne interwove his writing with talk about the writing of the young John

Harrington.[16] The reason Donne gave for writing to Lucy was structured as a kind of moral imperative, which argued that had he failed to write he would have incriminated her brother. The letter consisted of philosophic speculation peppered with a little gritty pragmatism. Apologizing for not having written to Lucy at the same time as her brother, Donne argued that:

> It makes no difference that this [letter] came not the same day, nor bears the same date as his; for though in inheritances and worldly possessions we consider the dates of evidences, yet in letters, by which we deliver over our affections and assurances of friendship, and the best faculties of our souls, times and days cannot have interest nor be considerable, because that which passes by them is eternal, and out of the measure of time.[17]

Yet even as he spoke of 'the best faculties of … souls' and of the 'eternal', financial issues were not far from his mind as talk of 'inheritances' and 'worldly possessions' crept into the verse.

The wording of the letter was highly controlled. Donne had clearly burnt the midnight oil in his library to get it absolutely perfect, and his care over its wording is reminiscent of a letter he wrote some years later to introduce himself to Robert Carr, Viscount Rochester and the Earl of Somerset. In the letter to Carr, Donne explicitly called upon the support of another person, in this case Lord Hay, as a means of introducing himself in much the same way as he used John Harrington as a means of contacting Lucy:

> My Lord, I may justly fear, that your Lordship hath never heard of the name which lies at the bottom of this Letter; nor could I come to the boldnesse of presenting it now, without another boldnesse, of putting his Lordship [Hay], who now delivers it, to that office.[18]

In no other of Donne's surviving letters does he so obviously use this device, so lending weight to the view that, like the letter to Carr, the letter in which he referred to John Harrington was his first written approach to Lucy.

The circumstances of Donne's meeting with the younger Harrington are unknown, but the two may have been introduced by Goodyer. John Harrington was a precocious and educated youth, well versed in logic, philosophy, mathematics and languages, and his membership of Prince Henry's court would have made him an interesting and attractive figure to Donne, who was keen to enter the glittering circle gathered around Henry. By 1606 Prince Henry's court was evolving in a manner conducive to Donne's interests and temperament. Among other things, Henry was a passionate collector of books from both national and international sources, and a voracious reader like Donne would have jumped at the opportunity to peruse the Prince's ever expanding library. Donne may have viewed a friendship with John as a double blessing: enabling access to Lucy and perhaps also an entrée to Henry's court.

Having sent his letter to Lucy, Donne awaited a response. What kind of reception would she give it? Would she place it alongside the other letters in her 'Cabinet'?[19] To retrieve it would 'she o'r skip the rest'?[20] Persuing the lines would she 'read them twice', perhaps even 'kisse the name' of he who sent it?[21] In fact, Lucy did nothing of the kind. Despite all the time and energy expended on careful composition and the agonized waiting, Donne's letter did not lead to any sustained contact with Lucy. She accepted his 'best wishes, and ... noble love' but took his approach to her no further.[22] If John Donne wanted to attract Lucy's attention he would have to try a different approach.

Lucy Russell and John Donne were widely separated by rank and personal circumstance, but one quality they did share was ambition. Attitudes toward ambition were viewed differently in the early modern period, and talking about one's aims and attempting to achieve them was not automatically frowned upon by society. Indeed, according to Donne, ambition formed an integral part of the individual's religious duty, because when a man had 'kneaded up riches, and honor, and favour in a settled and established fortune' he was in a position to offer himself to God.[23] As Richard Hooker observed, ambition had consistently attracted negative ideas, for ambition 'as wee vnderstand it hath beene accompted a vice which seeketh after honours inordinately'.[24] But Hooker was at pains to make clear that:

> we ought not therefore with the odious name of ambition to traduce and draw into hatred euerie poore request or sute wherein men may seeme to affect honor; seeing that ambition and modestie do not alwaies so much differ from the mark they shoote at as in the manner of their prosecutions. Yea euen in this may be error also if we still imagine them least ambitious which most forbeare to stirre either hand or foote towards their owne preferments.[25]

Yet as Hooker argued for a more charitable view of ambition, some of his less enlightened contemporaries still enjoyed condemning any sign of it in others, so Anne Harrington was dismissed as 'an ambitious woman' by some of her peers.[26]

Raised in a household that assiduously pursued every advantage God had bestowed upon it, Lucy shared the same ambitious traits as her mother and her father, and it was this ambitiousness coupled with steely determination and a modicum of good fortune that brought her success. By the time she and Donne formed a friendship around late 1607, she was a powerful courtier. Lucy's successful pursuit, and acquisition, of power was probably one of the attractions she held for Donne, for although he derided those who gathered at court as 'vaine ... witlesse, and ... false'[27] he too was ambitious for his 'owne preferments' and needed the influence of friends at court to help him achieve them. In any event Donne was a pragmatic man who knew that in order to achieve one's aims it was sometimes necessary to find ways of overcoming personal objections:

> ... To make
> Courts hot ambitions wholesome, do not take
> A dramme of Countries dulnesse; do not adde
> Correctives, but as chymiques, purge the bad.[28]

Indeed, Donne made just such a distinction for his great friend and sometime court dweller, Henry Goodyer, telling him, 'for you living at Court without ambition, which would burn you, or envy, which would divest others, live in the sun, not in the fire'.[29]

In large part Donne's ambition originated in pressing economic need. His secret marriage to Ann More, which took place some time around the end of 1601 or early 1602, had incensed Ann's father Sir George More who took his revenge by attempting to thwart his unwanted son-in-law's career at every possible turn.[30] Donne was repeatedly denied positions for which he was qualified and by which he might earn his living. Even more galling was the fact that Sir George More was a chief officer, and therefore a major power broker, at Prince Henry's court and in addition to making the acquaintance of the younger John Harrington, Donne made strenuous attempts to enter this glittering circle. Yet despite all Donne's best efforts in this direction his way remained permanently barred. With his career options blocked and an ever-growing family to support, Donne desperately needed employment. Sympathetic friends like Henry Goodyer and Ann's sisters helped the Donnes in various ways, but John's inability to secure a position appropriate to his intellectual abilities took a physical and psychological toll on him. No evidence exists of how Ann felt about the situation caused by her marriage, but her husband's letters indicate that the couple experienced difficult times.

By 1607 Donne was dividing his time between Mitcham and London. He took lodgings in the Strand, a move which placed him on the most important and fashionable thoroughfare in London. As well as housing some of the most socially prominent families in the kingdom, the Strand was beginning to emerge as a commercial centre for luxury goods. A number of china shops located on the street were joined early in 1609 by the Burse, an upmarket shopping centre developed by Robert Cecil, Earl of Salisbury, on the site of the former stables of Durham House. Taking lodgings in the Strand enabled Donne to locate himself at the very epicentre of power, wealth and influence, but it did not in itself put an end to his difficulties.

Yet around mid-1600 John Donne was not the only Londoner with problems; Francis Bacon had a few worries of his own. In the early 1580s Francis had, along with his brother Anthony, been a friend and employee of the Earl of Essex, and the Bacon brothers had derived considerable benefits from this relationship. But as Essex began to fall from Elizabeth's favour, Francis took steps to distance himself from his friend and former benefactor. After the abortive uprising and Essex's execution, Bacon cooperated with Cecil by writing and disseminating anti-Essex texts. These accounts of the actions of his former friend and benefactor were often spurious, and their content profoundly disturbed friends of the disgraced Earl. On the accession of James, Bacon began to suffer the consequences of his actions, because the new king was sympathetic to Essex and his former supporters and viewed Bacon with suspicion. One consequence of this wariness on James's part was that potentially lucrative appointments were not offered to Bacon and, over time, his financial problems deepened. One measure he took to resolve his monetary problems was to dispose of a property he owned at Twickenham and which for years he had used as a place of retreat from the pressures of the court and his political life in London. This created a fortuitous opportunity for Lucy as taking a leaf out of Bacon's own thinking on the workings of fickle fortune – 'the folly of one man is the fortune of another'[31] – she acquired Twickenham Park for herself. Acting on Lucy's behalf, Henry Goodyer arranged the lease of Twickenham Park in 1607. Tellingly, Edward's name was never mentioned in relation to the property.

Twickenham Park spanned two parishes and consisted of nearly one hundred acres of land, part of which bordered the Thames. It was conveniently located close to Hampton Court, so within easy reach should Anna or James be resident there and suddenly demand Lucy's presence. It was also to prove close to where John and Anne Harrington would attend Princess Elizabeth, who was moved from Combe Abbey to a new establishment at Kew in 1608. Twickenham was also convenient for Richmond Palace, where Prince Henry kept a country court and where Lucy might easily visit her brother, John.

Surviving plans show that the Twickenham property was dominated by a garden which was considerably larger than the house. Lucy was no stranger to beautiful gardens. She had spent her childhood amid the dazzlingly colourful parterres and carefully tended lawns and walks at Combe Abbey. When she married and moved to Bedford House, her new London garden was located on the site of a former convent garden. The grounds at Bedford House were well laid out and intersected by pleasing walks. But the garden at Twickenham Park was on a different scale altogether from those at Combe or Bedford House. A surviving plan of Twickenham Park drawn by Robert Smythson around 1609 shows that the garden was surrounded by a brick wall within which lay rows of hedges. The outermost hedge was comprised of quickthorn, the next of topiary trees cut into the shape of animals, the third made up of rosemary and the innermost hedge planted with fruit trees. In the centre of the garden there was a circle around which lay other circles; three of these circles were planted with birch trees, two with limes and the outermost with fruit trees. At each corner of the garden a flight of steps led to a raised platform planted with trees and from these elevated points the whole garden could be viewed. The arrangement of the garden was clearly emblematic and represented the pre-Copernican universe. The circle in the centre of the garden represented the 'Earth followed by Luna, Mercury and Venus (birch circles), Sol and Mars (lime circles), Jove (fruit trees circle) and Saturn (beyond)'.[32] Who exactly was responsible for the design and planting of the garden at Twickenham Park is not clear. Bacon, the former occupant of the house, was a keen gardener and it has been suggested that the raised platforms at the corners of the garden are in fact mounds, landscaping features of which Bacon was particularly fond.[33] However, that the layout of the garden at Twickenham was probably the work of Lucy rather than Bacon is suggested by its close similarities to a garden created by her friend, William Herbert, at Wilton. A visitor to Herbert's garden described how the gardener had:

> made walks, hedges and arbours, of all manner of most delicate fruit trees, planting them and placing them in such admirable art-like fashions, resembling both divine and moral remembrances, as three arbours standing in a triangle, having each a recourse to a greater arbour in the midst, resemble three in one and one in three; and he hath there planted certain walks and arbours all with fruit trees, so pleasing and ravishing to the sense ... Moreover, he hath made his walks most rarely round and spaceous ... and withal the hedges betwixt each walk are so thickly set one cannot see through from one walk who walks in the other ...[34]

The Wilton garden, with its trees arranged in 'art-like fashions' and the 'divine and moral remembrances' contained within its geometric shapes strongly echoes Smythson's plans of Twickenham. Given Lucy and William Herbert's close relationship it was natural that they shared ideas, plans and plants, as they set about creating their respective gardens. When she developed her other famed garden, Moor Park, Lucy eagerly sought plants from friends. She wrote to Jane:

> This monthe putts mee in mind to intreate ... som of the litle white single rose rootes I saw att Broome, & to challinge Mr Bacons promis for som flowers, if about yow ther be any extraordinary ones, for I am now very busy furnishing my gardens.[35]

But she was equally willing to return the favour, telling Jane, 'thus yow see itt is not good being to free an offerer to a free taker, but be not discouraged, for I shall be as free a requiter whensoever yow shall make mee know itt is in my power'.[36]

The creation of a garden was both time-consuming and expensive, but for the individual fortunate enough to possess one it served the 'two commodities' of 'vtilitie and delight: the vtilitie, yeeldeth the plentie of Herbes, floures, and fruytes right delectable: but the pleasure of the same procureth a delight, and ... a iucundite of minde'.[37] The idea of 'vtilitie and delight' was directly analogous with the idea of 'profit and delight', the words Philip Sidney had used to describe the function of poetry in his highly influential work, A Defence of Poetry. Gardens provided 'profit' in the form of 'Herbes' and 'fruytes' and like poetry they also soothed the mind. As with poetry's sister arts – music and dance – gardens were actively concerned with the 'wittie ordering' of their component parts and the imposition of order on a blank space.[38] Standing upon the raised pavilions at the corners of a garden and watching the patterns created by the plants and trees was the same as looking down upon the steps taken by the dancers in a masque. Both were art and both had a positive mental influence on the viewer.

Lucy's development of the garden at Twickenham coincided with works Anna had commissioned for Somerset House and Greenwich under the direction of the garden designer and engineer Salomon de Caus. The career of de Caus exemplifies how at the time a garden was not separate from, but formed an integral part of, the artistic spectrum. As an engineer, de Caus was 'an artist and an artisan, a military man, an organizer of court festivities'.[39] Inigo Jones might as easily design a set for a court masque as collaborate with de Caus and an architect on designing a magnificent garden. For Lucy, Anna, Prince Henry, Princess Elizabeth, William Herbert and others, a garden created an exceptional opportunity to display wealth and power as well as advertise their artistic credentials.

Where Francis Bacon had used Twickenham as a bolt hole, Lucy used it to entertain friends. Resident with her at Twickenham, and indeed her London houses, at various times were two of her kinswomen: Bridget Markham and Cecilia Bulstrode. A third woman who lived with, and waited upon, Lucy was Jane Meautys, the daughter of Hercules and Philipa Meautys of Essex. Jane was to marry twice – first to Sir William Cornwallis and, after Cornwallis's death, Nathaniel Bacon – and she and Lucy maintained a close, lifelong friendship. Bridget, Lady Markham, was the daughter of Sir James Harrington, Lucy's uncle. In 1598 Bridget married Sir Anthony Markham but he died in 1604 leaving his widow with three young children to raise. Bridget was one of the ladies of Anna's Bedchamber, a position which Lucy may have had a role in obtaining for her. Lucy certainly offered her cousin and her children hospitality and kindness, providing them all with a home in her household.

Cecilia Bulstrode was related to Lucy through the Keilway branch of the family, and, like Bridget, she was a lady-in-waiting to Anna. But where Bridget appears to have been a quiet figure, Cecilia seems flamboyant and mischievious. Few firm facts about Cecilia can be recovered, but her name appeared in connection with a libel about James which circulated in early 1605. Precise details as to the nature of this text are sketchy but it greatly exercised Sir Edward Coke and Cecil, who attempted to track down the author of the offending work. Despite grilling several witnesses, including a Mistress Russell who served in Lucy's household, Coke and Cecil drew a blank. Mistress Russell could tell them only that she didn't know who wrote it nor anybody who had a copy 'saving only Mrs. Boulstrode, that waits on the Countess of Bedford'.[40] Cecilia may simply have been doing nothing more than amusing herself by reading the latest anti-James tract, but she was playing a dangerous game in possessing an 'outrageous and unchristian' work which was deeply upsetting to the King.[41]

Yet Cecilia seems to have had scant regard for how her behaviour was viewed. Around mid-1600 she was widely alleged to be the lover of Sir Thomas Roe. Roe had served Queen Elizabeth as an Esquire of the Body, a position which primarily involved him guarding the monarch by night. After Elizabeth's death, he proved adept enough to secure a good position in the new reign, and soon after James's accession he received a knighthood. His connections with the new court were cemented by the friendships he forged with Prince Henry and Princess Elizabeth. Roe served Princess Elizabeth at Combe Abbey and was therefore a familiar figure to the Harringtons and to Lucy. He was also a close friend of Donne, Jonson and Southampton. Given Roe's relationship with Cecilia and his friendship with Lucy, he almost certainly visited the ladies at Twickenham and probably spent time with Cecilia there, although a much more likely venue for the couple's liaisons was the chamber Cecilia occupied at court. Cecilia's chamber might provide a discreet love nest, but it was also used for a quite different purpose, for the playing of a sophisticated writing game known as 'News'.

Games were a common pastime among the women who formed Queen Anna's court, even if not all the ladies found them as enjoyable as the Queen. Arbella Stuart famously wrote to her uncle complaining that Anna had her ladies out playing games from ten in the evening until two or three o'clock the following morning.[42] Popular indoor games often revolved around the subject of love, such as those in which the players chose booklets to foretell their romantic futures.[43] But there were other indoor games which had a quite different purpose and were designed to place intellectual demands on their participants to devise witty sayings that 'obliquely incorporated gossip and political intrigue'.[44] These games were not only enjoyable for their own sake; they were also an important part of the social fabric of the court because 'through them moved information, innuendos, reputations, and the makings of useful or possibly harmful ties among courtiers'.[45]

The 'News' game was enjoyed by a group of men and women that included Cecilia Bulstrode, Sir Thomas Roe, Sir Thomas Overbury, Lady Southwell, John Donne and probably Henry Wotton and Anne Clifford. There is no firm evidence that Lucy herself played but she may well have done; the game would have provided her with an excellent opportunity to 'devise' texts of her own. But even if Lucy did not play herself, she was almost certainly aware of the existence of the game and the identity of its players, not only because most of them were her close friends, but because Cecilia's participation in the game led to tensions between her and Ben Jonson.

Although Cecilia waited on Anna she was not a high-ranking courtier and her modest place within the court hierarchy meant that she spent a great deal of time removed from royal activity. Cecilia's distance from the centre of power at court meant that her chamber would have been located away from those of the Queen and courtiers of higher rank like Lucy. Potential 'News' players could visit Cecilia without going near the main court, and as they gathered at leisure in her room somebody suggested playing a round of the game.

The game commenced with a player being given or selecting a theme, perhaps 'the sea', 'the court' or 'the country'. The chosen player then constructed a sequence of witty sayings which consisted of news appropriate to the location from which they were writing. Each of the clauses began with the word 'That' or 'it is said here' or 'it is thought here'. Players intially composed their sayings on paper and then read their work aloud to the assembled group. Players on the opposing team then attempted an 'answer' in the form of an antithetical response.

So John Donne wrote *Newes from the very Countrey* which began:

> That it is a Fripery of Courtiers, Marchants, and others … The Iesuits are like Apricockes, heretofore, here and there one succour'd in a great mans house, and cost deere … That Women are not so tender fruit, but that they doe as well, and beare as well vpon Beds, as plashed against walles.[46]

Donne's contribution to the game exemplifies how the news items ranged over such diverse themes as the court, city, religion and sexuality while using imagery appropriate to where the passage was located, in this case the country. Donne's 'News' was countered by an *Answere to the very Countrey Newes* which was probably penned by Anne Southwell:

> That Nature too much louing her owne, becomes vnnaturall and foolish. That the soule in some is like an egge, hatched by a young Pullet, who often rigging from her nest, makes hot and cold beget rottennesse, which her wanton youth will not beleeue … That I liuing neere the Church-yard, where many are buried of the Pest, yet my infection commeth from *Spaine*, and it is feared it will disperse further into the Kingdome.[47]

Topically, Anne claimed that she feared the threat posed by Spain far more than falling victim to the more immediate threat of 'infection' by plague. This witty turn of phrase would have played well to the vehemently anti-Spanish politics of the assembled group. Men like Roe were close to Prince Henry, who advocated militant Protestantism and strongly opposed the overtures that James, who was inclined to pacifism in matters of foreign policy, was making to the Spanish.

Jonson's difficulties with Cecilia originated in a deeply disparaging poem he wrote about her which related directly to the 'News' game. Many years later, in 1619, when he was visiting his friend William Drummond, Jonson revealed that he had written a poem about Cecilia that had been stolen out of his pocket when he was drunk and presented to Mistress Bulstrode: 'that piece of the Pucelle of

the Court, was stollen out of his pocket by a Gentleman who drank him drousie
& given Mistress Boulstraid, which brought him great dispeasur'.[48] Entitled *An
Epigram on the Court Pucell*, Jonson's verse was a vicious and highly personal
attack on Cecilia in which, amongst other things, he made specific reference to
her ability to play the 'News' game well:

> Do's the Court-Pucell then so censure me,
>   And thinkes I dare not her? let the world see.
> What though her Chamber be the very pit
>   Where fight the prime Cocks of the Game, for wit?
> And that as any are strooke, her breath creates
>   New in their stead, out of the Candidates?
> What though with Tribade lust she force a Muse,
>   And in an Epicoene fury can write newes
> Equall with that, which for the best newes goes,
>   As aerie light, and as like wit as those?
> What though she talke, and cannot once with them,
>   Make State, Religion, Bawdrie, all a theame? / ...
> Shall I advise thee, *Pucell*? steale away
>   From Court, while yet thy fame hath some small day ...[49]

In branding Cecilia a 'Pucell' Jonson was calling her a prostitute and he went
on to employ even more disparaging sexual imagery. Cecilia was a whore who
surrounded herself in her chamber with the self-explanatory 'Cocks'. She was also
accused of forcing the literary muse – always represented as a woman – in the
manner of a lesbian, that is, with 'Tribade lust'. The image of Cecilia engaged in
the lesbian rape of the muse of poetry was considerably more than just a snide
remark and related to the fact that the ladies of the 'News' group were given
to greeting one another with the salutation, 'my worthy Muse'.[50] Jonson may
therefore have been making a crude sexual allusion, accusing Cecilia of some kind
of physical relationship with one of her fellow lady players. Not only was Cecilia
sexually suspect she was, according to Jonson, woefully lacking in literary talent,
unable to achieve the necessary integration of the themes of state, religion and
bawdry which was the desired result of all the best 'News'.

Such a vicious poem would have caused upset, distress and anger for
Cecilia and her friends. And Lucy was a fiercely loyal friend. When Lady
Roxburgh, a lady-in-waiting to Anna, displeased the Queen it was made clear
that she would be expelled from the royal Bedchamber. However, despite Anna's
obvious displeasure with Roxburgh, Lucy remained a staunch supporter of the
unfortunate lady, telling her friend Jane:

> of the Queens court I can say litle good, for her [Anna's] resolution to part with
> Roxbrough still continues w[hi]ch makes her looke big vpon all shee thinkes loves that

good woeman … I am one, that price her favor [Anna's], but vpon such an occasion can not be sorry for her frowns, w[hi]ch are now litle to mee.[51]

Lucy's loyalty to her friend and relative Cecilia would have caused her to view Jonson's behaviour with distaste, and one wonders what Cecilia had done to Jonson to deserve such an outpouring of vitriol. The anger that induced Jonson to write the poem may have originated in the ladies of the News group mocking him for his efforts on behalf of his friend, Sir Thomas Overbury. Overbury had allegedly fallen madly in love with the Countess of Rutland, Philip Sidney's daughter, and had expressed his feelings in a poem which he had Jonson recite to her. News of Jonson's role as a go-between for the love-struck Overbury made him look like a 'pander', and the ladies of the News group, no doubt encouraged by Cecilia, soundly mocked him. Jonson was more than capable of distributing wounding insights on people he knew, but he was less sanguine when the same was done to him. Cecilia paid a heavy price for upsetting Jonson. Yet despite all the unpleasantness surrounding the poem, Jonson remained fond of it even years later. Listing the pieces of poetry he most enjoyed reciting, he confessed to his friend Drummond that one of them was 'Verses on the Pucelle of the Court Mistriss Boulstred'.[52]

The possibility that Lucy reacted in some way to Jonson's attack on Cecilia is suggested by a letter which Jonson wrote to Donne. Bearing the contemporary title 'A Letter from Ben. Johnson to Doctor Donne, in clearing himself upon a former accusation', the letter is undated and refers to an unnamed woman who may well be Lucy.[53] Jonson complains of being 'misunderstood' and is clearly concerned that this lady has heard disparaging things about him. He tells Donne that 'My Lady may believe whisperings, receive tales, suspect and condemn my honestie; and I may not answer, on the pain of losing her; as if she who had this prejudice of me, were not already lost'.[54]

The lady in question has promised not to do Jonson any 'hurt'; she will 'think and speak well of any faculties' he possesses, but Jonson is still uneasy. One of his greatest fears is that he will lose Donne's friendship – 'the losse of you my true friend' – something which in fact never happened.[55] If Lucy did rebuke Jonson over his poem and refuse to believe his protests that he never intended it to leave his pocket, the rift between them was not a permanent one.

Yet as Jonson was enjoying the sometimes tumultuous friendship and patronage of Lucy, John Donne still sought her good offices. Lucy knew about Donne's situation and activities through various sources including his fellow 'News' players and friends, but in all likelihood it was Henry Goodyer who initiated the contact between them. Goodyer was actively employed by Lucy around 1607 – as evidenced by his undertaking the Twickenham property transaction on her behalf – and was therefore in a good position to make the necessary introductions between his two friends. At the time of their meeting Donne was simply one man among many seeking powerful friends to help him. He was not a professional writer like Jonson or Daniel, and the circumstances of his marriage would have caused some courtiers to be cautious in their dealings with him. It would not do to upset a powerful man like Donne's father-in-law, Sir George More. Lucy's brother was a member of Prince Henry's court, a group within which Sir George More was a major figure. There is no doubt that if there was any possibility that her brother's position might be jeopardized by her contact with Donne, Lucy would never have entered into the friendship.

If Goodyer felt hesitant about introducing Donne to Lucy, his instincts were sound. As Ben Jonson made clear, Lucy could be exceptionally generous:

> Madame, I told you late how I repented,
> I ask'd a lord a buck, and he denyed me;
> And, ere I could aske you, I was preuented:
> For your most noble offer has supply'd me.[56]

Yet she was not always receptive to every demand made on her good offices. There was no sign she responded to Donne's earlier letter to her and she studiously ignored the overtures of no less a man than her relative John Harrington of Kelston to write epigrams on her behalf. She also turned a deaf ear to the desperate pleas of her cousin, Henry Harrington, who was imprisoned for debt and called upon her for help. Henry responded by writing a poem in which he made it clear that Lucy's behaviour toward him had a direct influence on the behaviour of others who might have been in a position to offer him assistance:

> Sublunary things do move
> As the celestiall do,
> And if you'd begin to love
> The world would do so too.
>
> But if you should once begin
> To frown upon my state,
> The world would then account it sin
> To cherish what you hate.[57]

Prefixed to the poem was a short note explaining the origins of the verse:

> Mr H. Harrington to the Countess of Bedford, he being her kinsman and in prison for debt; his friends neglecting him for fear of displeasing her in regard of her distasting and being angry at some of his unthrifty courses.[58]

The idea that the profligate and permanently indebted Lucy might be 'angry' at some of Henry's 'unthrifty courses' is frankly comic and indicative of both a hypocritical and judgemental streak in her nature. Lucy not only had the choice of denying help; she could also cause others to withhold their assistance. Her power and influence were such that 'fear of displeasing her' was a potent enough reason to deny help to a friend.

Just as Lucy knew about Donne through her friends, he too had a good sense of various aspects of her character from those same friends. Ben Jonson, Cecilia Bulstrode, Thomas Roe, Edward Herbert, and of course Goodyer could tell him what interested her, how she liked to be addressed, what amused her, vital details that could make all the difference in attempting to win a patroness. Goodyer gave Donne careful advice on how best to approach Lucy and other powerful persons of rank. In an undated letter, Donne makes it clear that Goodyer has made helpful suggestions to him. He speaks of Goodyer's 'counsaile' and of how he has 'obeyed you thus far, as to write'.[59] But Donne did not follow Goodyer's advice unthinkingly; he might also choose to decline it if after careful consideration he felt so inclined.

Having 'swallowed' Goodyer's opinion of Lucy's 'worthiness' Donne appears to have written a complimentary verse letter for her in the hope once again of winning her patronage. In December 1607 both Lucy and Henry Goodyer were immersed in rehearsals for an upcoming masque and Donne realized that the effort involved in preparing for a masque would distract her from any other matters, so Goodyer was charged with choosing the right moment to deliver the letter.

Donne's letters to Lucy, and indeed to his other friends and acquaintances, are of paramount importance because he repeatedly made it clear that for him the writing of a letter amounted to a great deal more than an opportunity to pass on news and information. For Donne, writing a letter was tantamount to a spiritual activity, and he consistently associated letter writing with the soul, 'I make account that this writing of letters, when it is with any seriousness, is a kind of extasie, and a departure and secession and suspension of the soul, w[hi]ch doth then com[m]unicate it self to two bodies' and again, 'more then kisses, letters mingle Soules; / For, thus friends absent speake'.[60]

Such sentiments were hardly surprising in a man who wielded the pen as a poet and, for a time, worked as a secretary. Years later, long after he had left Mitcham behind and entered holy orders, Donne's ideas about what it meant to write a letter persisted, transformed by:

> The Spirit of God that dictates them in the speaker or writer, and is present in his tongue or hand, meets himself again (as we meet our selves in a glass) in the eies and eares and hearts of the hearers and readers.[61]

Donne's views on the spiritual dimension of letter writing meant that he was deliberately casual about dating his correspondence:

... in letters, by which we deliver over our affections and assurances of friendship, and the best faculties of our souls, times and days cannot have interest ... because that which passes by them, is eternal, and out of the measure of time.[62]

When a confused Goodyer complained about the lack of dates on the letters Donne was sending him, Donne apologized to his friend for 'writing ... without dating' and for having 'made the chronology and sequence of ... letters perplexed to you'.[63] Yet despite Goodyer's plea for clarification, Donne remained unrepentant about not dating letters because 'in the offices of so spiritual a thing as friendship, so momentary a thing as time must have no consideration'.[64] For Donne 'houres, dayes, months' were nothing more than 'the rags of time'[65] and so the chronology of what he wrote when did not cause him to be the least bit 'perplexed'.

The absence of firm dates for many of Donne's letters creates enormous difficulties in tracing the chronological development of the friendship between Lucy and Donne with any degree of accuracy. Imposed dates are always arbitrary and highly susceptible to error. Like the muddled Goodyer it is sometimes necessary to be content with accepting Donne's letters on their own terms, observing the 'affections, and assurances of friendship' he offered to Lucy and listening to these two 'absent' friends 'speake' outside the constraints of time.

The first verse letter Donne may have sent Lucy, 'Reason is our Soules left hand', was a work of praise in which Donne revealed how he had watched Lucy, learning about her friends and activities from people like Cecilia, Roe, and Goodyer:

> ... I study you first in your Saints,
>> Those friends, whom your election glorifies,
> Then in your deeds, accesses, and restraints,
>> And what you reade, and what your selfe devize.

Donne must have fervently hoped that Lucy would also glorify him with 'election' to her friendship. He quickly realized the futility of trying to understand why she was so loved: 'But soone, the reasons why you'are lov'd by all, / Grow infinite, and so passe reasons reach'.[66] Furthermore, she was the 'first good Angell ... / That ever did in womans shape appeare'.[67] In fact she was 'Gods masterpeece' and implicit in the closing lines of the poem was a request for her help:

> ... you are then Gods masterpeece, and so
> His Factor for our loves; do as you doe, / ...
>> For so God helpe mee, ...
>> For all the good which you can do me here.[68]

Lucy was referred to as a 'Factor', a word which carried several meanings all of which could be applicable to how Donne viewed Lucy. In a primary sense 'Factor' denotes a person who makes or does something, including a performer or the author of a literary work; the word also carries a secondary meaning which refers to an individual who acts as an agent or representative for another. In choosing the word Donne could simultaneously allude to Lucy's role as a masque performer and perhaps as a writer, as well as the role he hoped she would assume for him – as an agent of patronage.[69] As an agent and as a patroness, Donne made it abundantly clear in his poem that Lucy could do him considerable 'good'. Yet there existed a tone beneath the standard language of compliment which suggested that Donne was still not entirely comfortable with having to seek patronage. So Lucy, a staunch Protestant, was treated to theologically loaded phrases like 'Catholique' and 'Heretique'[70] as Donne wove a sense of ambivalence into his writing. This sense of an undercurrent occurred frequently in poetry Donne wrote for Lucy and yet in spite of, or perhaps because of, such piquancy Lucy liked what she read. What lady could resist being likened to an angel or thought of as a 'masterpeece' of God? Lucy responded to Donne so that he gained a personal knowledge of her. Sometime around the end of 1607 or early in 1608 he finally managed to attract the good offices of a patroness powerful enough to assist him in achieving his long frustrated ambitions.

Many of Donne's letters concerning Lucy fell into a category of letter writing commonly used at the time, which has been termed 'for showing', as distinct from letters which were for the strictly private perusal of the addressee.[71] A letter intended 'for showing' represented 'a degree of intimate plain-speaking which is nonetheless carefully tailored to the sensibilities of the third and more powerful reader to whom the whole performance is finally directed'.[72] An elaborate and complex network of primary and secondary readers participated in establishing and cultivating the friendship between Lucy and John Donne. So Donne sometimes wrote to Goodyer aware that Lucy would also read the letter that he had in fact carefully crafted for her eyes. The difference between the two kinds of letter writing appears in two letters Donne wrote to Henry Goodyer at various times. The first was a late letter for Goodyer's eyes only and Donne ordered his friend to destroy it after it had been read:

> Of my Lady Bedford, I must say so much as must importune you to burn the letter; for I would say nothing of her upon record, that should not testify my thankfulness for all her graces. But upon this motion, which I made to her by letter, and by Sir Thomas Roe's assistance ... she was somewhat more startling, than I looked for from her ... I would you could burn this letter before you read it; at least do when you have read it.[73]

The second letter intended 'for showing' to Lucy was written to Goodyer and carried a copy of a second, enclosed letter which Donne had already sent to Lucy. Donne provided some witty social chit chat and then concluded:

These, sir, are the salads and onions of Micham, sent to you with as wholesome affection as your other friends send melons and quelque-choses from Court and London. If I present you not as good diet as they, I would yet say grace to theirs, and bid much good do it you. I send you, with this, a letter which I sent to the Countess. It is not my use nor duty to do so, but for your having of it there were but two consents, and I am sure you have mine, and you are sure you have hers. I also wrote to her Ladyship for the verses she showed in the garden ... I would write apace to her, whilest it is possible to express that which I yet know of her, for by this growth I see how soon she will be ineffable.[74]

Donne's letter was filled with the imagery of exchange fundamental to his patronage relationships with both Lucy and Goodyer, while the country analogies from Mitcham recall the imagery he had used in News from the Very Countrey. The news Donne conveyed to Goodyer was termed 'salads and onions', good honest rural produce rather than the more upmarket 'melons and quelque-choses' which court friends were in the habit of exchanging with one another. Goodyer was invited to read a copy of the letter Donne had written directly to Lucy. Goodyer was therefore cast as the intermediary in the letter writing and reading chain. Moreover, he was instructed to show the letter Donne had written directly to him to Lucy. In fact it was important to Donne that Henry did just that. Lucy would then discover, by artful accident, just how eagerly he awaited the arrival of some of her own poetry which she had shown him as they walked together in her garden at Twickenham. She would also read the complimentary words about herself, of how she would soon become 'ineffable'. Donne's letter was intended to impersonate an idealized conversation Lucy's friends might have about her in her absence. But the conversation was an elaborate fiction: firstly because her friends might not be so effusive in private and secondly because Lucy participated in the impersonation by overhearing, or more correctly, overseeing a discussion of herself.

Lucy was not the only lady with whom Donne corresponded. Around the time he was becoming personally acquainted with Lucy, Donne was in regular contact with Magdalen Herbert. Mrs Herbert was a widow whom Donne had met in the late 1590s when she was resident in Oxford while her two sons attended university there. A friendship developed between Donne, Magdalen and her eldest son, Lord Edward Herbert. After her sons left Oxford, Magdalen moved to London and took a house near Charing Cross where Donne was a frequent visitor. Magdalen and her sons were the distant relatives of the better known Herberts – William and Philip – and in 1606 Edward resigned his rights to Montgomery Castle after Philip Herbert was created Earl of Montgomery. Lucy also knew Edward Herbert, perhaps through his relative William Herbert, and the relationship between the three was obviously close. In his autobiography Edward recalled an incident in which his tailor demanded half a yard more of satin than was usual for making him a new suit, claiming that the extra cloth was needed because he had grown taller. Edward told the tailor:

> I knew not how this hapned but howsoeuer he should haue halfe a yard more and that when I came into England I would cleare the Doubt, for a litle before my departure thence I remember That William Earle of Penbrooke and my selfe did measure haights together at the request of the Countesse of Bedford and hee was then higher then I by about the Breadth of my litle finger: At my returne ... I measured againe with the same Earle and ... found my selfe taller then hee by the Breadth of a litle Finger.[75]

But Lucy did more for Edward than just measure how tall he was. She also used her position as a court insider, privy to gossip, to confirm some alarming news that Robert Sidney had for Herbert. According to Edward, Robert Sidney:

> sent mee word that Sir John Aers intended to kill mee in my Bed and wisht mee to keepe a Guard vpon my Chamber and person, the same ... was confirmed by Lucie Countes of Bedford ... shortly after.[76]

In a society given to outrageous and overblown claims, the threat to Edward's life was remarkable for its being real. Sir John Ayers claimed that Edward 'had whored his wife' and he intended to take his revenge.[77] While Edward protested that he was 'not ingaged in any affection towards her',[78] Ayers' wife revealed herself to be totally besotted. Wearing an enamelled miniature picture of Edward strung on a chain and hidden 'vnder her brests' he came upon her in her chamber one day lying on her bed looking at the aforesaid picture.[79] She then turned her gaze upon him 'with more earnestnesse and Passion than I could haue easily beleiued'.[80] Consumed by jealousy Ayers did make an attempt on Edward's life and inflicted a flesh wound; the matter was sufficiently serious for it eventually to be referred to the deliberations of the Privy Council for resolution.

Lucy's friendship with Edward meant that she was well aware that Donne wrote to his mother. But what Donne wrote to Magdalen was rather different from what he wrote to Lucy. The most obvious difference between the letters Donne sent to the two women was that he always wrote directly to Magdalen and never employed the strategy of the 'showing' letters that were such a dominant feature of his written communications with Lucy. The 'showing' was part of an elaborate patronage strategy which was unnecessary in his relationship with Magdalen, for although Donne consistently associated her with 'goodness' and she clearly offered him practical assistance during difficult times, she could not provide him with the contacts and influence that a power broker like Lucy could. Donne was grateful for Magdalen's many kindnesses, her 'favours ... are everywhere; I use them and have them. I enjoy them at London, and leave them there, and yet find them at Mitcham'.[81] With no need to impress a patroness Donne's letters to Magdalen were less studied than those he wrote to Lucy.

Donne recognized the lightness of his tone and enjoined Magdalen not to burn the letters he sent her, arguing that though each in itself was lightweight, they became substantial when read together:

> I would not burn my first letter; because as in great destiny no small passage can be omitted or frustrated, so, in my resolution of writing almost daily to you I would have no link of the chain broken by me, both because my letters interpret one another, and because only their number can give them weight.[82]

Donne's relationship with Magdalen meant that on occasion he was able to raise potentially sensitive issues like flattery. Flattery was something Florio had broached with Lucy in his dedication of his *A Worlde of Wordes*, and it was something Donne discussed rather more frankly in a letter to Magdalen, telling her to 'remember that nothing is flattery which the speaker believes; and of the grossest flattery there is this good use, that they tell us what we should be'.[83] He then promptly flattered Magdalen claiming, 'But, madam, you are beyond instruction, and therefore there can belong to you only praises'.[84] Beneath the slightly flippant tone, Donne revealed himself prepared to use flattery if it helped him gain the good offices of a patron or patroness. Like Magdalen, Lucy was a recipient of Donne's flattery and like Magdalen she was shrewd enough to see it for what it was.

Despite the differences between how Donne addressed himself to Magdalen and to Lucy, there were some common links. He compared both women to royalty. Magdalen was saluted as 'you, who are not only a world alone, but the monarchy of the world yourself'[85] while Lucy's house at Twickenham was deemed a 'commonweal', the domain of a king or queen. Perhaps more importantly, Donne viewed both women as representatives of virtue. To Magdalen he paid the compliment 'the greatest virtue in the world, which is you'[86] and he consistently wrote of Lucy as the epitome of virtue. Donne conceived virtue as 'light': 'Vice and her fruits may be seen, because they are thick bodies, but not virtue, which is all light'.[87] This association coincided happily with Lucy's name which derived from Lucina, meaning light, and which poets, including Donne, delighted in playing upon in the poetry they addressed to her. Lucy Russell was variously the bright, the light, the shining.

As 1608 slipped by, Donne badly needed the help of powerful friends. He mentioned Lucy in a letter that described her 'despatching in ... haste for Twicknam' and of how she had given 'no word to a letter' which he had sent her.[88] The lack of a reply to his letter was perhaps less troubling now he was assured of her interest in him, but it still worried him sufficiently for him to mention it to Goodyer. Donne's anxiety was closely related to his mood upon taking up his pen. Donne usually wrote letters in his library surrounded by his books; sometimes he wrote as he rode along the highway, but this particular letter was written in a thoroughly domestic location. Donne told Goodyer, 'I write from the fireside in my parlour, and in the noise of three gamesome children'.[89] But the pleasing image of a man sitting down to write to a good friend surrounded by his playful children was shattered as he went on to recount that he sat 'by the side of her, whom ... I have transplanted into a wretched fortune'.[90] Beside him sat his pregnant wife, suffering the consequences of the 'wretched fortune' as Donne's spirits began to fall. Even the arrival of spring could afford no comfort:

> Because I am in a place and season where I see everything bud forth, I must do so too ... The pleasantness of the season displeases me. Everything refreshes, and I wither, and I grow older and not better, my strength diminishes, and my load grows ...[91]

Ann gave birth to a daughter and in early August Donne wrote to Goodyer and told him that Lucy had agreed to give her name to the new baby and act as her godmother. Donne invited Goodyer to attend as well. He was at pains to point out how grateful he was to Lucy, 'I covet any occasion of a grateful speaking of her favours'.[92] Lucy's role as a godmother suggests considerable intimacy with Donne and his family. Perhaps Donne's mind was already racing ahead to the benefits that might befall his daughter with the Countess of Bedford as a friend and protector, because like any father Donne had high hopes for his children, later claiming that if he 'had fixt a Son in Court, or married a daughter into a plentifull Fortune, I were satisfied for that son and that daughter'.[93] Talk at the christening extended to literary matters as four days after the event Donne wrote to Goodyer enclosing a 'translation' of some kind for Lucy:

> I spoke of this to my L[ady] of Bedford, thinking then I had had a copy which I made long since at sea, but because I find it not I have done that again: when you find it not unseasonable, let her see it ...[94]

Yet if Donne was gladdened by Lucy's attendance at his daughter's christening, and as he busied himself with making a translation for her, his mood was not to last. He reported illness within his family and that his wife had fallen into 'discomposure' as his mood of introspection and melancholy deepened:

> I have often suspected myself to be overtaken ... with a desire of the next life; which though I know it is not merely out of a weariness of this ... I would not that death should take me asleep. I would not have him merely seize me, and only declare me to be dead, but win me and overcome me.[95]

Around this time Donne completed work on *Biathanatos*, a prose treatise on suicide which he may have written as an attempt to rationalize and confront the feelings he was experiencing. In the preface to the work he described a failed suicide attempt by the Calvinist Theodore de Beze, adding:

I haue often such a sickly inclination. And, whether it bee, because I had my first breeding, and conversation with Men of a suppressed and afflicted Religion, accustomed to the despite of death, and hungry of an imagin'd Martyrdome … whensoeuer my affliction assayles me, me thinks I haue the keyes of my prison in myne owne hand, and no remedy presents it selfe so soone to my heart, as mine owne sword.

Often Meditation of this, hath wonne me to a charitable interpretacion of theyr Action, who dye so …[96]

It is extremely unlikely that Donne seriously intended to take his own life. The graphic image of a man holding the keys to his life in his 'owne hand' formed part of the rhetorical structure of the preface and should not be taken as a statement of intent. However, the exploration of suicide in the work was wholly compatible with what Donne was writing to Goodyer at the time. Many years later Donne was at pains to make clear that *Biathanatos* was a product of an earlier part of his life, before he entered the ministry when he was simply 'Jack Donne, and not … Dr. Donne'.[97] His attitude toward the work was deeply ambivalent. Prior to his journey to Germany with James Hay in 1619, he sent a copy of it to his friend Robert Carr, later Earl of Ancrum, instructing him, 'Reserve it for me, if I live, and if I die I only forbid it the presse and the fire; publish it not, but yet burn it not, and between those do what you will with it'.[98] Part of the ambivalence was no doubt related to Donne's fears for his personal safety in his forthcoming travels, but part of it was concerned with his anxieties over how such a piece of writing might be received.

Despite his melancholy Donne continued to visit Lucy. Around the end of September he planned to 'sup with the good Lady' and a little later he informed Goodyer that having just arrived in London he had not as yet 'offered to visit my Lady Bedford'.[99] Lucy therefore saw and supported John Donne at one of the lowest points in his life and she understood very clearly the great benefits that friendship could bring in moments of personal crisis:

I … affectionatly desier to … have my selfe the comfort of a freind [sic] by mee (when any opression lies heavie on my hart) to whom I might trust my cares, & be shuer they should not only be safely lodged, but beget a desier as farre as wear possible, or att least advise how to make them lightest.[100]

Sympathetic yet pragmatic Lucy would have had no hesitation in advising Donne on how to make his cares 'lightest'. She would have urged him to 'not loose [sic] couradge … as to yeald vp the strength of … resisting reason, & consent to sincke vnder that melancoly' and, most importantly of all, to place his trust firmly in God believing, 'yett doe I not doubt but by the assistance of almighty God I shall ear long ouercom all those difficulties [which] att the present contest with mee'.[101] But Donne's troubles increased as his melancholy became compounded by physical illness. He wrote of having:

contracted a sickness which I cannot name nor describe. For it hath so much of a
continual cramp, that it wrests the sinews, so much of a tetane, that it withdraws and
pulls the mouth, and so much of the gout ... that it is not like to be cured ...[102]

At the time illness was believed to betoken spiritual sin and the sufferer was
enjoined to take the opportunity presented by illness to 'sift through one's
spiritual inventory, to test one's faith, to engage and to exemplify tolerance,
patience, and humility'.[103] And this was exactly what Donne did, claiming that if
'I continue thus, I shall have comfort in this, that my B. Saviour, exercising His
justice upon my two worldly parts, my fortune and body, reserves all His mercy
for that which best tastes it and most needs it, my soul'.[104]

In November 1608 Donne rallied himself sufficiently to make yet another
attempt to secure employment, this time as a secretary for James in Ireland, a
position which had become vacant on the death in October of Sir Geoffrey Fenton.
Donne was in London and had been to 'sup' with Lucy and other company at
Bedford House.[105] The dinner conversation that evening revolved around the
King's departure for Royston to engage in some hunting, and of how he had left
instructions with Anna to begin thinking about a masque for Christmas. Over
dinner Lucy and her guests were already beginning to give serious consideration
to the forthcoming masque and although she had planned to visit Edward at
Chenies within the next week or so, the necessary arrangements for the upcoming
masque meant she would not be able to spend as long with him as she had
planned. The projected masque turned out to be a work by Jonson called *The
Masque of Queens*. Anna had taken James's command seriously and expressed her
own ideas of what should be incorporated into the masque, because when the
text of the masque was published Jonson complimented '*Bel-Anna* ... of whose
dignity, and person the whole *scope* of the *Invention* doth speake throughout'.[106]
The masque was a continuation of *The Masque of Blackness*, which had been
performed three years earlier.

Lucy's role in the *Queens* masque was as Penthesilea, Queen of the Amazons,
and a sketch of the costume she wore which was designed by Inigo Jones showed
her clothed in a transparent fabric which revealed her right breast and stomach,
while her left breast was lightly covered by a sash which was intended to refer to
the Amazonian practice of removing a breast in order to optimize the warrior
woman's ability with a bow and arrow. The costume was clearly erotic, but the
public exposure of a woman's breasts and nipples, often with the veins in the
breast painted for added emphasis, was by no means an uncommon practice
in masque performances, which were always presented to a privileged and elite
coterie audience. The court 'allowed its women to display their breasts, [but]
other areas of the female body, such as the arms and shoulder, could not be
shown without breaking with decorum'.[107] As a courtly woman, Lucy's breasts

and stomach were displayed to the view of the King and other male and female courtiers and probably to masque makers like Daniel, Jonson and Jones who oversaw the productions of their work. But Lucy's aristocratic body was never exposed in such a way publicly. So, when she invited friends to 'sup' with her she may have worn a dress which featured a deep décolletage, but which limited the sight of her breasts and stomach.

Donne used the dinner at which *The Masque of Queens* was first mooted as an 'occasion to employ all my friends' assistance in gaining the position of Irish secretary.[108] Lucy and James, Lord Hay, promptly offered him their help. At first Donne was somewhat suspicious of the ebullient Hay who 'promised so roundly, so abundantly, so profusely' to assist him, but Donne soon came to the happy conclusion that Hay was not like so many of his ilk for 'having spoke like a courtier, [he] did like a friend'.[109] Donne's comments about Hay reveal the deep uncertainty involved in asking courtiers to put in a good word on one's behalf, an activity that more often than not brought forth fulsome promises that were never fulfilled. It was difficult for Donne to overcome his prejudices against the inhabitants of the court and to accept the need for pragmatism: to 'awake and stare the Court in the face'.[110] But he was eased toward this by the ever helpful Goodyer who arranged contacts for Donne, something Donne was quick to acknowledge, telling Goodyer, 'I owe you what ever Court friends do for me'.[111]

Lucy's pre-eminent position in Anna's Bedchamber and her contacts with James and members of his court made her an ideal person to approach in order to promote Donne's interests. She had, after all, helped John Florio to become Anna's Italian tutor and enabled Daniel and Jonson to find employment as writers of court masques. It was a simple matter for her to remind her royal mistress or master of Donne's existence and suitability for a position. For those about whom she cared, Lucy was quite willing to put in a good word with the Queen and to push Anna along if she proved slow in performing what she had promised. As she assured Jane:

> I have not forgotten to putte the Queen in mind of her promis to yow, but in that as all others shee is slowe in performance, I will not bee so in soliciting her till yow have yo[u]r desier ...[112]

But the powerful combined influence of Hay and Lucy was not enough. Donne failed to obtain the position of secretary. Despite this disappointment, his fortunes finally began to take a turn for the better, not least because Sir George More was finally forced to relent in the matter of Ann's dowry and the couple received the money that had been so long withheld because of the unorthodox circumstances of their marriage.

It is clear that various literary friends visited and perhaps stayed with Lucy at Twickenham – most obviously John Donne and probably Ben Jonson, Samuel

Daniel, George Chapman, the musician John Dowland and others – but there is no evidence that she established any kind of formal salon for writers there.[113] At the time a circle of writers associated with an influential woman patroness was most obviously exemplified by the activities of Lucy's relative Mary Sidney, the Countess of Pembroke. At the family home of Wilton, Mary had provided support and encouragement for an earlier generation of writers and had herself collaborated in some of the works written by her brother, Philip. As a Sidney relative Lucy may well have visited Wilton as a child and observed some of the writers Mary supported. If so, Lucy would have viewed this as a further manifestation of the patronage example set by her own parents. The hope that Lucy might follow in the footsteps of Mary and actively encourage writers was certainly uppermost in the mind of John Harrington of Kelston when in late 1600 he sent her a book as a gift. Binding together some of Mary Sidney's translations of the psalms with verses of his own, Harrington told Lucy:

> I have sent you heere the devine, and trulie devine translation of three of Davids psalmes, donne by that Excellent Countesse, and in Poesie the mirrois of our Age; whom, as you are neere unto in blood, of lyke degree in Honor; not unlyke in favore; so I suppose none coms more neere hir then your self in those, now rare, and admirable guifts of the mynde, that clothe Nobilitie with vertue.[114]

At Twickenham, Lucy was involved in writing just as Mary Sidney had been at Wilton. Donne wrote to Lucy with respect and enthusiasm asking to see some verses she had showed him:

> Happiest and Worthiest Lady, – I do not remember that ever I have seen a petition in verse. I would not therefore be singular, nor add these to your other papers. I have yet adventured so near as to make a petition for verse, it is for those that your Ladyship did me the honour to see in Twicknam [sic] garden, except you repent your making; and having mended your judgment by thinking worse, that is, better, because juster, of their subject. They must needs be an excellent exercise of your wit ... I humbly beg them of your Ladyship ... Here therefore I humbly kiss your Ladyship's fair learned hands, and wish you good wishes and speedy grants.[115]

Around the same time Donne wrote in similarly enthusiastic terms to Goodyer about Lucy:

> I also wrote to her Ladyship for the verses she showed in the garden ... I would write apace to her, whilst it is possible to express that which I yet know of her, for by this growth I see how soon she will be ineffable.[116]

In the great garden at Twickenham Park surrounded by plants and trees that replicated the iconography of the stars and the moon, John Donne and Lucy walked and talked and exchanged poetry. Moving through the garden they contemplated the art of poetry within the work of art that was the garden. Perhaps Donne stopped to gaze carefully at the lady who walked by his side. If he did, such a concentrated focus on his companion was for a specific purpose which was 'for no other end but to know how to present you to God in my prayers, and what to ask of Him for you'.[117] Walking through the trees of Twickenham, John Donne and Lucy Russell must have made a fascinating pair. Donne claimed, perhaps disingenuously, that he had a 'hoarse voyce'[118] but his friend Isaac Walton gave a rather different view of him. Walton spoke of 'Mr. *Donne's* merits, together with his winning behaviour (which when it would intice, had a strange kind of elegant irresistible art)'.[119] Walton's choice of language, with the illicit connotations of 'intice' and the sense of lure in 'irresistable art', gives an impression of Donne as capable of casting a spell upon people which they were powerless to resist. But, blessed with both power and beauty, the 'bright and amiable' Lucy had plenty of charms of her own.

For Donne, Lucy's house at Twickenham was a world in its own right; to him it was a 'Commonweale'.[120] In contemporary usage the word 'commonweale' carried specific meanings:

> A common weale is deuided into the state of people whiche beare rule, & also into that powre where the beste, and wisest haue gouernaunce, and thirdly into ones hande whiche alone beareth the stroke and is chief magistrate.[121]

Poetry is not a factual record of actual events, but like the drama of the period it was sometimes used as a means of expressing ideas and sentiments that could not be openly articulated. At the time the word 'commonweal' had a powerful resonance because it played directly on ideas of kingship, rule and power. The commonweal was literally what the king ruled and in a verse letter addressed to Lucy, Donne relocated that commonweal to Twickenham, so imaginatively transferring power to her residence, making it in effect her state. In making such an association Donne was creating a replica of the idealized action of society with benefits flowing from the head of state, the king, down to his subjects. He was in effect alluding to Lucy as the head of state at Twickenham in an alternative corporate body of her own. Donne was not alone in taking this view: some of Lucy's contemporaries compared her home at Twickenham to the royal residence which had been established for Princess Elizabeth at Kew. Perhaps it was around this time of growing friendship and intimacy that Donne presented Lucy with the gift of a Latin book, *Auctores Latinae linguae*, which had been published in Geneva in 1595.[122] But Donne's gifts to Lucy may not always have been so weighty. It is possible that it was around this time he wrote a verse which has come to be known as 'Twicknam Garden'. This title was never given to the poem by Donne himself; it became affixed in various manuscript copies of the text and this may reflect the fact that contemporary readers knew that it was connected in some way with Lucy's house at Twickenham. 'Twicknam Garden' is a Petrarchan love poem:

> Blasted with sighs, and surrounded with teares,
>   Hither I come to seeke the spring,
>   And at mine eyes, and at mine eares,
>   Receive such balmes, as else cure every thing;
>   But O, selfe traytor, I do bring
>   The spider love, which transubstantiates all,
>   And can convert Manna to gall,
>   And that this place may thoroughly be thought
>   True Paradise, I have the serpent brought.[123]

If, indeed, Donne wrote the poem for Lucy, she is not figured within it: she is not the woman the speaker of the poem claims to be in love with. It is more than possible that the poem was written as a result of conversations between Lucy and Donne about the nature of this kind of verse.

As the relationship between Lucy and Donne blossomed she was keen to explore his earlier writing. She asked Jonson to obtain a copy of Donne's satires for her. Donne had never published any of his poetry; it was transmitted by manuscript between a group of readers who would copy verses they particularly liked into a commonplace book. Jonson may have had a set of Donne's satires of his own, or he might have gone to various friends and patrons, examined their books and copied the necessary poems. He duly sent a set of the satires to Lucy and, in friendly competitiveness with Donne, enclosed with them a verse of his own:

> Lvcy, you brightnesse of our spheare, who are
> Life of the Muses day, their morning-starre!
> If workes (not th'authors) their own grace should looke,
> Whose poemes would not wish to be your booke? / ...
> Rare poemes aske rare friends.
> Yet, *Satyres*, since the most of mankind bee
> Their vn-auoided subiect, fewest see:[124]

Donne's first three satires were written around 1593–94 so when Lucy read them she was reading poetry he had written as a young man of around twenty years of age. As she perused the work Lucy would have discovered amongst it poetry that derided the court world of which she was so much a part:

> ... I have beene in
> A Purgatorie, such as fear'd hell is
> A recreation to, 'and scant map of this.
> My minde, neither with prides itch, nor yet hath been

Poyson'd with love to see, or to bee seene,
I had no suit there, nor new suite to shew,
Yet went to Court ...[125]

Jonson was fully aware that Donne's satires included a scathing criticism of the court, and in his epistle to Lucy he spoke of 'They, then, that liuing where the matter is bred', that is, the poetic matter 'Dare for these poemes, yet, both aske, and read'.[126] Jonson expressed his respect for people like Lucy who had the courage, or who dared, to read verses which mocked their world. To Jonson these individuals were special; for 'though few' they were 'of the best'.[127]

Ben Jonson appears to have been recalling Lucy's activities at Twickenham and London when sometime in 1609 he began work on a play called *Epicene, or The Silent Woman*. The play was not performed until early in 1610 because the theatres were closed due to an upsurge in plague. When it was finally staged it caused Jonson difficulties, most notably because of a protest from Arbella Stuart, King James's cousin, who claimed that she had been misrepresented in the play. Jonson responded to Arbella's complaints by writing a prologue in which he claimed:

... poet never credit gained
By writing truths, but things (like truths) well feigned.
If any yet will, with particular sleight
Of application, wrest what he doth write,
And that he meant or him or her will say:
They make a libel which he made a play.[128]

Jonson stated, somewhat disingenuously, that he didn't write 'truths, but things (like truths) well feigned', therefore close to reality but with sufficient differences to make it difficult for anyone who felt they had been unfairly characterized to point to a specific example. However, Arbella was not the only person portrayed in *Epicene*. The character of Truewit, a witty man about town, is believed to represent Donne, while his friend Clerimont is thought to represent Herbert, and the character of Lady Haughty appears, at least in part to be based on Lucy. In the play Lady Haughty is described as running a 'new foundation':

Truewit: A new foundation, sir, here i' the town, of ladies that call themselves the Collegiates, an order between courtiers and country madams, that live from their husbands and give entertainment to all the Wits and Braveries o' the time, as they call 'em: cry down or up what they like or dislike in a brain or a fashion, with most masculine or rather hermaphroditical authority, and every day gain to their college some new probationer.
Clerimont: Who is the president?
Truewit: The grave and youthful matron, the Lady Haughty.

Clerimont: A pox of her autumnal face, her pieced beauty! There's no man can be admitted till she be ready, nowadays, till she has painted and perfumed and washed and scoured, but the boy here: and him she wipes her oiled lips upon like a sponge.[129]

The collegiate ladies who live apart from their husbands are a cross between 'courtiers and country madams', accurately described Lucy and her friends who spent some of their time as courtiers waiting on Anna and some time as country ladies at Twickenham. The idea that these ladies possessed a 'masculine or rather hermaphroditical authority' is closely linked with the idea of the learned woman as a masculine figure, precisely the kind of imagery that was so frequently associated with Lucy. The masculine woman was often presented in a complimentary sense. Daniel considered Lucy to have escaped the 'prison of her sex' and Jonson himself had applauded Lucy on her 'manly soule'.[130] Masculine imagery was also used by Mary Wroth, herself a writer, to describe Lucy as one who 'excelled her sexe so much, as her perfections were stiled masculine'. But there was a deeply negative side to the manly woman that became expressed through the Hermaphroditus myth. The story of Hermaphroditus occurs in Book IV of Ovid's *Metamorphoses*. Briefly summarized, the myth tells of how a son was born to Mercury and Venus. Named Hermaphroditus after his divine parents, the boy is raised by the naiads on Mount Ida until the age of fifteen. Attracted by the delights of travel, Hermaphroditus journeys to Caria where he spies a beautiful pool. Salmacis, the nymph who lives in the pool, spends her time bathing and caring for her appearance. Out gathering flowers one day she sees Hermaphroditus and overcome by his beautiful appearance and longing to possess him she tells him that if he is not already married she would like to be his bride. Embarrassed and annoyed by the nymph's persistent attempts to kiss him, Hermphroditus threatens to leave. At this, Salmacis withdraws and hides herself in some bushes from where, barely able to contain her desire, she observes the naked Hermaphroditus. When Hermaphroditus enters the pool, Salmacis leaps in after him, twining herself around his struggling body. Salmacis appeals to the gods to keep them together forever. The gods grant her wish and the bodies of Salmacis and Hermaphroditus become united as one.

This myth invited various literary interpretations during the period. A few writers took a positive view of the hermaphrodite. In the original ending of Book III of *The Faerie Queene*, Edmund Spenser alluded to the union of two loves as a 'faire *Hermaphrodite*'.[131] More commonly, however, the Hermaphroditus myth with its portrayal of an effeminate man attacked by an aggressive female played very directly on male fears of emasculation and feminization.[132] The figure of the hermaphrodite took on a frightening reality as around the mid-1600s London witnessed an upsurge in women assuming male attire and carrying weapons. Throughout the Elizabethan period there had been intermittent instances of women cropping their hair and dressing as men, for which they earned the scorn of writers like Phillip Stubbes who was of the view that 'these Women may not improperly be called *Hermaphroditi*, that is, Monsters of bothe kindes, half women, half men'.[133] But by the Jacobean period mannish women had become a much more common sight on the streets of London. The reasons why women chose to adopt this form of dress were complex. The pacifist foreign policy pursued by James meant that men were no longer engaged in waging war, which led to a perception that society had become dominated by effeminate males. This perceived effeminacy led to a blurring of the sexual roles, and some women felt that in order clearly to delineate the differences between male and female they themselves were forced to assume manly attire and behaviour. The idea of the mannish woman was also closely related to the autonomy that many of the women who lived in London enjoyed. Far more so than their sisters in other European countries, the women of London were relatively free to shop, socialize and visit the theatre without the supervision of their menfolk. By early 1620 the situation had become such that official steps needed to be taken. James ordered that in sermons preachers should 'inveigh vehemently and bitterly ... against the insolencie of ... women, and theyre wearing of brode brimd hats, pointed dublets, theyre haire cut short or shorne, and ... stillettaes or poinards, and such other trinckets of like moment'.[134] There is no evidence whatever that Lucy ever adopted male clothing or habit and if she had it would certainly have been remarked upon by her contemporaries. Yet Lucy's personal autonomy, the fact that she was far more powerful and influential than Edward, would inevitably have led to the view that she resembled a hermaphrodite in some way, even if only by exercising 'hermaphroditical authority', that is, by controlling or ordering her own life in the way that a man might order his life. Lucy did not strut down the Strand with her breasts bared and a pistol tucked into her breeches as some Jacobean women did, but she did move beyond the normal role assigned to a female of the period by asserting her own independence of thought and action. In his characterization of Lady Haughty, Jonson was perhaps playing with the idea of Lucy as a pseudo-hermaphrodite, revealing how she differed from her contemporaries, yet stopping short of vilifying her as an unnatural 'monster'. The difference between how Jonson tempered his allusion to Lucy in *Epicene* can be illustrated by the experience of Mary Wroth. When, in 1621, Mary published her prose work *The Countess of Montgomery's Urania*, Lord Denny believed she had made unwelcome references to events within his own family. Specifically, Denny was of the view that Mary was commenting on his attempt to murder his daughter Honora – the wife of James Hay – as a punishment for her adultery. Denny brought a court action against Mary and when it failed, he contented himself by writing a deeply disparaging poem about her:

Hermaphradite in show, in deed a monster
     As by thy words and works all men may conster
Thy wrathfull spite conceived in Idell book.[135]

Mary was portrayed as a 'hermaphradite', a 'monster', as Denny used exactly
the same language Stubbes had nearly forty years earlier. Yet most telling of all
was Denny's view that Mary should 'repent of so many ill spent years of so vain
a book' and instead follow the example of her famous aunt, Mary Sidney, and
'redeem' her 'time with writing as large a volume of heavenly lays and holy love
as you have of lascivious tales and amorous toys'.[136]

There are many passages in *Epicene* which suggest that Lady Haughty was
modelled on Lucy. In the play Haughty is described as being over fifty years old,
although when Jonson was writing Lucy was only about twenty-eight. Jonson
may have been deliberately misleading about the woman's age in order to ensure
that the true identity of the lady was 'feigned'. He certainly appears to have been
similarly vague about Lucy's age in another context. In a copy of Martial which
he purchased sometime in 1619 he wrote next to Epigram IX – 'In Gallam', a
poem which depicts an older woman making unwanted and highly inappropriate
sexual advances to a writer – the initials 'vel Lu. Co: B'.[137] The initials both mask
and identify Lucy. It is, however, extremely unlikely that Lucy would have made
any advances – either flirtatious or overtly sexual – to Jonson around or after
1619, when she was dealing with the deaths of Anna and her mother, and because
as she grew older she adhered closely to religion and such sexual impropriety
would have been wholly out of character. When Jonson inscribed his copy of
Juvenal with Lucy's initials, he may have been thinking of her flirting with him
years earlier. Jonson was certainly not averse to such advances, admitting to
Drummond that in his youth he was 'given to Venerie' and 'thought the use of a
maide, nothing jn comparison to ye wantonness of a wife & would never haue
ane other Mistress'.[138]

In *Epicene* the characters of Lady Haughty, Truewit, and Trusty discuss books
and diseases:

Haughty: And one of 'em (I know not which) was cured with *The Sick Man's Salve*, and
the other with Greene's *Groat's-worth of Wit*.
Truewit: A very cheap cure, madam ...
Haughty: Oh, Trusty, which was it you said, your father or your mother, that was cured
with *The Sick Man's Salve?*
Trusty: My mother, madam, with the *Salve*.
Truewit: Then it was *The Sick Woman's Salve*.[139]

The Sick Man's Salve was an enormously popular religious tract written by
Thomas Becon which instructed Christians on how best to conduct themselves
in illness and death. However, in the mid-1590s a Puritan divine called William

Perkins dedicated a book to Lucy also entitled *A salue for a sicke man*, perhaps in an attempt to capitalize on the success of Becon's work. For a contemporary reader who knew that Lucy had received a dedication from Perkins, Jonson's reference to the 'Salve' would have been a private joke.

In the course of the play the character of Morose describes how his wife is being moulded into a 'Penthesilea',[140] the Amazon queen Lucy had so recently played in Jonson's *Masque of Queens*. Perhaps Jonson was also thinking of Lucy when he had Truewit warn of the evils of marriage. According to Truewit a wife will:

> go live with her she-friend or cousin at the college ... be served in silver; have the chamber filled with a succession of grooms, footmen ... besides embroiderers, jewellers, tire-women, sempsters, feathermen ... while she feels not how the land drops away, nor the acres melt ... so she may censure poets and authors and styles, and compare 'em, Daniel with Spenser, Jonson with the tother youth, and so forth; or be thought cunning in controversies or the very knots of divinity ...[141]

If Jonson was making reference to Lucy it would seem she gathered women about her – as it is known she did at Twickenham – and invited 'wits' to her house in London to discuss poetry, divinity, mathematics and other subjects and voiced her opinions on such subjects forcibly. Lucy and her 'she-friend[s]' were also guilty of indulging in the womanly art of cosmetics, spending large amounts of money and living apart from their husbands. Of the women with whom Lucy associated – Cecilia Bulstrode, Bridget Markham, Jane Meautys – none were married and Lucy, though married, lived apart from Edward for extended periods of time.

As John Donne's fortunes began to improve around 1609, for Lucy the opposite was true: the year was marked by illness and great personal loss. Yet the year began promisingly enough. In January her brother John – who was travelling abroad with his tutor, John Tovey – visited Venice and was introduced to the Doge. Donne's old friend, Henry Wotton, was ambassador to the court there and presented John Harrington as the 'right eye' of Prince Henry.[142] This introduction must have been a source of great pride within the Harrington family as too would have the letters in which John corresponded with the future king, Prince Henry.

But by early May the mood changed abruptly with the death of Bridget Markham at Twickenham. Bridget's body was taken from the Park and interred at Twickenham church where Lucy had an epitaph erected in her memory. The epitaph was inscribed in Latin, possibly with a composition by Lucy herself, and represented a very public expression of her feelings of grief and loss. According to the inscription Bridget was '*inclytae Luciae comitissae de Bedford sanguine/ (quod satis) sed et amicitia, propinquissima*';[143] she and Lucy were bound together by both blood and friendship. Donne was among those of Lucy's friends who responded to Bridget's death by writing an elegy:

> Man is the World, and death the ocean,
> To which God gives the lower parts of man.
> This Sea invirons all, and though as yet
> God hath set markes, and bounds, twixt us, and it,
> Yet doth it rore, and gnaw, and still pretend,
> And breaks our bankes, when ere it takes a friend.[144]

But Donne also appears to have written another poem for Lucy around this time. Neither poem was dated, but in a book of manuscript poetry collected and arranged by an individual in some way connected to the Essex family the two poems follow one another. The first is called 'An Eligie vpon the death of the La: Markham' and the next is given the title, 'An Elegie to the La: Bedford'.[145] The ordering of the poems and the addition of a title to the second verse by someone who knew Lucy and saw Donne's verses is significant because it suggests that the second elegy was written for Lucy and that it related specifically to Bridget's death. The elegy for Lucy was a deeply personal poem in which Donne celebrated the friendship which existed between her and Bridget. For Donne, friendship was of paramount importance and he spoke of it as his 'second religion'.[146] In his elegy for Lucy he argued that rather than she and Bridget being two distinct individuals their bond of friendship meant that they were in fact a single entity:

> You that are she and you, that's double shee,
> In her dead face, halfe of your selfe shall see;
> Shee was the other part, for so they doe
> Which build them friendhips, become one of two;[147]

Donne's emphasis on the closeness between Bridget and Lucy echoed the 'amiticia', the friendship between the two women which Lucy had had inscribed on Bridget's epitaph.

Bridget's sudden death robbed Lucy of a relative and an intimate friend and she was still grieving when she herself fell ill in early June and although the nature of her illness remains obscure it was probably exacerbated by sadness over the death of her friend. However, despite illness and bereavement she still had court duties to fulfil. Anna was on a progress and by the beginning of July Lucy was waiting on her. She planned to pay a visit to her Sidney relatives at their house at Penshurst. Sir Robert wrote to his wife Barbara indicating that Lucy also wanted to meet with Sir Robert's daughter, Lady Mary Wroth:

> I doe not thinck my Lady of Bedforde will bee at Penshurst till after the progress, because she and your dowghter and I cannot meet althogether there.[148]

As events transpired, Lucy's visit was postponed. Sir Robert told Barbara he felt unsure as to whether or not he could guarantee being at Penshurst at the time arranged for Lucy's visit and considered that 'it would not bee well taken if I were away when my Lady of Bedforde were there'.[149] Robert Sidney was a stickler for doing the right thing and he was also deeply conscious of how his actions and the affairs of his family were interpreted, and perhaps misinterpreted, by his friends and peers. A typical instance of this sensitivity occurred when he sensed difficulties emerging between his newly married daughter, Mary, and her husband, Lord Wroth. Writing to Barbara he told how he had met with Wroth and that there was:

> somewhat that doth discontent him: but the particulars I could not get out from him: onely hee protests that hee cannot take any exceptions to his wife ... It were very soon for any unkindness to begin; and therefore whatsoever the matters bee, I pray you let all things be carried in the best maner til wee all doe meet. For mine ennimies would be very glad for such an occasion to make themselves merry at mee.[150]

In the wrong hands such information could become a potent weapon which might be used against him and he urged Barbara to keep quiet. His feeling that his absence during Lucy's visit might 'not bee well taken' related to his desire to act properly toward her, but it also suggests that Lucy might be easily offended and view his absence from Penshurst at the time of her visit as a personal slight. From Robert's letter to Barbara it seems that it was also of some importance that their daughter Mary was at the house when Lucy visited. Whether this was because Lucy had wanted to see Mary or Mary wanted to see Lucy is unclear. Mary and Lucy were certainly well known to each other. They had probably known each other since childhood and they certainly danced in masques together. Mary had married her husband Sir Robert Wroth in 1605 and after his death in 1614 she embarked on an affair with her cousin William Herbert, third Earl of Pembroke, and bore him two illegitimate children.

The year wore on and in August Cecilia Bulstrode fell ill at Twickenham. Donne visited the ailing Cecilia and kept himself informed of the progress of her illness and with the situation through messages. Writing to Goodyer he was deeply pessimistic about her chances of recovery:

> I fear earnestly that Mistress Bolstrod will not escape that sickness in which she labours at this time. I sent this morning to ask of her passage of this night; and the return is that she is as I left her yesternight, and then by the strength of her understanding and voice (proportionally to her fashion, which was ever remiss), by the evenness and life of her pulse, and by her temper, I could allow her long life, and impute all her sickness to her mind. But the history of her sickness makes me justly fear that she will scarce last so long as that you, when you receive this letter, may do her any good office in praying for her; for she hath not for many days received so much as a preserved

barbery but it returns, and all accompanied with a fever, the mother, and an extream ill spleen.[151]

Donne's close observation of Cecilia's health – her steady pulse, her vomiting and her fever – verges on the interest of a professional. Yet this sustained, almost gruesome focus was a practical expression of what Edward, Lord Cherbury, advocated as the kind of knowledge necessary to a gentleman:

> It will become a gentleman to have some knowledge in Medicine, especially the Diagnostick part, whereby he may take timely notice of a disease ... as also the prognostick part whereby he may judge of the Symptnomes either increasing or decreasing in the disease, as also concerning the Crisis or Indication thereof. This art will get a Gentleman not only much knowledge but much credit, since seeing any sick body he will be able to tell in all human probibility [sic] whether he shall recover, or if he shall die of the disease ...[152]

Donne also mentioned, and dismissed, the possibility that her sickness lay in her 'mind'. The troubled state of Cecilia's mind or conscience seems also to have occupied Lord Herbert of Cherbury, who claimed that the need for repentance occupied the last days of her life. Perhaps Cecilia was troubled by the way in which she had been conducting her life.

Donne's prognosis was correct: on 4 August 1609, Cecilia died at Twickenham. As he had for Bridget, Donne wrote an elegy for Cecilia. Ten days after Cecilia's death he wrote to Goodyer telling him of how he had sent a letter to Lucy:

> who did me the honour to acknowledge the receipt of one of mine by one of hers; and who only hath power to cast the fetters of verse upon my free meditations: it should give you some delight, and some comfort, because you are the first which see it, and it is the last which you shall see of this kind from me.[153]

Donne's view that Lucy was the only person who had the 'power to cast the fetters of verse upon my free meditations' suggests that he wrote the poem for Cecilia at Lucy's request. Her influence over him at this point was therefore considerable because she possessed sufficient 'power' to get him to do something he preferred not to do, as indicated by the prisoning connotations of 'fetter'. George Garrard, a cousin to Thomas Roe and a friend to both Donne and Jonson, gathered verses in memory of Cecilia. Even Cecilia's old foe, Ben Jonson, was prevailed upon to pen a verse to mark her death. He wrote the required verse and enclosed it with a letter as Garrard's servant stood waiting, adding:

> If it [the elegy] be well, as I thinke it is, for my invention hath not cooled so much to iudge, show it, though the greater Witts haue gone before ... Would God, I had seene her [Cecilia] before that some yt liue might haue corrected some preiudices they haue had iniuriously of mee.[154]

Jonson's letter to Garrard was written as the ink was still drying on the verses he had written for Cecilia. Fresh from composing he trusted Garrard to 'iudge' whether the verses were acceptable or not. He was conscious too of his timing, of how the 'greater Witts', presumably Donne, had already 'gone before' him. Jonson's *Epitaph on Cecilia Bulstrode* began with an arresting call to:

> Stay, view this stone: and, if thou beest not such,
> Read here a little, that thou mayst know much.[155]

But as the verse progressed there was a sense that either Jonson was trying too hard or holding his tongue very firmly in his cheek while he was composing. The woman who he had claimed could not write 'News' and was a slut was suddenly transformed into one who 'might haue claym'd t'have made the Graces foure; / Taught Pallas language; Cynthia modesty'.[156]

Cecilia's death would have caused Lucy a great deal of distress. As a woman of strong religious belief, her faith would have offered her comfort and solace in the face of sudden death. There was certainly no shortage of texts which dealt with death and how best to respond to it. Confronted by the passing of two friends Lucy could reread the tract written for precisely such situations, *A salue for a sicke man*, in which William Perkins advised that there are 'many things happen farre more heauie & bitter then death' and that 'death is ... sleepe'.[157] Donne wrote to Garrard that he had 'left Sir Thos. Roe so indulgent to his sorrow, as it had been an injury to have interrupted it with my unuseful company'.[158]

Donne wrote poetry for Cecilia, and Lucy wrote a reply to his verse. Lucy's verse was written from the perspective of a person who had just experienced the unexpected deaths of two people to whom she was very close. In the only surviving example of Lucy's poetry she was defiant toward death:

> Death be not proud, thy hand gave not this blow,
> Sinne was her captive, whence thy power doth flow;
> The executioner of wrath thou art,
> But to destroy the just is not thy part.
> Thy comming, terrour, anguish, griefe denounce;
> Her happy state, courage, ease, joy pronounce.
> From out the Christall palace of her breast,
> The clearer soule was call'd to endlesse rest,
> (Not by the thundering voyce, wherewith God threats,
> But, as with crowned Saints in heaven he treats,)
> And, waited on by Angels, home was brought,
> To joy that it through many dangers fought;
> The key of mercy gently did unlocke
> The doores 'twixt heaven and it, when life did knock.
>   Nor boast, the fairest frame was made thy prey,

Because to mortall eyes it did decay;
A better witnesse than thou art, assures,
That though dissolv'd, it yet a space endures;
No dramme thereof shall want or losse sustaine,
When her best soule inhabits it again.
Goe then to people cursed before they were,
Their spoyles in Triumph of thy conquest weare.
Glory not thou thy selfe in these hot teares
Which our face, not for hers, but our harme weares,
The mourning livery given by Grace, not thee,
Which wils our soules in these streams washt should be,
And on our hearts, her memories best tombe,
In this her Epitaph doth write thy doome.
Blinde were those eyes, saw not how bright did shine
Through fleshes misty vaile the beames divine.
Deafe were the eares, not charm'd with that sweet sound
Which did I'th spirit-instructed voice abound.
Of flint the conscience, did not yeeld and melt,
At what in her last Act it saw, heard, felt.
     Weep not, nor grudge then, to have lost her sight,
Taught thus, our after stay's but a short night:
But by all soules not by corruption choaked
Let in high rais'd notes that power be invoked.
Calme the rough seas, by which she sayles to rest,
From sorrowes here, to a kingdome ever blest;
And teach this hymne of her with joy, and sing,
The grave no conquest gets, Death hath no sting.[159]

In Lucy's public writing, public at least in the sense that it would be passed from hand to hand within a carefully controlled circle of readers, she was defiant toward death. Yet alone and in private she may have felt somewhat differently. The deaths of Bridget and Cecilia had a profound effect on her, if only because she was suddenly deprived of two friends with whom she had been closely involved. These women had lived in her houses, helped her dress, talked, gossiped, laughed and danced with her, and in an instant they were both gone. Lucy's response at the time was very publicly expressed – in erecting the monument to Bridget – and putting her feelings into poetry. Yet some sense of how she responded to the deaths of Bridget and Cecilia on a very private level appeared in a letter she wrote about the death of another person who meant a great deal to her. Years later she wrote to Jane Bacon about another unexpected death, that of her great and much loved friend the Marquis of Hamilton. Her response to Hamilton's death was raw and intensely personal. She wrote:

I acknowledge that I feele so to the quicke this last affliction God hath pleased to lay vpon mee, as no worldly comfort will euer be able to prevaile against itt ... this hath made mee see that I must haue the best freinds [sic] in the world but to lose them I know not how soone, for he that was so sodainly taken from mee, both for his years, strength, health, & temper, was like to have lived to much greater adge ...[160]

God may have laid the 'affliction' of her friend's death on Lucy for a reason, but that did not alter the fact that it hurt her 'to the quicke' and that she felt nothing would ease her grief. There is no reason to believe that Lucy did not feel a similar profound sense of loss when Bridget and Cecilia died.

Some kind of distress on Lucy's part is apparent in a verse letter Donne wrote to her which although undated was probably written in 1609 soon after the deaths of Bridget and Cecilia. The date is suggested by the contents of the letter as Donne wrote that:

> We'have added to the world Virginia,'and sent
> Two new starres lately to the firmament;
> Why grudge wee us (not heaven) the dignity
> T'increase with ours, those faire soules company?[161]

In February 1609, Donne had applied unsuccessfully for the secretaryship of the Virginia Company and the 'two new starres' may represent Bridget and Cecilia.[162] Donne implied that his verse was a direct response to a letter or a verse letter from Lucy and he began with an explanation of the timing of his own verse:

> T'have written then, when you writ, seem'd to mee
> Worst of spirituall vices, Simony,
> And not t'have written then, seemes little less
> Then worst of civill vices, thanklessnesse.[163]

Donne may have been slow in replying because, if the poem followed his vow to Goodyer that Lucy was the only person who could 'cast the fetters of verse' on him, he may in fact not have wanted to write it at all. If Robert Sidney's veiled comment about things not being taken well implied that Lucy could take offence easily, this might explain the lengths Donne went to in order to explain his delay in responding to what she had 'writ' to him. He was on very dangerous ground with a patroness who may have felt her poet did not sufficiently demonstrate his 'beholdingnesse' to her:

> ... I seem'd to shun beholdingnesse.
> But 'tis not soe, *nothings*, as I am, may
> Pay all they have, and yet have all to pay.[164]

He then returned to issues of virtue:

> I have been told, that vertue'in Courtiers hearts
> Suffers an Ostracisme, and departs.
> Profit, ease, fitness, plenty, bid it goe,
> But whither, only knowing you, I know;
> Your (or you) virtue two vast uses serves,
> It ransomes one sex, and one Court preserves.[165]

The discussion of virtue was a further instance of the iconography with which Lucy had habitually been associated, particularly in the work of writers like Daniel. Donne went on to discuss ideas of virtue, specifically of how an understanding and appreciation of virtue cannot exist without the corresponding experience of vice:

> Even in you, vertues best paradise,
> Vertue hath some, but wise degrees of vice. / ...
> And ignorance of vice, makes vertue lesse, / ...
> But in your Commonwealth, or world in you,
> Vice hath no office ...
> Take then no vitious purge, but be content
> With cordiall vertue, your knowne nourishment.[166]

Donne's view of the close connection between virtue and vice was not a sop hastily manufactured to make Lucy feel better. Years later, exactly the same ideas emerged again in his conviction that 'vertues and vices are contigiuous, and borderers upon one another'. Donne's prolonged consideration of the nature of virtue may have been in response to Lucy's feeling that her lack of virtue, or the lack of virtue on the part of herself, Bridget and Cecilia had somehow invited tragedy. Did the sudden and shocking deaths of Bridget and Cecilia cause Lucy to reflect on how she conducted her life? The imagery of taking physic for the soul – the 'vitious purge' – and Donne's suggestion that Lucy should not embark upon such an aggressive course of action suggests she was evaluating her conduct and considered that some kind of reformation in her life was necessary. The ideas of purging that Donne responded to in his verse recall Psalm 51, in which David calls out to God for purification:

> ... wipe o lord my sinnes from sinnfull mee
> O clense, o wash, my fowle iniquitie: / ...
> with Hisop, lord thie Hisop, purge me soe:
> and that shall clense the leaprie of my mynde.[167]

John Harrington of Kelston had written a poem in which he admonished a court lady of his acquaintance:

> Tell *Leda* ...
> That till she get a mind of more submission,

And purge that corps with Hysope of contrition,
And wash that sinful soule with saltish teares,
Though Quailes she eates, though Gold & Pearle she weares,
    Yet sure she doth …
    But feed and clad a Synagogue of Sathan.[168]

Harrington equated the court lady – to whom he gave the pseudonym Leda and who professed herself to be a Puritan – with a whore. Lucy would have been thoroughly familiar with the psalm, but perhaps she knew too the 'shalowe meditations' of her disingenuous relative and then sought the advice of her friend Donne to assure her that she had not fallen victim to the temptations of the 'Court, which is not vertues clime'.[169] In a period of confusion and great sadness John Donne offered Lucy 'compassion' in her 'wrechednesse'[170] just as she had supported him in his own dark moments so lately passed.

Lucy decided against taking the radical step of a spiritual purge but by the middle of September she sought physic of a different kind. Perhaps hoping to 'repair' her 'fort' and relieve an attack of gout which had increasingly begun to trouble her, she travelled to Bath to take the waters. But as Lucy spent time away from the court and followed a course of treatment the woes of the year were not yet over. In late September her mother fell dangerously ill at Kew and was not expected to survive. What illness Anne suffered from is unknown and despite the dire predictions of her imminent demise she made a full recovery as gossip again proved wildly inaccurate. For Lucy there was at least the relief that she was not to be robbed of her mother as well as Bridget and Cecilia.

The events of 1609 and Lucy's reflection upon them led her to make changes in her life. She certainly spent some time with Edward because in 1610 she fell pregnant again. An advanced state of pregnancy prevented her from taking part in *Tethys Festival*, a masque written by Daniel and presented at Whitehall on 5 June 1610 to celebrate the investiture of Prince Henry as Prince of Wales. A keen masquer, Lucy probably attended the masque as a spectator and watched as Anna led a performance that featured Princess Elizabeth and Prince Charles, the Duke of York. Unable to walk unaided due to weakness in his legs, the ten-year-old Charles was escorted onto the stage by two men disguised as '*Neptune's* Servants' and his legs were thereafter screened from the eyes of the spectators by the dancing forms of '*twelve little Ladies*, all of them the Daughters of Earls or Barons' who encircled him.[171] *Tethys Festival* depicted Anna as a sea-goddess and her ladies as British rivers, but the masque was unmistakably concerned with Anna's role as a royal mother. Prince Henry watched the masque with his father, James, in full view of the assembled audience, and the presence of Elizabeth and Charles on the masquing stage was a highly visible reminder of the other royal children that the fruitful Anna had borne. The design of the masque included a golden tree, an image which pointed back to the first time a tree of fertility had

appeared in one of Anna's masques when the heavily pregnant queen had danced
in the *Masque of Blackness* shortly after her accession. Now a heavily pregnant
Lucy watched the offspring of her queen and the young children of her fellow
'Earls or Barons' and her thoughts must inevitably have turned toward the child
she carried. Could she, too, finally be considered a fruitful branch? Would she
soon be able to call herself a mother?

Hopes in the Bedford and Harrington households were high as Lucy succeeded
in carrying the baby to term. In early September she gave birth to a daughter,
but tragedy struck again as the little girl lived only two hours. Lucy was left 'very
weake and much greeved for the loss of the childe'.[172] But her desire for a child
was strong and in October the following year she miscarried yet again. Once more
she faced the all too familiar heartbreak of gazing upon the 'formless eyes' of 'the
embryo, whose vitall band / Breaks ere it holds'.[173] Almost exactly a year after
the death of her 'lady infant', Lucy was still without the child she so desperately
wanted and on whom the succession of the Bedford family depended. After
1611 there was no mention of any further pregnancies and as she grew older
Lucy attempted to become reconciled to her childlessness, accepting it within
the terms of her religious faith by reasoning that 'God had [not] continued
mee a Mother'.[174] But she was conscious of what she missed as a result of her
childlessness. In a letter to Jane she added a postscript: 'I am very glad to hear
... that yo[u]r children are so well; he that hath given them yow, give yow with
them all the comforts children can bee to a Mother'.[175] Lucy's desire for a child
became channelled into a focus on the children of relatives and close friends.
She took a vital and genuine interest in Jane Bacon's son, Frederick. Named after
the heir apparent, Prince Henry Frederick – at whose court both his mother and
father had been active – Frederick Bacon was the recipient of frequent gifts and
messages from Lucy.

But in 1611 the absence of a child was a source of pain and great sadness. Mary
Wroth provided an intimate insight into what miscarriage meant for a woman.
It was a cruel:

> Faulce hope which feeds butt to destroy, and spill
>   What itt first breeds; unaturall to the birth
>   Of thine owne wombe; conceaving butt to kill, [176]

As Lucy came to terms with her loss, Anna was sympathetic and supportive. At
this most sad and difficult of times, Lucy 'was the queen's only favourite'.[177] But
as she retained the affection and good offices of the Queen she was confronting
a major change in her relationship with Donne. John Donne had decided to end
his patronage relationship with Lucy. Characteristically, he did not approach
her directly; instead he wrote to Goodyer, asking his friend to do the impossible.
Goodyer was to maintain Donne 'in the same room in my Lady Bedford's

opinion, in the which you have placed me [sic]', while simultaneously ending the patronage relationship.[178] Donne did not express himself so bluntly to Goodyer, but his intent was clear:

> I profess to you that I am too much bound to her for expressing every way her care of my fortune, that I am weary before she is; and out of a lothness, that so good works should be bestowed upon so ill stuff, or that so much ill-fortune should be mingled with hers, as that she should miss anything that she desired, though it were but for me; I am willing to depart from further exercising her endeavors in that kind. I shall be bold to deliver my poor letters to her ladyship's hands, through yours, whilst I am abroad ...[179]

Lucy no longer needed to exercise her 'endeavors' on Donne's behalf because he had secured himself a new patron to replace her, in the person of the wealthy Sir Robert Drury. Donne had endeared himself to Drury by writing a series of poems called the *Anniversaries* for Robert's daughter, Elizabeth. These intensely personal poems were written for a girl of fifteen whom Donne never met and who died a year before he wrote his first poem about her. Jonson considered the first of these poems, known as the 'First Anniversary', blasphemous and thought it would have meant something if it had celebrated the Virgin Mary but not Elizabeth Drury.[180] But Donne defended the poems on the grounds that he was writing about the idea of a woman, not about a particular woman: an argument that had strong echoes of his conversation with Magdalen Herbert on the nature of flattery. For Lucy, Donne's severing of their relationship was tantamount to a personal slight. A pragmatic woman well versed in the ways of patronage, she could easily see that she had been passed over for a more attractive benefactor. Donne's disingenuous claims that he did not want his 'ill-fortune' to mingle with hers were meaningless. She had plenty of 'ill-fortune' of her own. As he indicated in the letter, Donne left England to travel 'abroad' with Drury and his wife in late November 1611. He lived in France with the Drurys and during this time he sent some French verses to Lucy. Even stranger was the fact that for the first time in his career, under intense pressure from Drury, Donne agreed that the poems could be published. This decision was to become a source of deep regret to him, 'Of my *Anniversaries*, the fault which I acknowledge in myself is to have descended to print anything in verse ... I confess I wonder how I declined to it, and do not pardon myself'.[181]

Donne's relationship with the Drurys and the poetry he had written about their daughter called into question the nature of his patronage relationship with Lucy. Donne was the poet who had vowed to be Lucy's muse and with whom she had spent time socially and to whose child Lucy stood as godmother. Now he had written sublime poetry about a dead girl. What was Lucy to think of the poetry Donne had written for her? Had their relationship been nothing more than a clever pretence, an intellectual game? Did Donne's verses for Lucy amount to nothing more than a means of securing her influence and winning her favour? While Donne may have regretted publishing the poems, he was defiant in the face of the displeasure of Lucy and his other friends which was being communicated to him by Garrard. Writing to Garrard from Paris, Donne answered the aspersions robustly:

> but for the other part of the imputation of having said too much, my defence is that my purpose was to say as well as I could; for since I never saw the gentlewoman, I cannot be understood to have bound myself to have spoken just truths, but I would not be thought to have gone about to praise her, or any other in rhyme; except I took such person as might be capable of all that I could say. If any of those ladies think that Mistress Drury was not so, let that lady make herself fit for all those praises in the book, and they shall be hers.[182]

Donne did not take the displeasure felt by Lucy and others in England meekly. If any woman lived up to the 'praise[s]' depicted in the 'Anniversaries' then 'they shall be hers'.

Lucy was not absent from Donne's thoughts while he was in France with Drury. Around this time he began writing a poem for her that was never completed and which she may never have seen. The poem dwelt on ideas associated with Easter as Donne appears to have sought forgiveness from Lucy and the renewal of their former relationship:

> This season as 'tis Easter, as 'tis spring,
> Must both to growth and to confession bring
> My thoughts dispos'd unto your influence; so,
> These verses bud, so these confessions grow.
> First I confess I have to others lent
> Your stock, and over prodigally spent[183]

The mercantile aspect of the client–patron relationship was evident in Donne's use of language like 'stock', 'spent' and 'prodigally'. There was also an implicit acknowledgement of his movement to Drury away from Lucy – 'I have to others lent / Your stock'. Spring is traditionally the season of regrowth, renewal, perhaps also the renewal of the relationship between the two. Early in April Donne wrote, probably to Goodyer, and again felt the need to defend himself over the Drury poems. He added:

> Therefore give me leave to end this, in which if you did not find the remembrance of my humblest services to my Lady Bedford, your love and faith ought to try all the experiments of powders and dryings and waterings to discover some lines which appeared not; because it is impossible that a letter should come from me with such an ungrateful silence.[184]

Fully aware that he could not simply resume communicating with Lucy after such a long 'ungrateful silence', Donne appeared to urge the recipient of the letter to seek other verses of his which could be sent to her. Lucy was not as rich as Sir Robert Drury, but she was powerful in the circles where such power counted, and Donne could still benefit from her patronage and he clearly still cared about what she thought of him. Perhaps he genuinely believed that the poems he wrote for Elizabeth Drury wouldn't offend her. In 1612 Donne accompanied the Drurys to Spa, spending June and July there before traveling on to Maastricht.[185] Near the end of his stay at Spa, Donne wrote perhaps to Goodyer or Garrard:

> I can glory of nothing in this voyage but that I have afflicted my Lady Bedford with few letters. I protest earnestly to you, it troubles me much more to despatch a packet into England without a letter to her than it would to put in three. But I have been heretofore too immodest towards her, and I suffer the purgatory for it.[186]

Perhaps Donne was thinking of how matters would stand on his return to England. The friendship he had shared with Lucy had fundamentally changed and he knew it; he knew too that he was not the only person who would like to enjoy the benefits of her patronage and influence. In 1611 Lucy was one of a number of women presented with a dedicatory sonnet by Aemilia Lanyer in a work entitled *Salve Deus Rex Judaeorum*. Aemilia was the daughter of one of Queen Elizabeth's court musicians and, as a young woman, susceptible to the attentions of an experienced courtier, she became the mistress of Elizabeth's Lord Chamberlain, Henry Hunsdon. Courtiers were notoriously duplicitous creatures and no more so than when they professed to be in love:

> Each greedy hand doth catch and pluck the flowr / ...
> But leaves the Tree to fall, or stand alone: / ...
> Believe no Vows, nor much-protesting men,
> Credit no Oaths, nor no bewailing Song;
> Let Courtiers swear, forswear, and swear agen,
> Their hearts lye ten Regions from their Tongue:
> And when with Oaths thy heart is made to tremble,
> Believe them least, for then they most dissemble.[187]

When Aemilia gave birth to Hunsdon's illegitimate son, he quickly married her off to a court musician called Alfonso Lanyer. Aemilia was an intelligent and attractive woman and she is mentioned in the diary of the Elizabethan magus, Simon Forman, who seems to have wanted to engage in a physical relationship with her. Forman's coded reference for sex was 'halek'[188] and although it appears that Aemilia allowed him some liberties there was no sex. Forman noted that on one of her visits, Aemilia:

staid all night. and she was familiar & friendlie to him in all thinges. But only she wold
not halek. Yet he tolde all parts of her body willingly. & kyssed her often but she wold
not doe in any wise.[189]

Aemilia's work was a long poem on Christ's Passion in which the dedicatory
material was exclusively addressed to women. The work contained dedications to
Anna; Princess Elizabeth; Lady Arbella Stuart; the Countess Dowager of Kent; the
Countess of Pembroke; Lucy; the Countess of Suffolk; Anne Clifford; and Anne's
mother Margaret Russell Clifford, Countess of Cumberland and also contained
a verse entitled 'To all vertuous Ladies in generall'.[190]

Like any woman of her time Aemilia knew that Lucy was influential at Anna's
court, but she may well have known Lucy personally, from when Lucy visited
Anne Clifford and the Countess of Cumberland in whose household Aemilia
lived. The sonnet addressed to Lucy is an acknowledgment of the power she
wielded at Anna's court and her personal involvement with her female Clifford
relatives, and was probably a bid for patronage.

In the dedicatory poem Aemilia wrote for Lucy she invoked the imagery of
the learned woman and the ideas of virtue, and her work shared similarities with
Samuel Daniel's poem in its presentation of knowledge as a type of key:

> Me thinkes I see faire Virtue readie stand,
> T'unlocke the closet of your lovely breast,
> Holding the key of Knowledge in her hand,[191]

Aemilia appears to have been aware of Daniel's work – and of the significance of
the imagery of the learned woman – probably because Daniel was a tutor to Anne
Clifford in the household in which Aemilia was resident. Aemilia was herself well
educated, having studied in the household of the dowager Countess of Kent, Susan
Bertie. Like Daniel, Aemilia invoked the idea of virtue and learning in relation to
Lucy and in so doing signalled that as a learned woman, Lucy could stand for a
great deal more than mere 'tokenism'. The female dedicatees of Lanyer's work – all
of them educated – did at some level further women's writing by helping a woman
like Aemilia venture into the new and potentially hostile world of print.

In 1612 there was much to look forward to. The court and country were
animated by the news that Princess Elizabeth was to marry Frederick, the Elector
Palatine. The marriage was planned for the end of the year and the necessary
preparations for an elaborate royal wedding began to be made. Towards the end
of October, Frederick landed at Gravesend to be greeted on behalf of the King
first by Hay and the following day by the Duke of Lennox. But barely ten days
after the arrival of Frederick, Prince Henry fell ill. Overcome by a fever Henry
was initially treated with cordials and seemed to recover. But the recovery was
only temporary. Theodore Mayerne was appointed to take charge of the case and

supervise the team of doctors attending the Prince, but nothing – from purging, repeated blood letting to cupping – proved to be any use. As Henry grew sicker the attempts to save his life became ever more desperate. Unsurprisingly, treatments of a highly unusual nature such as covering his body with freshly killed pigeons proved ineffective and on 6 November 1612, the unthinkable happened: the eighteen-year-old heir to the throne died. Henry's death, probably from measles, stunned the nation. The Prince's tutor and friend, Adam Newton, wrote to his brother-in-law, Sir Thomas Puckering, and gave some sense of the terrible shock the death had been to members of Henry's court: 'This late loss of our master came so suddaine and so unexpected, even when we were preparing for nuptials and jollity that the blow astonished the more'.[192] In a fraught atmosphere of grief, confusion and recrimination Mayerne's rivals promptly accused him of poisoning his patient. The country went into mourning for a prince who had promised to restore England's military glory and who had espoused religious sentiments which gave great encouragement to Protestants. With Henry's untimely death England's 'rising sun … set ere scarcely he had shone, and … with him all … glory lies buried'.[193] For Lucy and her family the death struck very close to home. Both John Harrington and his son had been active in Henry's court. John Harrington senior's responsibilities to Princess Elizabeth had frequently brought him into contact with members of Henry's entourage as the devoted brother and sister visited one another. His son, who had been so carefully groomed to act as a companion to the Prince, had at a stroke lost his position and a close friend. But, as the Harringtons were still reeling from the shock of Prince Henry's death and the sense of deep uncertainty that came with it, Lucy fell seriously ill. The Earl of Dorset wrote to Sir Thomas Edmondes on 23 November 1612 and reported that 'My Lady Bedford last night, about one of the clock, was suddenly, and hath continued ever since, speechless, and is past all hopes, though yet alive'.[194] Dorset added that his wife, Anne Clifford, was 'full of sorrow' at the news and had gone immediately to visit Lucy.[195] The exact nature of Lucy's illness is not known. All that is clear is that she was gravely ill and not expected to live. As the country was wracked by an unusually stormy and rainy winter Lucy hovered between life and death. During her illness she was attended by Mayerne, who had been cleared of the false accusations made against him after Henry's death. Lucy was also tended by Dr John Burges. Burges had been educated at St John's College, Cambridge, a well-known hotbed of Puritanism in England, and after leaving Cambridge he entered the ministry. The strength of his religious views brought him into various conflicts with authority, most notably with King James in 1604. On 19 June 1604, Burges preached a sermon before James at Greenwich and had the temerity, or foolhardiness, to take it upon himself to instruct his monarch on the behaviour appropriate to princes or rulers. He very pointedly discussed the misfortunes that might befall princes:

what is the misfortun of a Prince, It is not … to take a fall off a horse, or to be smitten with a sharp ague … What is it then? When God will not suffer him to reigne … the Prince is so farre in Gods disgrace, that he flyeth the company of the wise, and advanceth fooles, oppressours and flatterers and such as sooth him in all his sayings.[196]

James's court had been widely criticized for its hangers-on and its susceptibility to flatterers and Burges's sermon hit much too close to home. After preaching the sermon before the king, James so objected to its content that he had Burges imprisoned in the Fleet. From his cell, Burges wrote letters to the Privy Council and the king professing himself to be 'amazed at that distaste' which James took of his sermon.[197] Burges was eventually released from prison and tactfully left the country for a time, spending part of his overseas sojourn studying medicine at the staunchly Calvinist city of Leyden. In 1612 he returned to England and based himself around Isleworth where he set about building up a highly successful medical practice. His expertise was sought by men and women of social standing, some of whom took houses in the area and pushed property prices up in order to be close to their doctor. John Chamberlain wrote of journeying to 'Thistleworth'[198] with his friends Sir Ralph and Lady Winwood to see a house they had rented in the area. Chamberlain thought the new residence a:

litle reasonable convenient house, with a handsom garden and orchard: for my part I should have thought halfe the monie a more indifferent rent, but they are willing to have a retiring place, and geve the more for Doctor Burges neighbourhoode.[199]

Although trained in medicine, Burges's true calling was the church and it was there that he came into conflict with the authorities.

During her illness Burges was 'much about' Lucy and reportedly did 'her more good with his spiritual counsel than with natural physic'.[200] The difference between the physician and the minister was not always distinct in the period, and attending to the spiritual needs of a patient was considered just as efficacious as many of the medical treatments available at the time. It was of course preferable that an individual came to God through a sermon rather than through an illness: 'Hadst thou rather a sickness should bring thee to God, than a sermon? hadst thou rather be beholden to a Physitian for thy salvation, than to a Preacher?'[201] If illness was visited upon a person that person did not automatically reject conventional medicine. Furthermore, addressing the spiritual needs of a patient could at least not do the damage that medical care often did as patients risked bleeding to death as a result of inexpert blood letting or suffered the detrimental effects of the over zealous use of purges. An honest doctor of the time might have felt there was some truth in Harrington of Kelston's sharp epigram put into the mouth of a physician:

... I know too well, for want of skill,
My medcines [sic] many an honest man will kill.[202]

One of the pronounced effects of Lucy's illness was a re-examination of the way in which she conducted her life, as the same issues which seemed to trouble her after the deaths of Bridget and Cecilia resurfaced again. However, rather than John Donne pointing out that a knowledge of vice was essential to an understanding of virtue, she had the ministrations of Burges who took a much harder line and recommended severe spiritual physic as a means of redressing the spiritual problems which had become so obviously etched upon her body. During her illness Lucy vowed not to return to the court, possibly because she saw some kind of link between the manner in which she conducted her life there and the onset of her sickness. Perhaps Burges helped her to view her illness as a punishment from God for a life badly lived.

Theodore Mayerne was so impressed by what he saw of Burges's abilities as a doctor and a minister that he recommended him to James. Unfortunately Burges's second appearance before James was no more successful than the first. James deeply disliked Burges's style of preaching and was upset by the fact that the minister had taken it upon himself to 'dogmatize ... in his court'.[203] Mayerne also suffered the king's displeasure for making the introduction. The matter was passed into the hands of the archbishop who subsequently treated Burges 'somewhat roughly' and banned him from preaching within ten miles of London.[204] Just how highly Lucy thought of Burges was indicated by her attempts to help him after this debacle. By the middle of the following year Burges was allowed to preach again largely through the assiduous efforts of Lucy. In a letter to Villiers, Francis Bacon wrote 'concerning the restoring to preach of a famous preacher, one Doctor Burgess ... hath been laboured by my Lady of Bedford and put in good way by the Bishop of Bath and Wells'.[205] That Lucy 'laboured' on behalf of Burges suggests that her attempts to restore him to preaching were neither easy nor straightforward. Yet her endeavours must have been eased considerably by the fact that at the time the Bishop of Bath and Wells was James Montague, who just happened to be Lucy's cousin.

Lucy was busy using her influence and pulling strings for Burges in a way she had once done for John Donne and it was Donne who became the chief casualty of Burges's influence upon her. Lucy had fallen ill in late November 1612 just two months after Donne returned from his overseas travels and before he had had sufficient time fully to re-establish his friendship with her. When Cecilia Bulstrode was dangerously ill, Donne made a point of visiting her and would doubtless have visited Lucy had he been invited, or more importantly, had he been assured of a welcome. It would seem that no invitation was forthcoming. Perhaps the good doctor felt that Donne's presence about Lucy would be detrimental to her spiritual and physical recuperation. Donne certainly viewed Burges as a threat to his relationship with Lucy, claiming that Burges was not well disposed towards him and that he had urged Lucy to take note of Donne's 'past life', what Donne himself referred to as his 'giddiest dayes'.[206] What aspects of this 'past life' Burges was keen for Lucy to consider are unclear but they almost certainly centred on the activities of Donne as a young 'Jack the lad' around London. Prior to his marriage Donne had had affairs which would have troubled Burges, and he perhaps also cast a wary Puritan eye at the staunch Catholicism of the family from which Donne sprang. Unable to visit Lucy in person, John Donne may have attempted to show her he was thinking about her in her illness by writing *A Nocturnall upon S.Lucies Day, being the shortest day*. St Lucy's day fell on 13 December which was at the time erroneously believed to be the shortest day of the year. It would have fallen nearly three weeks after Lucy became ill and sharing the same name as the saint whom the day honoured, and the ideas of light and the imagery of decline consistent with a winter solstice approximated with the decline in her health due to illness.

> 'Tis the yeares midnight, and it is the dayes,
> *Lucies*, who scarce seaven houres herself unmaskes,
> The Sunne is spent, and now his flasks
> Send forth light squibs, no constant rayes;
> The world's whole sap is sunke:[207]

Lucy's recovery was long and slow. By February of 1613 she was still reported to be lying 'in weake case'.[208] Lucy's illness may have been the reason why she did not take part in the masque to celebrate the wedding of Elizabeth and Frederick, but she did recover sufficiently to participate in the marriage ceremony itself. She watched as her father led Elizabeth to the chapel while her mother followed behind the bride. With her hair studded with pearls and diamonds and falling down to her waist to symbolize her virginity, a crown of gold upon her head and a gown liberally scattered with priceless diamonds, Elizabeth made a stunning figure. The bridal train was carried by sixteen ladies and they in turn were followed by bridesmaids. Various members of the nobility were followed by the King and Anna, and behind the Queen came the married countesses. Dressed, as were her peers, in white satin richly decorated with embroidery, pearls and precious stones, a thin and wan Lucy walked in procession behind Anna. Lucy's attendance at the wedding must have required a tremendous physical effort on her part, but Elizabeth's wedding was a very special event.

By August Lucy was strong enough to propose visiting Spa, to continue with her recuperation. The waters at Spa together with its air were widely believed to confer health benefits and even prevent some illnesses, and the place was a popular destination with English travellers. The fact that a lengthy sea voyage was required in order to take advantage of the health-giving waters does not seem to have presented any problems and Lucy for one felt that there were 'litle ods betwixt crossing the Teams [Thames], & sea'.[209] Although Lucy was unconcerned by embarking on a sea voyage she was prevented from going to Spa for more prosaic reasons: the ongoing Bedford problem of a lack of money. But she was not alone in struggling with financial problems. Since the end of December 1611 her father had been attempting to be reimbursed for the expenditure he had incurred on behalf of Princess Elizabeth. But the money owed to him was slow in coming and the Harringtons' financial position was growing ever more desperate. John and Anne had been the recipients of valuable new-year gifts of gold plate from Frederick in 1612, allegedly worth £2000, while their servants received £400 apiece.[210] But despite Frederick's generosity, the Harringtons lacked hard cash. Out of affection for the Princess they had nurtured for so long, John and Anne Harrington wanted to travel to Germany to see her settled in her new life, but their finances were so disastrous that they could not raise the necessary funds to make the journey. Desperate to find a way out of his difficulties, John secured a royal patent to coin copper farthings, but no sooner had he secured it than the Duke of Lennox intervened with James to revoke the patent unless Lennox was allowed to share in the profits. Any hopes the Harringtons had of accompanying Elizabeth to Germany hung in the balance. At length John Harrington was granted the licence, but commentators were of the view that the limits placed on the number of farthings he could coin would severely limit the amount of money he stood to make, and that his venture was susceptible to being undermined by counterfeits. The Harringtons eventually raised the money they needed to make the trip to Germany and set sail with Elizabeth and Frederick. The long journey to Heidelberg began with a crossing from Margate to Flushing on board a ship called the *Prince Royal* (the construction of which had been a favourite project of Prince Henry), and the vessel now made its maiden voyage accompanied by another of Henry's new ships, the *Phoenix*. Naturally the hope amongst many was that the new court about to be formed by Frederick and Elizabeth would itself be phoenix-like. After the great sadness of Prince Henry's death perhaps at last something new, hopeful and good was about to emerge. Among the party that travelled with Elizabeth and Frederick were the Duke of Lennox, the Earl and Countess of Arundel, Lord Zouch, Robert Sidney, Inigo Jones and Henry Holland. As her parents took their leave, Lucy returned to the court and despite her vows during her illness never to set foot in that place again she did in fact return, but as a dramatically changed woman. One of her contemporaries reported that:

she is somewhat reformed in her attire, and forbears painting, which ... makes her look somewhat strangely among so many vizards, which together with their frizzled, powdered hair, makes them look all alike, so that you can scant know one from another at the first view.[211]

In rejecting 'painting' Lucy had dispensed with cosmetics. Female use of cosmetics was consistently attacked by clerics, because women who chose to adorn themselves in this way were viewed as usurping God's work. In applying makeup women took 'the pencill out of Gods hand'.[212] Given the lethal cocktail of arsenic and other chemicals that comprised the cosmetics of the day, Lucy probably did her health a favour by foregoing makeup, but from a social point of view her decision to enter the court devoid of paint was bold, because among her peers she looked so visibly different. Her rejection of cosmetics signalled not just her decision to retain the 'complexion'[213] God had given her it was also a studied rejection of the trappings and conceits of the court. Lucy had too many ties to totally turn her back on the court but she could make her own statement there. Her illness had, at least for a time, changed her.

5

Politician

… it is so busy a time here, both about what concerns the public and
my own private.

LUCY, COUNTESS OF BEDFORD

One morning in the summer of 1613 Edward Russell rose early to go hunting. In
the stableyard groups of horses and riders milled about and the hounds yelped
and bayed in anticipation of the coming chase. Edward must have contemplated
the day that lay before him with pleasure, for he was an experienced and
enthusiastic huntsman. But on this particular occasion he did not return home
from the woods soaked in the blood of his kill. During the course of the hunt
Edward's horse lost its footing, stumbled and fell, and he was thrown violently
against a tree. One person who heard about the accident was John Donne, who
noted that 'My Lord of Bedford, I hear, had lately a desperate fall from his horse,
and was speechless all Tuesday last; his lady rode away hastily from Twickenham
to him, but I hear no more yet of him'.[1] Donne's language in the letter is
noteworthy for two reasons: first, its somewhat dispassionate tone toward Lucy
who was simply referred to as a 'lady' rather than the more fulsome epithets he
was in the habit of using when speaking about her, and secondly, the sense that
Edward had received extremely serious injuries as a result of the accident.

Donne's reference to Lucy as a 'lady' may have resulted from his difficulties in
reestablishing a satisfactory client–patron relationship with her after his return
from the continent. Donne had, instead, begun to write for a new patroness, the
Countess of Salisbury. But attaching himself to a new patroness was not without
its problems, because Donne needed to achieve a balance between the addresses
he made to this new lady with what he had addressed to other women, including
Lucy. He confided to George Garrard about the problems confronting him, in
particular of how he would:

> be loath that in anything of mine, composed of her [Salisbury] she should not appear
> much better than some of those of whom I have written. And yet I cannot hope for better
> expressings than I have given of them … I would I could be believed when I say that all
> that is written of them is but prophecy of her.[2]

Donne's argument that what he had written for ladies prior to writing for the Countess of Salisbury were 'but prophecy of her' sounds much like the argument he had used in defence of the Drury poems: that the poems were about an ideal not an actual woman. Such dexterity in skirting around potentially contentious issues was something Donne had become expert at. Yet as Donne wrestled with the problem of what to say about which lady there was no confusion at all about his report of Edward's accident. The seriousness conveyed in Donne's letter was corroborated by Chamberlain who reported that:

> The Earl of Bedford hunting in a park of his own, by the fall of his horse, was thrown against a tree, and so bruised, that the report went that he was dead, and it is doubted yet that he is in daunger, for that his skull is said to be cracked.[3]

Lucky to escape with his life, Edward suffered severe head injuries and his recovery was long, slow, and never fully complete. The accident caused permanent neurological damage and he was left with impaired speech and difficulty in walking. On receiving word of the accident, Lucy dropped what she was doing at Twickenham, took a horse and rode to be with Edward as quickly as she could. With head injuries there was little a physician could do for a patient. Any open wounds would have been closed in order to control the bleeding and if Edward's skull was depressed it would have been lifted so as to relieve pressure on his brain. But beyond such basic measures physicians tended to leave nature to take its course. As a dutiful wife, Lucy stayed with Edward to oversee his recovery and supervise his care, and a year after the accident she wrote to Jane telling her that Edward was ill with a fever from which he was making a slow but steady recovery. According to Lucy one of the blessings of this most recent illness had been to cause some improvement in the injuries he had sustained in the hunting accident:

> … out of a very great, & almost hopeles danger, my Lord of Bedford hath recovered so much health & strength, as wee are out of all fear of him, doe conseave that the violent fever hee hath had, hath done him som good for his palsy, his speeach beeing better than itt was before hee fell sicke, though his lamenes bee nothing amended.[4]

Edward had never shown much inclination to assume an active role in the group around Pembroke or the court circles about James and Anna, preferring to live quietly in the country, content with his hounds and his hunting. But any interest he might have had in visiting the court, participating in London social life, or even attending parliament after the accident, would have proved difficult. Indeed, as Edward grew older he excused himself from his parliamentary duties by giving Pembroke his proxy vote in several parliamentary sessions, thereby conveniently relieving himself of his political responsibilities but still assisting

Pembroke in furthering an agenda that was staunchly Protestant and resolutely anti-Spanish.[5]

When Lucy felt that Edward's health was sufficiently improved for him not to need her presence she returned to London to resume her normal round of activities. But a month after she had left Twickenham to rush to Edward's side she received news that her father had died at the city of Worms on his way back to England from Heidelberg.[6] John and Anne Harrington had sailed from England in the party with Elizabeth and Frederick in optimistic mood. Their eventual destination, Heidelberg, was a sophisticated city boasting the third oldest university in the Holy Roman Empire which was 'known especially for its Protestant scholarship and magnificent library'.[7] At his palace Frederick had created a magnificent garden complete with 'elaborate geometric design, grottoes, fountains and statuary' which 'was regarded as a wonder of the world'[8] and his court welcomed thinkers and intellectuals. But the attractions of Heidelberg did not prevent members of its court from behaving like the members of any other court in Europe. Contemporaries knew full well that 'Most ... Courts, alas, are like to hell'[9] and Frederick V's court was a breeding ground for rivalries and tensions between those vying for power and influence. One such unfortunate incident touched John and Anne Harrington personally when Elizabeth decided she wished to pay a visit to Mannheim. Elizabeth and Lady Harrington duly travelled to Mannheim by coach, but on their return a heated argument broke out between Elizabeth's master of the horse, a man named Keith, and an esquire of John Harrington in which Keith accused Harrington of behaving improperly in choosing the horses to draw Elizabeth's coach. The disagreement was rather more than just a tiff. The following day it rumbled on as Keith ambushed Harrington's servant and set about beating him. Others joined the fray in support of one or the other side and several of the participants received serious injuries. Somewhat at a loss over what to do Frederick eventually referred the matter to his father-in-law for resolution, and James took the view that John Harrington had been dishonourably treated and ordered that Keith should be imprisoned. Shortly after the incident John and Anne Harrington departed for England. But the couple had not travelled far before John fell ill and died and contemporary gossip was of the view that his illness had developed as a direct result of the unpleasantness and stress he had experienced at Heidelberg. Anne Harrington was left with the unenviable task of bringing the body of her husband back to England for burial at Exton. Lucy's response to the death of her father was not recorded, but it must have been something of a shock as quite suddenly the man who had so carefully educated, guided and supported her was gone. In confronting the death of her father Lucy had the comfort of religion, and her belief in the goodness and wisdom of God would have sustained her through feelings of loss and grief. She was also acutely aware that very often in life 'itt pleased God to order [events]

... otherwise' than how she might wish them to be.[10] John Harrington's death was a terrible blow, but almost inconceivably there was worse to come. Barely six months after the death of her father, Lucy's brother, John, fell ill. In December 1613, Donne wrote to Sir Robert Drury telling him that John was sick but that he seemed to be recovering, adding 'This I heard yesterday; for I have not been there yet'.[11] Donne's letter makes it clear that he was on sufficiently good terms with the Harringtons to visit them, but his optimism that John would recover was misplaced. John Harrington died two months later at Lucy's Twickenham house.[12] The contemporary view was that John died either of smallpox or measles, which although separate and distinct diseases were frequently confused with one another at the time. There was, however, a school of thought that believed that this great Protestant hope had met his death by more sinister means: that he was the victim of Jesuit spite and had succumbed to slow poison administered during his travels on the continent. In this scenario John's death only went to show 'how dangerous a thing it is for religious Gentlemen to travel in these Popish countries'.[13]

It was easy to see why Jesuits might wish to eliminate John Harrington. He had set a strong example to Protestants, being cast in a mould close to that of his former master, Prince Henry. John was 'well grounded in religion and learning' and 'was eminent for sobriety and chastity'.[14] Clearly the Jesuits were well aware that there was no point in attempting to corrupt his mind so they turned instead to destroying his body. Yet the idea that John and his tutor had been given poison during their travels on the continent and that it had killed them both was far fetched. The very fact that such an idea might even be entertained as a credible explanation for John's death is indicative of the lively suspicion toward Catholics that flourished in some quarters of Jacobean society.

John died – or as one of his contemporaries delicately put it, was 'elevated hence' – two months short of his twenty-second birthday.[15] His death was widely remarked upon by his contemporaries and his passing called for universal lamentation:

> ... bid the night
> Extend her length, the day not come in sight
> ... Hang each Dorick Bell
> With numerous tongues, and a continued knell
> On every tongue; Command the beasts to roare,
> And each sad noyse be multiply'd a score,[16]

The close bonds which existed between members of the Harrington family were clearly demonstrated when it was revealed that John had left his estate to his two sisters, Lucy and Frances, rather than to a male relative outside the immediate family which would have been the usual practice. Two thirds of the estate went to Lucy and the remaining third to Frances, but the inheritance was a poisoned chalice because it was burdened by enormous debts.

Seated beside her mother and sister at John's funeral Lucy listened as the life and merits of her brother were recounted to the assembled congregation. John was an exemplary youth, chaste, godly and educated. Of his erudition there could be no doubt. During his travels on the continent, John had collected an impressive array of books on subjects ranging from religion to mathematics and science, many of which had been printed abroad and could not be obtained in England. After John's death Lucy and her mother donated the bulk of the library he had assembled to Sidney Sussex College. Lucy was deeply distressed by John's death. Jane was staying with Lucy at Twickenham when she received a letter from her suitor, Nathaniel Bacon, who wrote of how the 'unhappy news of the Lord Harrington's death had before possessed our country' and then noted that Jane's 'relation has added more, to my already conceived sorrow'.[17] Jane's physical proximity to Lucy meant that she could tell Nathaniel more about what Lucy was feeling. Although Nathaniel longed for his sweetheart to come and visit him he was content that she was supporting her friend in a time of grief, telling her:

> I do rest much troubled for your uncertainty in your coming down, but I must acknowledge myself so much endeared to the Lady of Bedford that I do account myself most happy in having interest in any which may be able to do her service.[18]

Some time after John Harrington's death, Donne wrote a moving elegy entitled 'Obsequies to the Lord Harrington, brother to the Countesse of Bedford'. For Donne, John's early death was decreed by 'Fate', because:

> ... had Fate meant to have his virtues told,
> It would have let him live to have beene old;
> So, then that vertue'in season, and then this,
> We might have seene, and said, that now he is
> Witty, now wise, now temperate, now just:[19]

Donne had known Lucy's brother personally and he was genuinely inspired to write verses in his memory. But equally, Donne probably also believed that in penning a fulsome verse to commemorate John's death he would bring himself closer to Lucy. This very personal aspect to the elegy was suggested by the fact that Lucy's name was directly coupled with that of her brother in the title to the poem and by Donne's dedication of the elegy to her:

> Madam, – I have learned it, by those laws wherein I am a little conversant, that he which bestows any cost upon the dead, obliges him which is dead, but not the heir; I do not therefore send this paper to your Ladyship that you should thank me for it, or think

that I thank you in it; your favours and benefits to me are so much above my merits, that they are even above my gratitude, if that were to be judged by words, which must express it. But, Madam, since your noble brother's fortune being yours, the evidences also concerning it are yours: so his virtue being yours, the evidences concerning that belong also to you, of which by your acceptance this may be one piece, in which quality I humbly present it, and as a testimony how entirely your family possesseth.[20]

Donne knew that John Harrington had dispersed his estate between his sisters for it was common knowledge, and despite his protestations of not wanting 'favours' or 'benefits' from Lucy, he was undoubtedly hoping that she would give him money. According to Donne, Lucy not only possessed her 'noble brother's … virtue', but also his 'fortune', and Donne must have had high hopes that some of that fortune might find its way to him. What is not clear is whether Donne knew how indebted the estate Lucy inherited from John was.

After her brother's death Lucy resumed her normal round of court duties but her health remained weak. Called to wait on Anna she attended the Queen with the result that she prolonged an illness which left her bedridden for six weeks. But as she relayed gossip to Jane she revealed that she was not alone in her sickness; many of her friends and acquaintances were also suffering from:

> the danger or canker of this sickly tyme, wherein my people every whear have binne vissitted [sic] with much sicknes, w[hi]ch hath concluded att Exton with the death of poor Francke Marckham, the newse whearof came to me yesterday, & brought me a greate deale of sorrow, having ever had cause to hope, if God had spared her lyfe she wold have repaid my care of her with honnor & comfort, whearin att her ende shee hath not deseaved mee, though my hope of seeinge her happely bestoed [sic] bee frustrate: had she lived till alhallondtyde shee had died a wyfe, for I had concluded such a match for her as I had reson to beleive [sic] shee should have led contentedly, but he that disposeth all things has prouided far better for her.[21]

Francke, or Frances, Markham was the daughter of Lucy's close friend and cousin, Bridget. Lucy had continued to take an interest in the care of the little girl after the death of her mother and as a surrogate parent to Frances, Lucy had busied herself making marriage plans which were 'frustrate[d]' by the girl's untimely death. There is a sense in which although Lucy literally had no choice but to accept that she could not change events willed by God she was irked by Frances's death because it ruined the plans she had so carefully arranged. Lucy appeared more provoked by the failure of the projected marriage than the death of Frances and this brusque, matter-of-fact attitude emerged in other snippets of gossip and news which she was in the habit of relaying to Jane. Such gossip frequently revolved around the perennial subjects of pregnancy, birth, illness and death. So Lucy wrote to Jane:

My La: Vvedale is becom the fonde mother of a sonne; My La: Marquess of Winchester is dead, & our noble freind [sic] my Lord Mounttagle very ill of a swelling in his throate; John Elviston died on Tusday [sic] last, to the great griefe of all good dawnsers; My La: of Roxbrough grows big, & lookes her for the latter ende of the next month ...[22]

Lucy was often dispassionate about death, particularly if it did not affect her personally, as in the case of the Marquess of Winchester. At other times she associated the death with what she perceived to be the talents or abilities of the deceased, so, as a dancer herself, she noted that John Elviston would be missed by 'good dawnsers'. Interwoven with the gossip and news for Jane, Lucy also revealed to her friend how crippling her financial problems had become. With Edward finally recovering from his fever she was again free to follow her usual business which was 'dayle ... multiplied' and made her 'heavily feel the burden of a broken estate'.[23] Her attitude to business was a curious blend of spirituality and hard-nosed pragmatism. At one moment she would invoke divine help – 'yett doe I not doubt but by the assistance of almighty God I shall ear long ouercom those difficulties [which] att the present contest with mee' – while at the next she would be completely hardheaded, claiming that she was unafraid of legal actions against her, taking the view that her opponent would 'gett nothing but lost labor' and that it would cost her no 'more than som few Lawyers fees & a litle troble'.[24]

Lucy was, however, solicitous for the welfare of her mother. Anne Harrington had been commanded to go to Elizabeth in Heidelberg and Lucy confessed to Jane how worried she was about her mother's fitness to undertake such an arduous journey given Anne's age and the inclement autumn weather:

... my mother goes presently into Germany, by my La: Elisabeths extreame earnest desier, & the K[ing]s comandment, w[hi]ch, the season of the yeare considered is so cruell a iourney, as I much feare how shee will passe itt: but her affection to her Highnes keepes her from being frighted with any difficulty. And her spiritt caries her body beyond what almost could be hoped att her years ...[25]

The bonds between Elizabeth and the Harringtons remained as strong as ever and there was no question that Anne would not go to Heidelberg as she had been commanded, but the experience of death within her immediate family seemed to make Lucy more than usually apprehensive about her mother's impending journey. In the event, Lucy's anxiety over the safety of her remaining family was not misplaced but it was not her mother who died. Early the following year Lucy lost her sister, Frances. Writing to Thomas Roe, Lord Carew noted that 'The Ladie Chichister, the onely sister to the countesses of Bedford, is dead, which gave a new wound to her and the olld [sic] ladye'.[26] Scarcely recovered from the loss of father and brother Lucy and Anne now lost a sister and daughter. More than ever there was a compelling need to cling to their faith, to the belief that life was temporary, a mere prelude for meeting again in a better and happier place where there was no such thing as death and where at 'the gates of heaven' all would meet 'and never part'.[27]

The years around 1613 and 1614 were exceptionally difficult ones for Lucy, and she turned to old and trusted friends like Jane for support. Once she might have approached John Donne but after the Drury business and his cultivation of the Countess of Salisbury as a new patroness, the relationship between the two had fundamentally changed. Furthermore, it is possible that a certain distance between them was exacerbated by Lucy's disapproval of the company Donne was keeping. Donne had, through the agency of James Hay, attracted the patronage of the highly influential courtier Robert Carr, later elevated to Viscount Rochester and eventually to Earl of Somerset. Carr was a young Scot who had travelled in Hay's train to England on the accession of James and initially found a place as a member of Prince Henry's Bedchamber. By 1611 he was made Viscount Rochester and quickly recognized by his contemporaries as a man of influence with James, but his power grew even greater after the death of Robert Cecil. After his accession James had relied heavily on Cecil to smooth and soothe the factional difficulties operating within his court. Although it is impossible to generalize about political groupings within the early Stuart court, two broad factions can be detected. One of these groups gathered around Pembroke and included men like the Archbishop of Canterbury, George Abbot, who were Protestant, anti-Spanish and staunch believers in parliamentary power. This group was pitted against one composed mainly of members of the Howard family who tended to be more amenable towards both Catholics and Spain. In addition to attending to the minutiae of state business, Cecil had held the aspirations of these two antagonistic groups in a delicate balance, but after his death in 1612 there was no person of like inclination, power or skill to assume his role. James decided to undertake the duties of secretary himself, but he was not the administrator Cecil had been and although he initially approached the task with enthusiasm, he lacked the discipline required to perform the work systematically. James was assisted by Carr, who by now had been appointed as a member of the Privy Council. Carr was influential with James not simply because he helped the King in attending to state business, but also because he was a handsome young man whom James found pleasing to have around. As one contemporary put it:

> Carr hath all favours ... The king doth much covet his presence ... for I tell you ... this fellow is straight-limbed, well-favoured, strong shouldered, and smoothfaced, with some sort of cunning and shew of modesty; though, God wot, he well knoweth when to shew his impudence.[28]

At first Carr did not favour any one court faction over another, but when he fell in love with Frances Howard, the daughter of Thomas Howard, Earl of Suffolk, he came within the political orbit of the Howard family. Frances had married the Earl of Essex with great ceremony in 1606, but the marriage had proved a failure and she was keen to encourage Carr's interest in her, even going so far as to visit Simon Forman to procure love potions to ensure Carr's continued interest. Suffolk and his uncle, Henry Howard, Earl of Northampton, viewed Carr's love for Frances as a unique and fortuitous opportunity to attract the King's favourite to their interests. The Howards soon began to reap the rewards of their association with Carr. After Northampton's death in 1614, Suffolk was named as Lord Treasurer and Carr himself replaced Suffolk as Lord Chamberlain even though the post had originally been promised to Pembroke. A further issue complicating the political landscape was James's plan to make positive overtures to Spain about marrying Prince Charles to the Spanish Infanta, daughter of Philip III of Spain, thus creating a strong ally for himself in the Spanish king and fulfilling his personal ambition to act as a peacemaker in a Europe riven by religious difference. James's reasoning was that having married his daughter Elizabeth to the Protestant Frederick, a Catholic bride for Charles would enable him to speak and act with authority on matters of religious tolerance and balance.

For men like Pembroke and George Abbot who 'detested Spain and preferred reliance on Parliament to subservience to a foreign, catholic power', both the 'Carr-Suffolk alliance and the pro-Spanish policy were an anathema', and to them it was clear that Rochester, by allowing himself to drift into the clutches of the Howard camp, lay at the root of the problem and therefore had to be got rid of.[29] But how? Any attempt abruptly to force Carr away from the King would serve only to drive the two men even closer together. Some subtlety was called for and it was eventually agreed that the best way to prise Carr away from James was to introduce a new favourite to the King. The candidate the group chose for this role was a handsome young man called George Villiers. Pembroke, Abbot, Hertford, Lucy and their like-minded sympathizers dedicated themselves to 'Somerset's removal, and finding King *James* his good nature loth to leave the bosom of one *Minion*, until he had reposed himself in another, made it their plot to advance' Villiers.[30] One evening:

> There was a great but private entertainment at supper, at Baynards Castle, by the family of Herberts, Hartford, and Bedford, and some others; by the way in Fleet-street, hung out Somersets picture, at a painters stall; which one of the lords envying, bad his footman fling dirt in the face, which he did; and gave me occasion thereby to ask my companion upon what score this was done. He told me that this meeting would discover: and truly I waited neer and opportune, and so was acquainted with the design to bring in Villiers.[31]

Lucy was fully involved in the political scheming that took place at Pembroke's London residence, Baynard's Castle, and the public abuse of Somerset's picture made it abundantly clear what the scheming aimed at – the removal of the hated Carr in order to smooth the way for the introduction of Villiers. According to one contemporary source, the day after the meeting at Baynard's Castle, Sir Thomas Lake led Villiers 'into Court, buying him the Cup-bearers place'.[32] Other sources suggest that Villiers was made a cup-bearer prior to the meeting at Baynard's Castle, but whatever the actual timing, the installation of Villiers in this post was a crucial step in the plan to bring him to James's attention. Every alternate month Villiers waited on the King at table and this gave James ample opportunity to see and converse with the young man at some length and the King very much liked what he saw and heard.

Despite James's interest in Villiers it was still Carr who had the King's ear and he was quite prepared to push for what he wanted, chief of which was to marry Frances. The only way for Frances and Carr to marry was for Frances to be granted a divorce. Carr's friend Sir Thomas Overbury, who had intially gone along with his friend when Frances was just a mistress, objected strongly to her becoming Carr's wife mainly because he feared he would lose his influence with Carr. He attempted to persuade his friend against marriage to Frances but to no avail, and he was shortly after offered a post as ambassador to Russia as Carr put pressure on James in order to rid himself of Overbury whose objections to the proposed marriage had become tiresome. But Overbury declined the offered appointment, being persuaded that it amounted to nothing better 'than an honourable Grave' and believing that it would be far more preferable to 'lye some days in the Tower, than more months in a worse Prison'.[33] Overbury duly went to prison, but he had made a fatal miscalculation, because while confined to the Tower his refusal of the Russian post was presented to James as an act of contempt and accordingly his imprisonment was made more restrictive with the result that he became far more vulnerable to his enemies. In the absence of Overbury, who had helped Carr compose letters – and allegedly love poetry – Carr now had the services of John Donne at his disposal. Donne had managed to align himself with a powerful favourite and that favourite needed to be carefully cultivated. Writing to Carr after a bout of illness Donne was effusive:

> Since your Lordship will not let me dye, but have by your favour of sending to me, so much prevaled against a vehement feaver, that I am now in good degrees of convalescence. I was desirous that my first sacrifice, to any person in this World for my beginning of health, should be to your Lordship, That I might acknowledge, that, as ever since I had the happinesse to be in your Lordship's sight, I have lived upon your bread; so I owe unto your Lordship now all the means of my recoverie, and my health it self: So must all the rest of my life, and means be a debt to your Lordship ...[34]

Eager to marry Frances, Carr persuaded James to call a commission of bishops and lawyers to look into the Essex marriage and as a result deeply intimate facts about the sex life of Frances and Essex became public knowledge, as Frances attempted to have the marriage annulled on the grounds that Essex was impotent and that she was still a virgin. In support of her claims Frances went so far as to submit to an examination of her virginity despite whispers in some quarters that she had a substitute take her place, while Essex faced the insult and humiliation of being branded a 'gelding'.[35] Over the objections of some members of the commission, including Abbot, Frances was granted a divorce toward the end of 1613, and in December she and Carr married. Despite the dubiousness of the divorce, Donne stoutly defended it and even went so far as to offer to write a legal justification of it:

> ... some appearances have been here, of some treatise concerning this Nullity, which are said to proceed from *Geneva*, but are beleeved to have been done within doors, by encouragements of some whose names I will not commit to this letter. My poor study having lyen that way, it may prove possible, that my weak assistance may be of use in this matter ...[36]

Donne also presented Carr, now elevated by James to Earl of Somerset, with a poem to celebrate his marriage, albeit some time after the wedding. In the poem he likened the newlyweds, somewhat incongruously, to swans: 'Blest payre of Swans, Oh may you interbring / Daily new joyes, and never sing'.[37] Donne was not alone in writing poetry for the Somersets. Ben Jonson was one of a number of writers who presented verses to the newly married couple, but for Lucy a complimentary verse from someone like Jonson would not be problematic because Jonson was a professional writer, whereas a piece of poetry from Donne, who was not a professional poet, was much more personal. However, not all the poetry prompted by the Somerest wedding was complimentary, and a very different view of the union, perhaps penned by Essex himself, was far from flattering:

> Ladye changed to Venus dove
> Gently guide your Carr of love.
> Lett your sporte from night to daye
> Be to make your Carre a waye ... /
> Plants ynough thene may ensue
> For Som-arsett where none ere grewe
> Som-arsett and Som are layde,[38]

The tweaking of Somerset's surname to 'Som' and 'arsett' was a clear and unambiguous debasement of the word 'arse'. Whoever the anonymous poet was, he or she had a very low opinion indeed of Frances's new husband.

Not only did Lucy personally dislike Somerset because of his partiality to the Howards and his undue influence over James, she was still friendly with, and loyal to, members of the Essex family and would necessarily have been troubled by the events overtaking the young Essex. Lucy had taken a prominent, and very public, role in the masque organized to celebrate his marriage to Frances, and she knew him personally. For Lucy, the idea that Donne was so publicly throwing in his lot with a man like Somerset, who had comprehensively humiliated and embarrassed Essex, was wholly unsatisfactory. Donne's involvement with Somerset was driven by his need to find secure and lucrative employment, and he no doubt hoped that his powerful friend could help him. But in this he was mistaken. Despite the personal backing of an influential political triumvirate comprised of Somerset, Hay and Egerton, John Donne failed to find a position. In fact James was of the view that Donne should not seek secular employment at all; rather, the King felt that Donne should enter the church and it was to a life devoted to the service of God that Donne eventually turned.

Lucy may have been displeased by Donne's association with Somerset but she was touched by the elegy he had written for her brother and she offered to assist him in repaying his debts before his ordination as a minister. Donne was not about to reject such a generous offer and he told Goodyer:

> ... it were an injury from me to the constancy of that noble Lady, if I should not, assoon [sic] as she promises, do some act of assurance of the performance; which I have done, as I say, in fixing times to my creditors; for by the end of next terme, I will make an end with the world, by Gods [sic] grace.[39]

But Lucy's own impecunious state meant that she sent Donne far less money than he had hoped for, a mere £30. Donne was disappointed by the gift and suspected that the reason why Lucy was less generous than he had anticipated was because of her memory of his 'past life' and the malevolent influence of Burges.[40] His sense of bitterness and disappointment were palpable in a letter he wrote to Goodyer:

> ... upon this motion, which I made to her [Lucy] by letter, and by Sir Thomas Roe's assistance, if any scruple should arise in her, she was somewhat more startling, than I looked for from her; she had more suspicion of my calling, a better memory of my past life, than I had thought her nobility could have admitted; of all which, though I humbly thank God, I can make good use, as one that needs as many remembrances in that kind, as not only friends but enemies can present, yet I am afraid they proceed in her rather from some ill impression taken from Dr. Burges, than that they grow in herself. But whosoever be the conduit, the water is the Holy Ghost's, and in that acceptation I take it. For her other way of expressing her favour to me, I must say, it is not with that cheerfulness as heretofore she hath delivered herself towards me. I am almost sorry, that an elegy should have been able to move her to so much compassion heretofore, as to offer to pay my debts; and my greater wants now, and for so good a purpose, as to come disengaged into that profession, being plainly laid open to her, should work no farther but that she sent me £30, which in good faith she excused with that, which is in both parts true, that her

present debts were burdensome, and that I could not doubt of her inclination, upon all future emergent occasions, to assist me. I confesse to you, her former fashion towards me, had given me a better confidence; and this diminution in her makes me see, that I must use more friends than I thought I should have needed. I would you could burn this letter before you read it; at least do when you have read it.[41]

Donne's letter was definitely not intended for showing and Goodyer was ordered to destroy it, not because Donne feared that Lucy might somehow stumble across it, but because at the time Goodyer was staying with the Countess of Huntingdon and Donne was afraid it might come to the notice of that lady and cause her to make unwelcome inquiries into the activities of his youth:

I am afraid out of a Contemplation of mine own unworthinesse, and fortune, that the example of this Lady, should work upon the Lady where you are [at the Countess of Huntingdon's]: for though goodnesse be originally in her, and she do good, for the deeds sake, yet, perchance, she may think it a little wisdome, to make such measure of me, as they who know no better, do.[42]

Lucy may well have been suspicious of Donne's motives for entering the church, because while there was no doubt that he possessed the necessary theological knowledge to engage in complex religious debate, for Lucy his personal commitment to his faith may have presented a greater problem. Burges loomed large in Donne's mind as the man responsible for influencing Lucy against him, but his view that it was Burges alone who stood between him and Lucy was overstated. Lucy was under the influence of clerics other than Burges. Most notably, around the time Donne was taking serious steps toward ordination, both Lucy and Edward were attending the services of the Puritan Nicholas Byfield who preached at Richmond. Over the years Byfield dedicated a number of highly Calvinistic texts to Lucy. The first of these was a work entitled *An Exposition Upon the Epistle to the Colossians*, which appeared in 1615 and was dedicated jointly to Lucy and Edward. The dedication revealed that, even some years after his accident, Edward still suffered from its effects and that his 'daily and affectionate respect of the word of God and prayer [was] in priuate, since the Lord hath made ... [him] lesse able to resort more frequently to the publike assemblies'.[43] Byfield also made it clear that Lucy and her household attended services both morning and evening on Sundays, thereby setting an admirable example for others to emulate:

Madam, what thanks can we euer sufficiently giue vnto God for that rare and worthy example, with which your Ladyship doth comfort and incourage the hearts of many, in your care of Gods sabaoths, and in your neuer-failing attendance vpon the ordinances of God, with the congregation, morning and euening, not only in your owne person, but with your whole familie.[44]

Byfield had good reason to feel indebted to Lucy, for just as she had for Burges, she also intervened directly with James on his behalf. Precisely why Lucy needed to intercede for Byfield is not clear, but it almost certainly centred on a hardline Puritan stance that brought him into conflict with the established church. Whatever the reason, Byfield was immensely grateful to Lucy's efforts on his behalf, telling her:

> what thanks can euer be sufficient, or what seruice can euer be enough for that incomparable benefit (which I haue and shall euer esteeme the greatest outward blessing did euer befall me; and which (Madam) by your Honors singular care and furtherance, after an admirable manner I obtained) I meane the clearing of my reputation from the vniust aspersions of my aduersaries, and that by the mouth and pen of the Lords Annointed, my most dread Soueraigne ...[45]

For Donne it must have been both frustrating and galling to see Lucy so ready to use her influence for others in matters of religion while she still appeared to harbour doubts about his own fitness for ordination. By the same token it may be that her support for stern Puritan preachers like Burges and Byfield was one of the reasons why she looked askance at Donne's desire to take orders. Donne might be able to speak eloquently and persuasively on the 'very knots of divinity', but was his heart really in what he was about to do? Did he have a calling?

What Lucy did not know was that at the same time that Donne was seeking money from her he was also seriously considering compiling a book of his poetry and printing it with a dedication to Somerset. Donne was fully aware that such an action would anger Lucy and he wrote to Goodyer floating the idea and at the same time urging absolute discretion on his friend:

> One thing more I must tell you, but so softly that am loth to hear it myself; and so softly that, if that good Lady were in the room with you and this letter, she might not hear. It is that I am brought to a necessity of printing my poems, and addressing them to my Lord Chamberlain. This I mean to do forthwith, not for much public view, but at mine own cost, a few copies.[46]

Still smarting from the negative responses to the Drury poems, Donne confessed that there were some 'incongruities' in this new 'resolution' and that in taking his poems to the press he predicted that his actions would 'suffer from many interpretations'.[47] Yet he seemed undeterred by a potentially hostile response. On the very verge of entering the church, Donne saw the publication of his poetry as 'a valediction to the world, before I take orders'.[48] In order to put the proposed book together Donne asked a favour of Goodyer:

> I am to ask you, whether you ever made any such use of the letter in verse, *A nostre Comtesse chez vous*, as that I may not put it in amongst the rest to persons of that rank; for I desire very very much that something should bear her name in the book ...[49]

The book was not to be made up of new compostitions but to comprise a collection of some of the verses Donne had already written, and he was clear that he wanted something in the book to honour Lucy. Yet despite all the planning and the flurry of letters to Goodyer it appears that Donne's proposed venture into print never materialized, perhaps because Goodyer managed to persuade him that such an undertaking would be an act of folly. Whatever the reason, Donne abandoned the plan and despite the doubts of people like Lucy concerning his fitness for the church, he was ordained as a minister on 23 January 1615. After the long years of false hopes, broken promises and bitter disappointment John Donne finally had a position.

By the spring of the same year there was good news for the Pembroke faction in their attempts to oust Somerset. Plans were afoot to place Villiers within the King's Bedchamber, a move which would certainly be resisted by Somerset but which might succeed if the plotters could enlist the help of Anna whom James, somewhat curiously, relied on for advice when deciding household appointments. George Abbot was influential in persuading Anna to support the plan, for although she detested Somerset, who treated her with undisguised contempt, she was shrewd enough to know that once a new favourite had found his feet he would not necessarily show any loyalty to those who had promoted him. Lucy, with her access to, and intimacy with, the Queen would no doubt have added her voice to those calling on Anna to help Villiers secure a place within James's Bedchamber. In the end Anna agreed to lend her support; according to Abbott:

> Upon importunity Queen Anne condescended, and so pressed it with the King that he assented; which was so stricken while the iron was hot that in the Queen's Bed Chamber the King knighted him with the rapier which the Prince did wear. And when the King gave order to swear him of the Bed Chamber, Somerset importuned the King with a message that he might be only sworn a Groom. But myself and others that were at the door sent to her Majesty that she would perfect her work and cause him to be sworn a Gentleman of the Bed Chamber.[50]

In a tense scene, Villiers's supporters stood just outside the door to Anna's Bedchamber and held their breath hoping and praying that she would prevail and that their carefully laid plans would not be derailed by Somerset's impassioned appeals to James. Lucy was a key player in this crucial moment as she literally propelled Villiers into the chamber; according to a contemporary report she ushered Villiers into 'the Presence-Chamber, entering him a Bed-chamber-man'.[51] Despite Somerset's predictably vociferous objections – that Villiers should be given the lesser position of a groom of the Bedchamber rather than the more elevated post of gentleman of the Bedchamber – Villiers was successfully placed within the King's most intimate space and in time grew to become a favourite without equal. But in the meantime Somerset's problems were beginning to prove far greater than dealing with a new man competing for the King's affection.

In the Tower Overbury had paid the ultimate price for objecting to the Somerset marriage: he was murdered. Writing to Thomas Roe in October 1615, Lord Carew brought his friend up to date on the latest news:

> by indirect and maillitious meanes, Sir Thomas Overburie was poysoned in the Tower. The Kinge, who is vnpartiallye just in all his wayes, (although the information pointed att the Erle of Somerset,) gave commandment for the enquirie of itt ... the Countesse of Somerset was the procurer of itt [the poison], who by Mrs. Turner ... att sundry times brought and sent vnto him poisons in tartes and gellye, which Overburye did eat; but those poysons not workinge ... a glister was administered vnto him by an apothecaryes boy ... which within a few howres dispatched him.[52]

After several unsuccessful attempts at poisoning, what finally killed Overbury was the administration of a mercury enema. This treatment, for therapeutic ends, was much favoured by Theodore Mayerne and so closely had he become associated with it that he was immediately implicated in Overbury's death. The enemies Mayerne had made in his handling of Prince Henry's illness had found a perfect opportunity to attack him anew, although he was eventually cleared of any wrongdoing. Overbury's murder became the talk of the land, and Lucy wrote to Jane telling her, 'I am shuer the busnesses now a foote hear flie over all the Kingdom, & therfore cannot bee unknown to you ... Whar & when this tragede will ende, I thinke God only knows'.[53] In contemporary usage, the word 'tragedy' referred to a play or drama and there is therefore a sense of detachment in Lucy's language, perhaps due to the fact that she had no love for either Somerset or Overbury.

Somerset and Frances were charged with Overbury's murder, and their trial which was held at Westminster Hall became the social event of the year. Additional seating for the anticipated public interest in the trial was built, but even this was not sufficient and tickets for a place in the public gallery rocketed in price. People were so:

> earnest for places, which at this time were growne to so extraordinarie a rate, that fowre or five peeces (as they call them) was an ordinarie price, and I know a lawier that had agreed to geve ten pound for himself and his wife for the two dayes, and fiftie pound was geven for a corner that could hardly containe a dousen.[54]

The fall of the Somersets was as dramatic as it was inevitable. The pair were found guilty of plotting Overbury's murder and there was a spate of executions and imprisonments as their accomplices were brought to trial and sentenced. But James spared his former favourite the death penalty and Somerset and Frances were imprisoned in the Tower. As the Somersets fell from power there was a gathering at Sir Ralph Winwood's house at Ditton in Buckinghamshire. According to Chamberlain, the meeting was attended by 'the Lord Chamberlain [Pembroke], the earle of Mongomerie [Philip Herbert], the countesse of Bedford and I know not how many … more'.[55] For the company assembled at Ditton, news of Somerset's fall must have been a cause for jubilation.

As the year wore on Lucy decided to spend some time at Spa and thereby combine a trip for health purposes with visiting her mother who was staying with Elizabeth at The Hague. Writing to Jane she outlined her plans for the summer of 1616:

> I thinke I shall … use the helpe of the spaw [Spa] for the confirmation of my health & prevention of som infirmities I haue of late years binne subiect to; for w[hi]ch Mayern counsells me to goe theather, w[hi]ch I shall do with much the more willingness that I may wayte by that occasion on my mother who crossed the sea thitherward on Thursday last …[56]

Lucy made it clear to Jane that before embarking on her journey she had settled her estate and that if anything untoward should happen to her during her travels abroad, Jane would receive the money Lucy had borrowed from her: 'I part not without so settling my estate, as whatsoever becom of mee, every on shall be shewer of ther owne; & you not be preiudised by yo[u]r kindnes to mee'.[57] Lucy's confidence in promising Jane that the debt would be repaid would have been all the greater because she had recently acquired a patent to coin copper farthings in much the same way as her father had, a privilege she shared with the Duke of Lennox. But Lucy's new income-earner was soon beset with difficulties as she came into dispute with a Gerard Malines, who protested to the Privy Council that as a result of Lucy and Lennox's business venture he stood to lose nearly three thousand pounds on farthings he had already coined. Such difficulties were not uncommon in the financial schemes Lucy undertook which ranged variously from being granted a tax on sea coal to holding shares in the Virginia Company.[58] Despite Lucy's letter to Jane there is no evidence she actually went to Spa.

Another plan of Lucy's which failed to come to fruition was her engagement of Nicholas Stone to create a monument to honour her family members. Lucy made arrangements for a monument to the deceased members of her family with the master craftsman Stone whose notebook recorded:

> A Bargen mad with mr Chambers for the ues [sic] of the Right honerabell Luce contes of Bedford for on far and statly tombe of Touch and whit marbell for har father and mother and brother and sister; for the wich I was to have 1020 £. and my lady was to stand at all charges for caregs and Iorn and Setting up.[59]

Raising a stone, or a tomb, on behalf of one's family was an important act because it was one way in which the dead could be remembered by the living. Jonson called attention to this practice when he wrote his elegy for Cecilia Bulstrode and used the device of the stone to engage the reader directly, with the premeptory command, 'Stay view this stone'. The aptly named Stone was a leading English sculptor who had trained in the Netherlands and was therefore an obvious choice for Lucy, who sought to engage the best craftsman she could find. But Lucy's decision to approach Stone may also have been influenced by his work for Thomas Howard, Earl of Arundel, in the previous year.

Lucy seems to have been both attracted and exasperated by Arundel's activities in equal measure. The Earl had grown up in a deeply troubled family, but despite his inauspicious beginnings he proved to be one of the most renowned art collectors of his generation. Around 1581 Arundel's father, Philip Howard, converted to Catholicism for which he was imprisoned in the Tower where he languished for seven years before eventually being executed. As a consequence of Philip's religious conversion his family suffered greatly under Elizabeth, and this experience had a profound effect on his son who grew up quiet, bookish and notably uninterested in religious matters. Although Thomas belonged by birth to the influential Howard clan, he was not particularly close to its other members, many of whom had callously abandoned his father to his unhappy fate. After the accession of James, Thomas hoped, like so many other men, that a change of monarch might lead to an improvement in his situation, but his hopes failed to materialize. He made little progress with James, but as the years went by he developed a close relationship with Prince Henry, with whom he shared a passion for art. Arundel married Alethea, daughter of the 7th Earl of Shrewsbury, an intelligent and independent woman and heiress to an immense fortune. With Alethea's money Arundel could finally afford fully to indulge his passion for collecting, an activity in which both he and his wife proved themselves to be knowledgeable and determined. Arundel and Alethea were of the party that accompanied the newlywed Elizabeth and Frederick to Heidelberg and, after their duties toward Frederick and Elizabeth had been fulfilled, Arundel, his Countess, and their friend Inigo Jones made their way to Italy where they travelled extensively. Arundel had travelled abroad before, but on his return from Italy late in 1614 he came back with an entirely new artistic vision which had been informed by the art and architecture he had seen during his travels; and he employed Nicholas Stone to incorporate these new ideas into a tomb he planned to erect in memory of his relative, Northampton. The monument Stone subsequently created for Arundel possessed a 'grace not found in English sculpture before'.[60] Eager to be at the cutting edge of new artistic trends Lucy also approached Stone; however, the crucial difference was that Lucy did not possess a vast fortune of the Arundels and the planned monument in memory of her family was never built.

By early 1617 Lucy was busily engaged in two of her favourite activities –

matchmaking and masquing – on behalf of her great friend James Hay. Hay's first wife, Honora, had died in tragic circumstances three years earlier when, returning home in her carriage from the theatre one evening, she was attacked and robbed. The robbery proved so unexpected and so deeply shocking for her that she lost the baby she was carrying and died shortly after. But by 1617, Hay had found a new love. He invited the French ambassador, De La Tour, to dinner and a masque at his house and it was Lucy who assumed the role of mistress of proceedings and she who was reported to be 'managing' Hay's love for Lucy Percy.[61] The fact that Hay was alleged to be so 'far ingaged in affection'[62] toward this new lady may have dictated the subject matter of the masque performed that evening. Nicholas Lanier, a fashionable musician, was engaged to design the scenery and compose the music for a short, sung, masque entitled *Lovers Made Men* written by Jonson. The masque depicted a group of men who had drowned as a result of love arriving at the river Lethe. It is subsequently discovered that the men are not in fact dead and they are commanded to drink of the river in order to return to their former selves:

> Doe, bow unto the reverend lake:
> And having touch'd there; up, and shake
> The shadowes off ...[63]

Near the end of the masque, Cupid, the god responsible for the pseudo-deaths of the lovers, appeared on stage and called on the masquers to choose partners to dance the revels. Amid the feasting and dancing Lucy was in her element and for a time at least the sadness and trials of the preceding years were assuaged. Although it appeared that Burley-on-the-Hill would soon slip from her grasp to her brother-in-law, Sir Edward Noell, who had already lent her money on it, there was good news a little later in the year as James granted Lucy and Edward the lease of a property called Moor Park which lay to the north of London in Hertfordshire.[64] Lucy wasted no time in taking over Moor Park. Selling the property at Twickenham she moved north and the year was one of great activity as she became absorbed in building a house and developing a new garden. The garden Lucy created at Moor Park was even more astonishing than the one at Twickenham. When Sir William Temple visited it in 1655 he described it, enthusiastically, as:

> The perfectest Figure of a Garden I ever saw, either at Home or Abroad ... It was made by the Countess of Bedford ... It lies on the side of a Hill, (upon which the House stands) but not very steep. The Length of the House, where the best Rooms and of most Use or Pleasure are, lies upon the Breadth of the Garden, the Great Parlour opens into the Middle of a Terras Gravel-Walk that lies even with it, and which may be ... about three hundred Paces long, and broad in Proportion; the Border set with Standard Lawrels, and

at large Distances, which have the Beauty of Orange-Trees out of Flower and Fruit: From
this Walk are Three Descents by many Stone Steps, in the Middle and at each End, into
a very large Parterre. This is divided into Quarters by Gravel-Walks, and adorned with
Two Fountains and Eight Statues in the several Quarters; at the End of the Terras-Walk
are Two Summer-Houses ... even with the Cloisters, which are paved with Stone, and
designed for Walks of Shade, there being none other in the whole Parterre. Over these
two Cloisters are two Terrasses covered with Lead and fenced with Balusters; and the
Passage into these Airy Walks, is out of the two Summer-Houses ... The cloister facing
the *South* is covered with Vines, and would have been proper for an Orange-House, and
the other for Myrtles ... From the Middle of this Parterre is a Descent by many Steps
flying on each side of a Grotto that lies between them (covered with Lead, and Flat)
into the lower Garden, which is all Fruit-Trees ranged about the several Quarters of a
Wilderness which is very Shady; the Walks here are all Green, the Grotto embellish'd with
Figures of Shell-Rock-work, Fountains and Water-works ... a Garden on the other side
the House, ... very Wild, Shady, and adorned with rough Rock-work and Fountains. This
was *Moor-Park* ... the sweetest Place, I think, that I have seen in my Life, either before
or since, at Home or Abroad.[65]

Precisely how much of the garden that William Temple saw was due to Lucy's
handiwork cannot be known with any certainty. Certainly the linking of the
house and the garden into a seamless unit and the arrangement of the statuary
within the garden was reminiscent of the new Italian style introduced by the
Arundels late in 1616 and may have been Lucy's attempt to keep pace with the
latest developments in garden design.

Features such as the shell grotto, however, may well have been much later
additions to the garden. What is clear is that in the time that she was working on
the garden at Moor Park, Lucy was totally absorbed in planning and planting.
The letters she wrote around this time contain a number of references to her
activities 'att the More' and they are infused with a sense of energy, contentment
and great happiness.[66] Throughout the summer Lucy was 'still adding ... trifles
of pleasure'[67] to her garden but it was an ongoing project and in addition to
begging plants from friends like Nicholas and Jane, she may also have acquired
plants from the many nurseries located in the low countries. As Lucy, her mother,
and various friends travelled back to England after taking the waters at Spa or
visiting Heidelberg, they may have carried new specimens to be planted in the
garden at Moor Park. For Lucy the garden was a central part of her life and to
enable Jane fully to understand how she felt about it Lucy compared her feelings
to the experience of being hopelessly in love, 'I am so much in love with [the
garden] as if I wear so fond of any man I wear in hard case'.[68]

The vagaries of love also emerged in a creatively related area when Lucy
arranged for a special masque, called *Cupid's Banishment*, to be written and
presented to the Queen at Greenwich Palace. The masque was performed for

Anna while she was enjoying a unique period of freedom from James, who was spending six months on a progress in Scotland. Few details exist as to who financed the performance but it may well have been the impoverished Lucy presenting a rather special gift to Anna. Written by Robert White, the masque was presented at Greenwich on 4 May 1617 and dedicating the text to Lucy, White made it clear that she had been instrumental in providing him with ideas and encouraging him to complete the work:

> I thought it injustice to devote the fruits which your honour first sowed, to any but yourself. Then from your honourable acceptance let this draw a perpetual privilege, that it may flourish in the fair summer of your gentle favour, and triumph in despite of Envy's raging winter.[69]

The characters in the masque included the mythological figures of Cupid, Diana, Hymen, Bacchus and Mercury, as well as representations of the concepts of Occasion and Fortune, and the story revolved around Diana, the goddess of chastity, in conflict with Cupid, the blind god of love. One of the more unusual aspects of the performance was that the amateur masquers were not ladies or gentlemen of the court but young girls who were students at Ladies Hall, a school in Deptford. In an unmistakeable reference to these young ladies, Cupid called upon the character of Occasion to 'Summon young spirits to a jubilee. / Invite fresh youth to some amorous scene'.[70]

Diana figured frequently in the poetry and drama of the period, but the inclusion of this goddess in the masque may also have been a nod toward Lucy, who due the etymology of her name was frequently associated with the imagery related to Diana. The name 'Lucy' derives from 'Lucina' – meaning 'the goddess who brings to light'[71] – and it was one of the many alternate names for Phoebe. As the poet Michael Drayton made clear, at the time Phoebe had many titles, and she could be known variously as:

> *Diana, Delia, Luna, Cynthia,*
> *Virago, Hecate,* and *Elythia,*
> *Prothiria, Dictinna, Prosperine,*
> *Latona,* and *Lucina,* most divine;[72]

In keeping with her chaste nature, in *Cupid's Banishment* Diana commands Cupid, to 'Steal to some amorous court and tutor / Wanton ladies how to woo'.[73] This command may have been taken as an in-joke by some of the audience who knew full well that after James and Anna acceded to the English throne they had presided over a court that became infamous for its sexual licence. But times had changed and by 1617 'Wanton ladies' were no longer welcome and the young women who danced in *Cupid's Banishment* were in effect 'younger versions of

their privileged adult counterparts' as the 'queen and her circle were being set
up as models of female virtue to which the young ladies could aspire'.[74] The
masques given by Anna had often been transgressive, whether in the appearance
of the Queen herself and her ladies disguised as blackamoors or Anna wearing
a costume which revealed her legs. Each of Anna's masques had in its own
way pushed at the boundaries of masquing decorum, and *Cupid's Banishment*
followed in that tradition because it was the first Stuart masque in which an
amateur masquer, as opposed to a professional player, spoke aloud on stage.
According to the cast list, one of the young ladies 'Mistress Ann Watkins acted
Fortune' and within the text Fortune delivered a short speech:

> We are engaged to Time for this occasion
> That meets our wishes with such good success.
> For this great courtesy I'll create
> Some unexpected joy to crown thy hours,
> Thy minutes, I'll so turn upon this wheel of mine
> That men hereafter shall call thee happy Time.
> Hymen, Mercury, how welcome you are hither.
> We can no more express than we already have.[75]

The strong links between the spheres of dance and language were fully expressed
toward the end of the masque when Anna's name was physically inscribed upon
the stage by nymphs who danced '[forming] Anna Regina [Queen Anne] in
letters; [in] their second masquing dance [forming] Jacobus Rex [King James];
[in] their departing dance is [the formation of] Carolus P [Prince Charles]'.[76]
At the end of the masque two of the young women, Ann Chalenor and Anne
Sandilands, approached the Queen and presented her with gifts of needlework.
Both girls were goddaughters of Anna and they were taken and presented to
their godmother by the character of Diana. Lucy was of course a spectator at the
masque and not a participant, but the figure of Diana was sufficiently associated
with her to raise the possibility that she was being represented in some way,
that the presentation of the needlework was a part of Lucy's gift of the masque
to Anna. In the eyes of a spectator like Anna, the chaste Diana of myth and the
childless Lucy could, for a brief moment, be conflated and she might be seen as
acting in *loco parentis* to Anna's goddaughters. Of the two pieces of needlework
presented to Anna one depicted an acorn, the other a rosemary plant, with the
initial letter of each plant – 'A' and 'R' – spelling out Anna's name. The plants
carried a wide range of symbolic meanings: acorns, for example, traditionally
represented renewal and may have been intended to point to a renewal of the
masquing association between Lucy and her mistress. Rosemary played an
important role in traditional medicine, but it was also a plant which flowered
twice, again suggesting that its appearance in the embroidery was linked to ideas

of renewal between Lucy and Anna.[77] *Cupid's Banishment* was an elaborate and special gift from Lucy to Anna, yet barely three weeks after the masque was performed Lucy was deeply unhappy at Anna's decision to dismiss Lady Roxburgh from her post as a lady-in-waiting. A disillusioned Lucy confessed to Jane that as her own court duties had been fulfilled for the present she was looking forward to some time to herself adding, 'I am grown to love my ease and liberty so well, as no measuer of favor could often invite mee theather [the court], whear ther is no hope of any good to bee donne'.[78]

John Donne seems to have been reflecting on his past when he delivered a sermon to Anna at Denmark House in mid-December. Taking as his text a verse from Proverbs, 'I love them that love me, and they that seek me early shall find me',[79] the sermon was a meditation on love. In a passage reflecting on the soul Donne took the view that the:

> soul, that hath been transported upon any particular worldly pleasure, when it is intirely turn'd upon God, and the contemplation of his all-sufficiency and abundance, doth find in God fit subject, and just occasion to exercise the same affection piously, and religiously, which had before so sinfully transported, and possest it.[80]

Donne was no longer the 'sinfully transported' writer of profane love poetry. Nor did he respect the selfishness inherent in ambition:

> ... doth any ambitious man love honor or office therefore, because he thinks that title, or that place should receive a dignity by his having it, or an excellency by his executing it? ... No, it is only himself that is within the definition, *vult bonum sibi*, he wishes well (as he mistakes it) to himself, and he is content, that the slavery, and dishonor, and ruin of others should contribute to make up his imaginary happiness.[81]

It is possible that Lucy was at Denmark House attending on Anna in the run-up to the Christmas festivities at court and that she joined the Queen in listening to Donne preach. If Lucy did hear the sermon she would have received ample evidence to allay any earlier misgivings she might have had about Donne's fitness for the church. Moreover there was much in Donne's sermon that was directly applicable to the experiences of many in the congregation, in particular his belief that Christ:

> loves us most for our improvement, when by his ploughing up of our hearts, and the dew of his grace, and the seed of his word, we come to give a greater rent, in the fruites of sanctification than before. And since he loves us thus, and that in him, this love is *velle bonum*, a desire that his beloved should be happy ...[82]

Personal bereavement had stalked Lucy for years and had quite thoroughly ploughed up her heart. But Donne's counsel that adversity must be experienced in order to achieve 'improvement' had a deeply personal resonance for him too, because God had clearly been at work in his life four months earlier when his beloved wife, Ann, had died.

As a representative of the established church, Donne was no friend to Catholics and many of his writings and public pronouncements made his standpoint abundantly clear. There could be no confusion whatever over Donne's position in a statement such as:

> And how knowes he, who lets a Jesuit scape, whether he let go but a Fox, that will deceive some simple soule in matter of Religion; or a Wolfe, who, but the protection of the Almighty, would adventure upon the person of the highest of all?[83]

Given Donne's unequivocal opposition to Catholicism, the fact that he was called upon to preach before Anna raises interesting questions about the Queen's religious beliefs. Anna is frequently described as being a Catholic, yet if she was so obviously Catholic how could she submit herself to listening to a sermon delivered by an enemy of her professed faith? Equally, if Anna was a practising Catholic, however discreet, how could the staunchly Protestant Lucy remain in her service? As a skilled courtier Lucy could quite easily look the other way in certain matters or make allowances for her royal superiors. So, when she became angry with Elizabeth's behaviour in Bohemia she could chastise her while simultaneously claiming that she 'will neuer omitte making good my professions to hir [Elizabeth] as becoms a faithfull & carefull servant'.[84] But after Lucy's severe illness in 1612–13 it was impossible for her in all conscience to evade or rationalize religious issues, in particular anything that might be connected with those she considered to be 'l[y]ing papists'.[85] Although Lucy withdrew from the court to some extent after her sickness, her withdrawal was not motivated by any religious difficulties with her mistress. Any differences she had with Anna revolved around the Queen's slowness in attending to business, to her being 'dilatory', or what Lucy considered to be her poor decision-making skills. Snippets of information that might be used to build a case either for or against Anna's supposed Catholicism are far from helpful in deciding where her true religious beliefs lay. It is perhaps most useful to adopt the view articulated by Piero Contarini who reported to the Doge that 'Some consider … [Anna] a Catholic because she would never go to the English church, but really her religion is not known'.[86] For Lucy it may well have been not knowing what lay deep in the Queen's heart which ultimately made it possible for her to obey both her mistress and her conscience.[87]

Religious differences between Protestants and Catholics were not confined to England. Many miles away in Bohemia, May 1618 saw the beginnings of a complicated religious conflict that would convulse Europe for close to thirty years and affect Lucy personally. In 1617, the sick and ailing Emperor Matthias of Habsburg recommended that his cousin Ferdinand of Styria should assume the rule of Bohemia. Ferdinand was a Catholic but he agreed to protect the rights of Protestants living in Bohemia; however, he proved incapable of keeping his word. The loss of Protestant rights led to resentment against Ferdinand and his representatives, and in 1618 a group of angry Protestant deputies gathered in Prague and, in an action which has become known as 'The Defenestration of Prague', overthrew their Catholic rulers and set up a Protestant government. Bold but vulnerable, this new government sought help from other Protestant states, particularly England and the Netherlands, as they clearly saw that Spain, in its role as leader to the Catholic, Habsburg confederation, would take steps to put an end to their rebellion. The Defenestration of Prague was seen by many as rather more than a little local religious difficulty; for James's son-in-law, Frederick, whose own lands bordered on parts of Bohemia, it was all about defending and upholding the integrity of the Protestant faith. However, James was more circumspect and, with one eye on a Spanish bride for Charles, he had no wish openly to antagonize Spain. Seeking a compromise he offered to mediate between the Bohemians and Ferdinand, an action which was welcomed by Spain who had no wish to see the English king take sides with Bohemia and for a time matters simmered uneasily on.

Conflict and competition were not confined to matters of international politics; they also emerged in the seemingly innocuous arena of art. The acquisition of great works of art – paintings, statuary, medals and coins – played an important part in Stuart high culture. The late Prince Henry, Anna, Pembroke, Buckingham and Arundel were all passionate collectors, and, although she did not possess the financial resources of her friends and contemporaries, Lucy was keen to assemble an art collection of her own. Lucy may have been helped in sourcing and selecting suitable pieces by Jane's husband, Nathaniel Bacon, who was himself a painter of some repute. One artist whose paintings Lucy was keen to acquire was Hans Holbein, but so too was the Earl of Arundel. Writing to Dudley Carleton, who acted as his agent in procuring artworks, Arundel informed him:

> I have received from your Lordship a very fine Bason of Stone ... for which I must give you very many thanks and am sorry you remember me so much to your charge; I hear likewise, by many ways, how careful your Lordship is to satisfy my foolish curiosity in enquiring for pieces of Holbein.[88]

Holbein had worked at the court of Henry VIII and painted kings, queens, princes, princesses, counsellors as well as commoners. Among the subjects Holbein had painted were some of Arundel's ancestors, and this provided the Earl with a powerful incentive to collect Holbeins. In addition to a personal interest in some of the subjects figured in the paintings, 'Arundel loved history, and Holbein provided wonderfully vivid images of the principal figures of his favourite period'.[89] Arundel had been steadily assembling a collection of Holbein paintings and he was a determined and highly competitive collector. Lucy appears to have come into competition with him for some paintings and she complained bitterly of his sharp practices to Jane:

> I had almost forgotten an earnest request I am to make by yow to Mr Bacon, but that a tricke of my Lo. of Arundell putt vpon mee yesterday to the cusning mee of som pictures promised mee, putte mee in mind of itt. I was told the last night that yo[u]r father in law was like to die, & that hee had som peeses of painting of Holbens, w[hi]ch I am shewr as soone as Arundell hears he will trye all means to gett ... I am a very diligent gatherer of all I can gett of Holbens or any other excellent M[aster's] hand; I do not care att what rate I have them for price ... when Mr Bacon coms to London hee shall see that though I bee butt a late beginner I have pretty store of choise peeses.[90]

For Lucy, acquiring the paintings before Arundel managed to was of paramount importance and any regard for Nathaniel's ailing father was an irrelevance. In the event, the illness of Bacon's father was not as serious as Lucy had been led to believe and the old man lived another six years and so presumably she did not acquire the paintings. Whether Lucy decided to begin collecting Holbeins because Arundel did, and she was motivated by a desire to emulate and compete with him, or because she genuinely prized them more 'than Juels',[91] and was prepared to pay any price for them is impossible to know. In truth it was probably a little of both. What is not in doubt is that Lucy would have seen and admired Holbein's skill every time she visited Whitehall Palace, because on the wall of the Privy Chamber hung a large fresco by Holbein depicting Henry VIII and Jane Seymour, while behind them stood Henry's parents Henry VII and Elizabeth of York.[92] Not only was the fresco an object of great beauty, it was also quite literally 'a speaking picture', a very potent visual reminder of royal power. Moreover, it advertised the great deeds of the two Henrys: Henry VII, who had founded a royal dynasty, and his son, who had banished Catholicism. As Lucy stood or kneeled before James and Anna, she saw behind them, as it were supporting and validating their power, the figures in the painting gazing down at her.

In early modern thought the visual image, as represented by painting, was closely associated with the workings of memory. Donne made this association clear when he compared memory to a 'gallery', the place where pictures were displayed: 'If these be too large pictures for thy gallery, for thy memory, yet every man hath a pocket picture about him, a manuall, a bosome book, and if he will turn over but one leaf, and remember'.[93] Lucy's attempts to secure the Bacon Holbeins indicates that she made efforts to acquire paintings in her own right, but in later years she also had access to a fine art gallery in Harrington House which had been assembled by her great friend the Marquis of Hamilton, who occupied part of the house as a tenant. Hamilton had gathered together an impressive collection of paintings that included works by Titian, Correggio, Tintoretto,

Palma Vecchio and Bassano, and there Lucy could wander at will noting and observing the lessons which these great painters had woven into their work.

In furthering her passion for collecting art, including ancient medals and coins, Lucy had two powerful international contacts: her old friend Sir Thomas Roe who was ambassador to India and later Turkey, and Dudley Carleton ambassador first to Venice and, from 1616, at The Hague. Roe often worked on behalf of Arundel to seek out antiquities, but he was especially fond of Lucy, telling her that he was her most 'antient seruant' and boldly declaring that he would 'euer profess and maynteyne' that he loved and honoured her 'aboue all weomen'.[94] Like Roe, Carleton soon realized that acquiring works of art for collectors back in England could provide a lucrative source of income for an ambassador who might be paid only intermittently if at all. Much of Lucy's correspondence with Carleton centred on political gossip, events concerning Elizabeth and Frederick, and accounts of her attempts to obtain a post back in England which Carleton so desperately sought. In one letter Lucy told Carleton 'I will shortly send yow over a picture of my Lo: Chamberlains [Pembroke] donne by Mittens w[hi]ch if to much of desire to do well make him not falle short of his late works'.[95] Precisely why Lucy proposed to send a painting of Pembroke to Carleton is unclear, but it is possible she had been acquiring paintings and antique coins and medals from Carleton, and she still owed him money for them. The painting may therefore have been presented as a gift in kind. If so, her action was remarkably similar to that of Arundel, who also appears to have sent portraits of himself and his wife Alethea, also painted by David Mytens, to Carleton as payment for debts he had incurred through his collecting and to advertise his fitness for housing and displaying the precious statuary Carleton was supplying him with.

While Carleton helped Lucy acquire artworks, she in turn made efforts to enable him to gain the promotion he so craved. What appeared to be an ideal promotion opportunity arose in 1618 when Secretary Lake was dismissed from his post. Lake had become the unfortunate casualty of the machinations of his wife and daughter, who had falsely accused the Countess of Exeter of infidelity with her step-son. The web of lies spun by Lake's wife and daughter about the Countess eventually came to the attention of James, who decided to take a personal interest in the matter. As the case went to trial James advised Lake to leave his wife and daughter 'to the *Law*',[96] but Lake steadfastly stood by his women who were eventually found guilty. When it became clear that Lake would be dismissed, Carleton was hopeful that the vacant post might become his and he approached Lucy to help him obtain it. She replied, telling him:

I have taken the more tyme to awnser yo[u]r letter because I wold faine have given yow by mine a better acounte of the effects of yo[u]r freinds good wishes ... for though wee forsee a sertain change, wee cannot make any iudgement when itt will bee, nor who is destined to the places will be void ... espesially who shall fille the secretaries roome ... not withstanding ...[97]

Predicting events required time, patience and experience. Lucy and her friends could see a 'sertain change' in the offing but could not decide precisely what that 'change' might be. Perhaps Lucy was circumspect so as not to raise Carleton's hopes unnecessarily; if so, she was proved right because the post of secretary eventually went to Sir George Calvert, who proved sympathetic to the Spanish position in respect of events in Bohemia. Consummate politician that she was, Lucy could in one breath claim herself to be of 'weake ... power'[98] while at the next, flex her muscles in attempting to marry her niece to the son of the Marquis of Hamilton. Speaking about the match that appeared to be in train for her niece, Anne, she told Jane that the:

offer being made mee for her [Anne] pleases mee well; & I doubt not will take effect if her vnreasonable father can be brought to do what he ought; w[hi]ch if love will not make him I hope fear will prevaile: but of this lett no speach passe yow, because itt is yett too early days, but as soone as it is setled to any sertainty, & that the K: hath declared himselfe whos work itt is, yow shall hear of itt more ...[99]

Far from being a 'weake ... power', in the matter of arranging marriages at least, Lucy was quite capable of using her considerable influence with James to try and intimidate her brother-in-law. In the event it made no difference. Chichester remained unmoved by such pressure and Lucy complained bitterly of his 'scurvie dealing'.[100] But Lucy was quite happy to arrange marriages even when the parents of the bride and groom were ignorant of the impending nuptials. A scandalized John Chamberlain noted that she had actively participated in a marriage between the son of Sir Thomas Smith and Lady Isabella Rich without the consent of the groom's father and that Pembroke was Lucy's co-conspirator in the deed:

Sir Thomas Smiths sonne ... maried the Lady Isabella Rich, without his fathers consent or privitie, and the affront is the more beeing don in so goode companie as the Countesse of Bedford with divers other Ladies and persons of account, wherof the Lord Chamberlain gave the bride, but not one of his frends of kinred present or made acquainted withall; which is thought a straunge thing that so great a man and a counsaillor shold geve countenance to such an action as the robbing a man of his only child ...[101]

For some time Anna's health had been failing, and on 2 March 1619 between two and three in the morning she died at Hampton Court. Her body was brought to Denmark House by barge and after embalming it lay in state for two and a half months. The very long delay in holding a funeral was as a direct result of James's financial problems, and it had a number of unforeseen consequences. While the Queen's body lay above ground, the theatres were forbidden to open and Anna's ladies were compelled by etiquette to take turns in keeping watch over her body. Chamberlain reported that 'the Ladies grow wearie of watching at Denmarke House, though all day long there is more concourse then when she [Anna] was living'.[102] A further consequence of the delay in holding the funeral was an unseemly row between the Countess of Arundel and the Countess of Nottingham over who would assume the role of chief female mourner when the funeral was eventually held. The Countess of Nottingham claimed that she had precedence because during his lifetime her husband had been the leading earl of England. In the event the chief female mourner at Anna's funeral was Alethea, with Lucy as her assistant. But after the weeks and weeks of interminable delay, Anna's funeral proved a disappointing event: it was a 'drawling, tedious sight, more remarqueable [sic] for number then for any other singularitie'.[103] Anna's death deprived Lucy of a woman who had been her close friend and mistress for nearly sixteen years. How Lucy responded to the death of the Queen is unknown, but a letter she wrote to Jane while waiting for a funeral date to be set was completely matter-of-fact: 'The K: is earnest to have the funeral hastened, & sayth itt shall be on saterday comsenight, but for all that I thinke itt will not be till this day fortnight'.[104] The death of the Queen meant that Lucy lost her formal role at court, but with friends like Pembroke, Montgomery, Hamilton and Hay, she still retained her power and influence.

With Anna's death, James's health began to deteriorate and this delayed the departure of James Hay, Lord Doncaster, who was about to leave on a diplomatic mission to Germany which aimed at settling the continuing unrest in Bohemia. Doncaster was to be accompanied by Donne, who would act as his chaplain. Before leaving England, Donne wrote to Sir Thomas Lucy, telling him that he was grateful to him 'principally, for keeping me alive in the memory of the noblest Countess, whose commandment, if it had been her Ladyship's pleasure to have anything said or done in her service at Heidelberg, I should have been glad to have received'.[105] Donne was keenly aware of Lucy's close links with Elizabeth, Queen of Bohemia, and he was offering to act as a go-between for the two women thus suggesting that there had been some kind of rapprochement between Lucy and Donne. As James began to recover, Doncaster and Donne finally set sail.

Towards the end of 1618 bitterly cold weather hit London and the Thames froze. Londoners had to cope with an unusually harsh winter and with it the added misery of an outbreak of smallpox which swept across the city. Chamberlain no doubt voiced the wishes of many Londoners when he reported that he hoped that something might 'stay the violence of the small pockes' which had spread so much that it was 'thought every third house in this towne hath ben infected with them'.[106] By the summer of the following year Lucy came down with the disease. Smallpox was relatively common in the sixteenth century and was not usually considered serious; however, by the turn of the century it had become both 'more prevalent and more lethal'.[107] Typically, the disease began with a fever, followed by a rash which formed pustules. When the pustules dried they formed scabs which then sloughed off to leave the ineradicable scars characteristically associated with the disease. It was to this disfiguring aspect of the disease that Ben Jonson addressed himself in a verse which he penned to smallpox, calling it an:

> Envious and foule Disease, could there not be
> One beautie in an Age, and free from thee?
> What did she worth thy spight? ...
> ... Thought'st thou in disgrace
> Of Beautie so to nullifie a face,[108]

The physical legacy of smallpox, in particular its ability to 'nullifie a face', had happened within Pembroke's family. When Queen Elizabeth I contracted smallpox, Pembroke's grandmother, Mary Sidney, was one of the women who cared for the ailing queen and as a result Mary too fell ill and for her the disease was nothing short of a catastrophe. In so far as she was able, Mary shut herself off from the world. Whenever it was necessary for her to appear in public she wore a mask to conceal the damage that smallpox had done to her face. Smallpox was not a disease to be trifled with.

At first Lucy's illness appeared to give no great cause for concern. She had been to Dover to meet her mother, who had returned to England after visiting Elizabeth in Heidelberg. On reaching Dover Lucy was informed that Anne was seriously ill in Calais and she sailed there to care for her mother. Lady Harrington recovered and she and Lucy made their way back to London. Having been in Heidelberg so recently, Anne could give Lucy first-hand news of the instability surrounding Elizabeth and Frederick. Frederick still hoped that his father-in-law might intercede in the defence of Protestantism and no doubt Lucy intended to convey this news to James and any other person of influence she might persuade to listen.

However, it was soon reported that Lucy was 'dangeroslye sicke', although her doctor hastened to assure her friends that it was 'only the Mesells, & some few small pockes'.[109] Lucy was sufficiently well enough to promise to write to Carleton in a few weeks once she felt stronger. But four days later Lucy's 'messells' had turned into 'small pockes, whereof she is full & hath those ordinary accidents y[t] accompanye that disease, a little feuerishe & some time ill rest ... wee hope she is in noe great daunger now. Majerne is in the house w[it]he her'.[110] Attended by Mayerne, Lucy and her friends awaited her recovery, but by the middle of July she lay within Harrington House close to death. Her friends – including Pembroke and Hamilton – gathered around her bed in order to support her as she received her last communion. John Chamberlain reported to Dudley Carleton that:

> The Countesse of Bedford was lately at the last cast and no hope of life left, insomuch that receiving [sic] the communion in companie of the Lord Chamberlain, Marquis Hamilton and others as her viaticum, she gave over the world and tooke her leave ...[111]

At the 'gates of death' Lucy focused her mind on the life to come but it was not her time to die. She eventually recovered, but not without some physical cost. She lost the sight in one eye and was left scarred in the face. Chamberlain wrote that 'the small pocks had seased on the Lady of Bedford, and so seasoned her all over, that they say she is more full and fowle then could be expected in so thin and leane a body'.[112] Chamberlain was puzzled as to why men and women of Lucy's age should fall victim to smallpox, thinking it 'somwhat straunge that this disease shold now adayes take such hold of persons that for yeares and other respects thought themselves privileged long since from the boyling and furie of maladies that follow younge bloud'.[113] Smallpox was not exclusively a disease of the young but Chamberlain was right to wonder why, after being in contact with the disease for many years, Lucy should suddenly catch it. It is possible that the increased ferocity of the disease which Chamberlain witnessed was due to it being a new and more virulent strain which had been introduced from Africa or the Orient.[114] As Lucy recovered from her illness she received some welcome news. James had granted her and James Hamilton £2,000 a year each in order to help them repay their debts. Such funding could not come a moment too soon for the perpetually penniless Lucy.

At the end of August, the Bohemians offered their crown to Frederick who was thrown into a quandary over whether to accept or not, but by September he had decided that it was his religious duty and declared that his 'only end' was 'to serve God and His church'.[115] Accompanied by Elizabeth, Frederick travelled to Prague to accept the crown while in London, Archbishop Abbot employed language plucked directly from the apocalyptic visions in the Book of Revelations:

> ... methinks I do in this, and in that of Hungary, forsee the work of God, that by piece and piece, the Kings of the Earth that gave their power unto the Beast ... shall now tear the whore, and make her desolate, as St. John in his revelation hath foretold ... Our striking will comfort the Bohemians, will honour the Palsgrave ...[116]

But as Abbot welcomed Frederick's decision, James was less enthusiastic, having been led to believe by the Spanish ambassador that the entire Bohemian crisis had been deliberately engineered to break the amity between England and Spain. John Chamberlain rightly saw the terrible events that lay ahead, believing that there was 'now no place left for deliberation, nor for mediation of peace till one side be utterly ruined', adding that the 'world thincks yt was a plot ... to draw in our king'.[117]

Frederick's decision to accept the crown of Bohemia immediately unleashed hostile forces against him as four armies led variously by Bucquoy, the Duke of

Bavaria, Spinola, and the Elector of Saxony began heading for Prague. In the face of such threatening and overwhelming force surely England would come to the help of Frederick and Elizabeth? Along with Pembroke and George Abbot, Lucy was a prime mover in attempting to encourage James to engage directly in the situation in Bohemia in support of the Protestant cause. But James had no desire to break with Spain and nor did he feel inclined to approach parliament to raise money for a war: he decided to use his influence with Spain and with the Emperor to try to arrange a peace treaty. Donne and Doncaster returned from what proved to be an unsuccessful diplomatic mission late in 1619. In February of the following year Henry Goodyer's daughter, Lucy, married Sir Francis Nethersole. Given the relationship between Goodyer and Donne it was natural that Goodyer would ask his friend to officiate at the service. The bride was Lucy's goddaughter and had lived in her house:

> Sir Fra: Nethersole was ... newly maried to Mistris Goodyeare that served the Lady of Bedford who gave her 500li or 700li, besides 500li she bestowed upon them in gloves, which brought in a great contribution of plate to make up a portion which her father Sir Henry could not geve.[118]

The perpetually importunate Goodyer was unable to provide a full dowry for his daughter and it is possible that some of the money Lucy had recently received from James made its way into the gifts she bestowed on Lucy Goodyer and her new husband. As Donne preached the marriage sermon before a congregation that would have included Lucy, he took as his text a verse from Genesis, 'And the Lord God said, it is not good, that the man should be alone; I will make him a helpe, meet for him'.[119] The occasion of the sermon was powerful for all involved: for Francis Nethersole and Lucy Goodyer it was a reminder of the solemn vows they were undertaking; for Donne it must have brought into sharp focus his own married life and the loss of Ann; for Lucy there must have been a sense that as she watched a bride who, having lived in her house and received a dowry from her, she was looking at a substitute for her own dead daughter.

No Jacobean sermon on marriage would be complete without at least a passing consideration of the appropriate role of the wife in the union and as he approached this part of his oration, Donne may well have looked at the frail and scarred woman who sat before him and preached directly to her:

> I know there are some glasses stronger then some earthen vessels, and some earthen vessels stronger then some wooden dishes, some of the weaker sexe, stronger in fortune, and in counsell too, then they to whom God hath given them; but yet let them not impute that in the eye nor eare of the world, nor repeat it to their own hearts, with such a dignifying of themselves, as exceeds the quality of a Helper.[120]

Even in her manifestly poor state of health Lucy was a far stronger 'vessel' than

Edward had ever been and Donne also knew that in the sphere of politics her advice, her 'counsell', carried a great deal more weight than that of Edward or indeed many of her male contemporaries. In warning against exceeding 'the quality of Helper', was Donne giving coded advice to Lucy to rein in her attempts to interfere in matters affecting Bohemia? That events overtaking Elizabeth and Frederick were already present at the gathering is implicit given the fact that the groom, Nethersole, had been appointed English agent to the princes of the Protestant Union and private secretary to Elizabeth at the end of the preceding year. Furthermore, Doncaster's failed mission and the Spanish view that he had not been impartial in his deliberations, that he had in fact been sympathetic to Frederick, had deeply displeased James. When Baron Achatius von Dohna, Frederick's ambassador to England, visited James early in 1620 to lobby support he was made less than welcome by a highly irritated King. As Dohna entreated the Mayor and Aldermen of London to lend Frederick money to finance war he laid heavy emphasis on Elizabeth being James's daughter:

> That which I so earnestly entreat is on the behalf of my master and of his Queen, the only daughter of the King your Sovereign, the most glorious mother and fruitful nursery of the royal plants, the only consideration whereof, and of those heavenly blessings which so clearly appear in her, will incite you to this holy enterprise.[121]

As news of Dohna's reception by James became public knowledge it prompted angry sermons and a proliferation of 'scandalous pamfletts'[122] and so tense did the situation become that speaking about the Bohemian crisis in public was considered unacceptable meddling, something which may account for Donne's circumspection in his sermon, and his coded advice to Lucy. In earlier years Donne had enjoyed discussions and debates with Lucy on such subjects as poetry and religion. But was he now discreetly objecting to Lucy usurping the place of the male? Did Donne consider that she was venturing too far into the political sphere? The prevailing contemporary view of the appropriate role of a woman was very clear:

> As it befits not Man for to imbrace
> Domesticke charge, so it's not *Womans* place
> For to be busied with affaires abroad:
> For that weake *sexe* it is too great a load,
> *And it's vnseemely, and doth but disgrace,*
> *When either doth vsurpe the others place:*[123]

Lucy had never been content to be merely 'a helper' and she had consistently bucked the trend for how a woman was expected to conduct herself by taking a prominent role in public affairs. Predictably Donne's attempts to give her some discreet advice had no discernible effect. For Lucy, the plight of Frederick and

Elizabeth was much more than a crisis confronting people she knew well; it also impinged very directly on her own beliefs. For many in England, including Lucy, the events taking place in Bohemia were a 'part of a pattern of Protestant apocalyptical history'[124] in which Frederick was destined by God to defend the Protestant faith. The war was therefore deeply personal.

Weighed down by anxieties about the fate of Frederick and Elizabeth there was yet more sadness in store for Lucy when a few months later Anne Harrington died. With the death of her mother, Lucy felt herself to be as 'fulle of iust sorrow as ... [a] hart can bear', telling Jane, 'What a Mother I have lost I need not tell yow, that know what shee was in hirself & to me'.[125] But Anne's death was not the only grief to befall Lucy. The night before Lucy wrote to Jane, Pembroke's son, Henry, died:

> My losse of a dear Mother camme not so vnexpectedly as my Lord Chamberlains did att this tyme, for to outward aparance his child mended, but my Mother so manifestly decayed dayle as I could not flatter myself with hope she could continue long, though I looked not her ende wold haue binne so sodaine, yett the disease she was subiect to threatened no lesse, w[hi]ch I sorting with that opinion she ever had since I knew her that her ende wold be sodaine, made itt I thanke God not so to her, who had left many testemonis how well she was prepared for itt, which is my vnspeakable comfort: it now rests for me to follow as well as I can her good exsample ...[126]

Added to Lucy's woes was the rapidly deteriorating situation in the Palatinate. In November 1620, the long expected assault on Prague began and the Bohemian forces were comprehensively defeated, a little outside the city, at the battle of White Mountain. The victorious Catholic League army followed up this success by marching into Silesia, Moravia, Austria and the Rhine Palatinate, and Frederick, Elizabeth and their children fled Prague, eventually taking refuge at The Hague. James had dispatched a small army to the Palatinate under the command of Sir Horace Vere in June with strict orders to act defensively and on no account to attack the Catholic troops, but after the defeat at White Mountain it became clear that this policy was wholly ineffective. Burges, who served as chaplain to Vere's troops, tried to make the best out of a disastrous situation, claiming that:

> The king and queen of Bohemia do bear their afflictions with such patience and piety as have added to them more true honour than a victory could have done, and makes me to hope that God, in his time, will lift them up again, to the astonishment of their enemies, and joy of his people.[127]

James attempted to arrange a peaceful settlement based on Frederick's surrender of his claims to Bohemia in return for his restoration to the Palatinate. But Frederick was in no mood to agree to such a plan.

By early November, Mayerne was treating Lucy for melancholy, which at the time also went by the name of *Hypocondriacus*. Mayerne's casebook recorded two separate entries for '*Hypochondr.*' or the symptoms of 'melancholia' in Lucy between 1620 and 1621.[128] '*Hipocondriacall*', also less charmingly known as 'flatuous Melancholy', was believed to originate from both inward and outward causes: inward sources might relate to problems with the spleen – something of which Lucy frequently complained – while outward causes might take the form of 'care, griefes' and 'most commonly … perturbation of the minde … in such bodies as are ill disposed'.[129] Lucy's experience over the preceding years of a series of seemingly endless disasters ranging from personal illness, the deaths of friends and relatives, financial difficulties, to the deteriorating situation in Bohemia which threatened both her friends and her faith would have provided ample cause for the development of melancholy. As with any illness the first recourse was to the healing offered by religious faith, but this could be taken in conjunction with medical remedies. Praying for the health of the body and mind might in itself be sufficient to effect a recovery; however, if the 'Patient of himselfe is not able to resist, or over-come these heart-eating passions, his friends or Physitian must be ready to supply that which is wanting'.[130]

On 7 January 1621 John Donne preached a sermon at Harrington House. Lucy had clearly invited Donne to deliver a sermon and such an invitation suggests that not only was she on good terms with her old friend, but that she was interested in what he had to say in his capacity as a servant of God and to hear his views on the situation in Germany. Within the walls of Harrington House Lucy listened as Donne took as his topic a verse from the book of Job, 'Loe, though he slay me, yet will I trust in him'[131] in order to explore how and why the individual must endure misfortune and adversity. Although Donne was circumspect in the sermon he did appear to make some discreet allusions to the Bohemian crisis by comparing the beleaguered individual to a town under attack and referring to a king embarking on a war. Furthermore, he almost certainly made an allusion to Lucy herself:

> … if there be such an irreparable *Devastation* upon us, as that we be *broken as an Earthen vessel, in the breaking whereof there remaines not a sheard to fetch fire from the hearth, nor water from the pit.* That our *estate* be ruined so, as that there is nothing left, not onely for future *posterity*, but not for the present *family*, yet still God and the calamity are together …[132]

The analogy of the earthen vessel was by no means uncommon in sermons of the time, but it was an unmistakable repetition of the imagery Donne had used in his sermon at the wedding of Nethersole and Lucy Goodyer. The description of the earthen vessel was particularly applicable to Lucy, who, scarred and partially blinded as a result of her bout of smallpox, was in a quite literal sense a site of 'Devastation'. Not only was she physically 'ruined', she was also financially crippled by a completely broken 'estate'. As a friend to Lucy, Donne seems to have attempted to address her melancholy in his sermon and she no doubt explored the range of other remedies commonly suggested to the afflicted sufferer. Burton was of the view that to 'expell griefe and procure pleasance, sweet smells, good diet, touch, taste, embracing, singing, dancing, sports, playes, and above the rest, exquisite beauties ... are most powerfull meanes'.[133] But these diversions alone were clearly no longer sufficient for Lucy to overcome her melancholy and Mayerne prescribed a course of physic for her. Following a course of treatment prescribed by Theodore Mayerne was not for the faint hearted. He was an enthusiastic dispenser of chemical remedies to his patients and for the spleen or melancholy he favoured the administration of 'steel'[134] in powdered form. He was also of the view that foul-tasting medicines were the most efficacious, and although Lucy probably did not have to drink or inhale some of Mayerne's more bizarre concoctions made variously from ingredients such as 'boiled bats ... suckling puppies ... earthworms, hog lard', she probably underwent bleeding in an attempt to correct perceived imbalances with her humours, specifically what she herself referred to as her 'rebellious ... spleene'. [135]

In his great work, The Anatomy of Melancholy published in 1621, Robert Burton depicted the typical posture of the Hypochondriac as that of a seated individual leaning on one arm. The accompanying explanatory verse explaining the arrangement of the picture noted that:

> Hypocondriacus leanes on his arme,
> Winde in his side doth him much harme,
> And troubles him full sore God knowes,
> Much paine he hath and many woes.[136]

The pose of Burton's melancholic bears a close resemblance to a portrait of Lucy which may have been painted about this time. In the portrait she wears a small coronet on her head and is dressed in black, probably because she was still in mourning for her mother and for Anna. She leans her head a little to one side, resting it on her hand, and stares directly at the viewer. In having herself portrayed in this manner Lucy was at a stroke treating her melancholy: by engaging a painter to create an object of beauty – a painting – while simultaneously advertising her state of health to anyone who viewed the picture.

In August Lucy had recovered sufficiently to pay a brief visit to Elizabeth at The Hague but the trip proved less than satisfactory, allegedly because of arguments and unpleasantness among Elizabeth's ladies-in-waiting over the correct order of precedence for Lucy. Lucy stayed at the English embassy with Dudley Carleton and his wife but left The Hague early to take advantage of a favourable wind for her journey back to England. Shortly after her return she wrote to Elizabeth and added a covering letter to Carleton. What Lucy wrote to Elizabeth is unknown, for as she told Carleton, 'of such newse as I found hear the Queen will ... give yow ... [it] is not worth a double wrighting'.[137] But she was expecting Pembroke and Hamilton to dine with her that evening, perhaps in order that she might relay to them news of events at The Hague, and she was clearly in close contact with her old friend and spiritual mentor, Burges, who:

> coming to me yesterday, told me that he was making all the hapy preparacion [sic] he could to send ... the youth he brought with him to The Haghe ... whom itt seemes the K. of Boehemia was resolved should have ... to Duke Charles ...[138]

Deeply committed to the Protestant cause, Burges was clearly instrumental in assisting Elizabeth and Frederick with the appointment of household staff for their children. But as the situation confronting Elizabeth and Frederick grew ever more disastrous Lucy wrote to Carleton urging him to encourage Elizabeth to write directly to Prince Charles and the pro-Spanish Secretary Calvert: 'she [Elizabeth] should wright to the Prince, & secretary Calvert, perswade her not to delay itt'.[139] Lucy's advice implies that she saw no point in attempting to change James's mind and that she felt it might be more profitable for Elizabeth to bypass her father and appeal directly to her brother, Charles. According to the French ambassador, Tillieres, James recognized Elizabeth's capacity to rally English Protestants to the Palatinate cause, claiming that the 'King is in the greatest fear that the Electress Palatine his daughter will arrive here [England] and favor the party of the Puritans'.[140] Indeed, many English Protestants would have been more than happy for Elizabeth to succeed to the English throne. The situation reached crisis point in September 1622 when cities loyal to Frederick fell to Catholic forces and rumour spread that a desperate Frederick was considering accepting assistance from Turkish forces. Many in England saw nothing wrong with adopting such a policy in a moment of dire need. This course of action was never explicitly mooted but often surfaced obliquely, so around this time Lucy received a literary dedication from a writer called Patrick Hannay who had served in an English foot regiment in support of Frederick in the Palatinate. Part of Hannay's work was a poem entitled 'Sheretine and Mariana' which purported to be based on Hungarian history and told of how 'Arch-Duke *Ferdinand*' was 'elected King of *Bohemia*'[141] and set about invading Hungary, the kingdom ruled by King John. Being militarily weak, John was forced to flee his country but was ultimately assisted by the Turk, Solyman, who defended him and restored him to his kingdom. Although primarily a love poem it is possible that Hannay introduced this particular piece of history in order to draw attention to a precedent for Turkish intervention in Bohemia. History was a site of knowledge and Hannay may have been persuaded that Lucy would read his poem and perhaps relate this historical lesson to the counsellors and advisers to Frederick who might encourage him to act on it.

While some of his citizens considered that the Bohemians should not scruple to seek help from such an unlikely quarter, James persisted in his plans for a Spanish bride for Charles and early in 1623, Prince Charles and Villiers, by now elevated to Duke of Buckingham, set sail for Spain intending to return with the Infanta. In a fraught environment in which careless words might easily be taken up and wilfully misconstrued, Elizabeth appeared to allude to the fact that because the Spanish regarded Charles as a future ally he would be safe in the country. Her comments were quickly seized upon by her enemies in England and so thoroughly twisted that they were put forward as evidence that Elizabeth would welcome the death of her brother in order to claim the English throne. This was clearly not Elizabeth's intention but it demonstrated that she needed to take much greater care in what she said. Lucy was horrified by the turn of events and wrote to Carleton begging him to speak with Elizabeth directly:

> I beseech yow doe me the favor to deliver or send the Queen this letter as soone as yow can ... & for Gods sake preach more warning to the Queen whom uses freedom to, else she will vndo her selfe, & make others afrayd how they interest them=selues [sic] in her servis ...[142]

Although the situation in the Palatinate was hopeless, Lucy and Pembroke had not abandoned the cause and late in 1624 Sir George Goring was warning Buckingham over the 'ill councils of Bedford House'.[143] The following, anonymous, ditty was probably penned around the same time:

> As I went to Bedforde Howse,
>   To that puritan shrine,
> Mett twise that begger Hamleton
>   And a freinde of mine.
> Mett I weake Lord Chamberlaine,
>   Doncaster there was he,
> Mett I proude Lorde Arundell,
>   Foolish Montgomery.
> In counsell thease undertakers breake
>   The Spanish matche and the truce.
> The puritans offer golde and pearle
>   With Sacrifices to St Luce.[144]

The poem alluded to contemporary political events, particularly those concerning the failed Spanish match, and the reference to Bedford House was probably rather more than a glance back to Edward's Puritan background, suggesting instead that the house had become a gathering place for those sympathetic to the Protestant cause. Lucy herself may be figured in the reference to 'Sacrifices to St Luce', perhaps in connection with some kind of finance-raising exercise. Lucy was active in furthering the cause of Frederick and Elizabeth. When Elizabeth's secretary, Nethersole, visited England late in 1624 he wrote to Carleton asking for news of the 'Low-countreys' and explaining that he:

went downe to Court at Cambridge; cheifly, in regard of a business of the Q[ueen]s. [Elizabeth] w[hi]ch the Countesse of Bedford putt me vppon; touching wh[ich] I haue written at this time to her M[ajes]ty: from whome y[ou]r L[ord]s[hip] may haue information. I humbly beseeche y[ou]r L[ordship] the letters, may be speedily delivered vnto her Ma[jes]tyes owne hands, and w[i]th some secrecy because I vnderstand by my Lady of Bedford shee is unwilling the matter should be vented forth in any sort.[145]

What exactly the secret business which could not be 'vented forth' actually amounted to is unknown.

In March of the following year, James, Marquess of Hamilton, died and his death left Lucy utterly bereft. Writing to Jane, Lucy told her old friend:

I acknowledge that I feele so to the quicke this last affliction God hath pleased to lay vpon mee, as no worldly comfort will euer be able to prevaile against itt, for I have lost the best, & worthiest freind [sic] that euer breathed …[146]

Hamilton's death robbed Lucy of a close friend and confidant and it also took away a person of considerable power and influence. With the loss of Hamilton, Lucy felt that Pembroke was 'the last person left of power that I can relie on for the worth of his affection & freindship [sic] to mee … the only honest harted man imployed that I know now left to God & his countrie'.[147] Although stricken by grief over Hamilton's death, Lucy realized the necessity of bowing before the harsh discipline God had imposed on her, because his 'will, as itt is euer best, whatsoeuer itt apear to our sence, so must wee submitt owr selues to itt in all thinges; though itt is the hardliest practised lesson of all wee learne in religion'.[148] But as she wrote to Jane about Hamilton, Lucy also told her friend that she had heard 'from Tibauls [Theobalds] that the King was this morning in so weak estate as ther was no hope of his life'.[149] James died four days later on 27 March 1625 and there could not have been a greater contrast between Lucy's responses to the two deaths. Where Hamilton's passing left her utterly heartbroken, the death of James seems barely to have registered. As the King's body was transported from Theobalds to London, two noblemen – Lord Morton and Lord Roxborough – chose not to attend the journey of their dead sovereign as so many of their peers did; rather, 'That efternoone thaye went to Moore Parke to my Ladye Bedfoords to pass the tyme and be mirrye their' and this unusual excursion did not go unobserved, being 'mutche remarked' upon.[150] Lucy had strongly opposed James's policy in Bohemia and she disliked his cavalier attitude toward parliament, but her merry-making with Morton and Roxborough while the rest of the country was going into mourning for a dead king may also indicate that after experiencing so much personal loss she had become desensitized to death.

Lucy had great hopes of Charles and some time after his return from Spain with Buckingham she wrote to Elizabeth, telling her:

> in the great affairs, now on the Stage of this our world ... none playes his part, with so due applause, as your Excellent Brother, who wins daily more and more upon the hearts of all good men, and hath begotten, by his Princelie and wise proceedings, such an opinion of his realitie, judgment, and worthie intentions for the publick good ... I am sure, the world hath not another parallel with him. He is, besides, most diligent, and Indefatigable in businesses, a patient Hearer, judicious in distinguishing counsells, moderate in all his actions, steady in his resolutions ... so civill, and accomplished withall, every way, both in mind and body ...[151]

With the accession of Charles, Lucy continued to work on behalf of those whom she favoured and she was once again busily engaged in matchmaking including encouraging a marriage for her friend Theodore Mayerne's son. She also spent time contemplating her collection of coins and medals. In a letter to Lucy written in late December 1626, Sir Thomas Roe wrote of how on a visit to London he had seen her 'marshalling ... antient coynes and medalls, delighting in the records of vertuous tymes, vertuous men, and uertuous actions'.[152] As Roe explained, such an interest in antiquities, although condemned by some censorious souls, was about far more than just bringing the viewer delight. Coins and medals represented:

> a kynd of lay humanitye, teaching and inciting deuotion to morall uertue, as well, and more safely then images among the new Romans, to the contemplation of diuine misteries. They propose a liuely cronologye on the one syde, and a representation of historye, heroicque or greate actions, on the other. They carry in them a shadow of eternitye, and kindle an emulation of glorye, by seeing dead men kept long among the liuing by their famous deedes.[153]

There is no doubt that Lucy would have shared Roe's assessment of the hidden functions of coins and medals in encouraging 'virtue' and inviting the 'emulation of glorye', and she positioned herself firmly within this interpretative tradition by commissioning a coin of her own from the French craftsman, Nicholas Briot. Lucy's decision to commission a coin was not dictated by a desire to emulate the practices of her contemporaries; in fact it was a highly unusual step because 'there was no real tradition of patronage of medals in Britain'[154] at the time. Because Lucy was fully conversant with the language of signs and symbols the representation she chose for her coin is illuminating. What view was she inviting her contemporaries, indeed, posterity to take of her? Could a consideration of her life incite a 'deuotion to morall virtue' in others? The design on the coin Lucy commissioned depicted a snake, with its tail coiled twice around its head, and it carried the Latin inscription 'IVDICIO NON METU', 'judgement, not fear'. It has been pointed out that the arrangement of the snake in this particular position – with the head of the serpent protected by its body – was unusual and probably derived from stories about the behaviour of animals.[155] Specifically, interpretations of serpents could be found in the work of Edward Topsell who compiled several influential books on the meanings to be derived from animal imagery. According to Topsell:

> whe[n] a serpent is set vpon and strooken ... she hideth her head, and exposeth all her other parts to blowes, reseruing that sound; so you, when you are persecuted by Tyrants, preserue your head, that is, your fayth, and deny not your God to death.[156]

The impresa Lucy chose appeared to signal her decision to follow her own beliefs and conscience in matters of religion and to advertise her absolute steadfastness to her faith. That Lucy might choose to project this particular image of herself was rather more than a histrionic gesture: she had given ample proof of her independence of mind and her religious sincerity as she clung to her faith while watching her fellow Protestant believers in Europe 'persecuted' by those she considered 'Tyrants'.

6

Post Mortem

Death hath no sting.

Lucy, Countess of Bedford, *Elegy for Bulstrode*

In early May 1627, Edward died. Reporting the death to Jane Bacon, her brother Thomas Meautys added that 'my lady's recovery is much doubted; her strength and spirits being, as they say, far spent, and wearing out daily by an untoward cough, which is almost continual'.[1] Physically exhausted by a persistent cough and once again beset by grief, a frail Lucy looked on as Edward was buried at Chenies. On very many occasions in her life Lucy had been seriously ill, yet each time she had made a remarkable recovery. This time it was different. She died on 26 May 1627, barely three weeks after Edward.

Lucy's body was taken north to Exton and laid to rest with her beloved family. With no son to inherit the Bedford title, the family name and what little remained of the ravaged estates passed to Edward's cousin, Francis Russell, who became 4th Earl of Bedford. Fittingly, it was Lucy's close friend and fellow gardener, Pembroke, who took possession of her great love, the garden at Moor Park.

Lucy Russell's life was not especially long but it was immensely rich. Drayton's bitter curse on her, that she should be utterly forgotten by the work of 'devouring time', failed to materialize; although she is not a familiar figure to modern audiences, nor is she lost or inaccessible. She shines as brightly as ever in the writings of the men and women who knew and loved her. In the lines of John Florio, John Donne, Ben Jonson, Samuel Daniel, Aemilia Lanier, Anne Clifford, Mary Wroth and others she is fully present, whether as a correspondent, benefactor, friend, or muse.

Notes

Notes to Chapter 1: Beginnings

1 Potter, G.R. and Simpson, E.M. (eds) *The Sermons of John Donne*, 10 vols (Berkeley and Los Angeles: University of California Press, 1953–62), V (1959), p. 172.
2 Collinson, P. *The Elizabethan Puritan Movement* (London: Jonathan Cape, 1967), p. 54.
3 *Alumni Cantabrigiensis*, 4 vols (Cambridge: Cambridge University Press, 1922), Part I, II, p. 310.
4 McClure, N.E. (ed.) *The Letters and Epigrams of Sir John Harington* (Philadelphia: University of Pennsylvania Press, 1930), p. 110.
5 Wright, J. *The History and Antiquities of the County of Rutland* (London, 1684), p. 28.
6 Norden, J. *Speculum Britanniae* (London, 1593), lists 'Sir *Io. Harrington* at Stepney' in a list of 'Noblemen, and Gentlemen, for the most part, hauing houses, or residence, within this Shire', sig. H1r and v.
7 Desainliens, C. *Campo di Fior* (London, 1583), sig. *ijr.
8 Adams, S. (ed.) *Household Accounts and Disbursement Books of Robert Dudley, Earl of Leicester 1558–1561, 1584–1586*, Camden Fifth Series Volume 6 (Cambridge: Cambridge University Press, 1995), p. 299.
9 Collinson, P. *English Puritanism* (London: The Historical Association, 1983), p. 28.
10 Stewart, A. *Philip Sidney: A Double Life* (London: Chatto & Windus, 2000), p. 3.
11 McClure, *The Letters and Epigrams of Sir John Harington*, p. 67, original italics.
12 Donne, J. to Mrs. M.H. ('Mad paper stay') lines 21–2 in Milgate, W. (ed.) *John Donne: The Satires, Epigrams and Verse Letters* (Oxford: Clarendon Press, 1967).
13 King James, cited in Oman, C.M.A. *Elizabeth of Bohemia*, rev. ed. (London: Hodder and Stoughton, 1964), p. 22.
14 On the history of Sidney Sussex see Beales, D.E.D. and Nisbet, H.B. (ed.) *Sidney Sussex College Cambridge Historical Essays* (Suffolk: The Boydell Press, 1996).
15 Wright, *The History and Antiquities of the County of Rutland*, p. 52.
16 Ibid., p. 52. Anne Herbert notes that this 'label is one of the earliest examples of a woman's gift plate', in Herbert, A.L. 'Oakham parish library', *Library History*, 6 (1982–84), p. 3.
17 Sidney, P. *A Defence of Poetry*, ed. Van Dorsten, J.A. (Oxford: Oxford University Press, 1984), p. 25.
18 Desainliens, *Campo di Fior*, sig. *ijr.
19 Ibid., pp. 366–7. Thomas Vautrollier printed a large number of the language manuals.

20 Boutcher, W.V. 'Florio's Montaigne: Translation and Pragmatic Humanism in the Sixteenth Century' (unpublished DPhil., Cambridge, 1991), p. 100.
21 Desainliens, *Campo di Fior*, sig. *ijr.
22 Ibid., sig. *ijv.
23 Florio, J. *A Worlde of Wordes* (London, 1598), sig. a3v.
24 'Of Women learned in the tongues', lines 1–6, in McClure, *The Letters and Epigrams of Sir John Harington*, pp. 255–6.
25 Anne Clifford was related to Lucy by marriage. Anne's mother was Margaret Russell Clifford, Countess of Cumberland, the daughter of Francis Russell, the second Earl of Bedford. The Countess of Cumberland was Edward's aunt.
26 Clifford, D.J.H. (ed.) *The Diaries of Lady Anne Clifford* (Gloucestershire: Alan Sutton Publishing, 1990), p. 51.
27 Plat, H. *The Garden of Eden* (London, 1659), pp. 31–2.
28 'Orchestra Or a Poeme of Dauncing', in Krueger, R. (ed.) *The Poems of Sir John Davies* (Oxford: Clarendon Press, 1975), p. 118.
29 Shuttleworth, J.M. (ed.) *The Life of Edward, First Lord Herbert of Cherbury written by himself* (London: Oxford University Press, 1976), p. 31.
30 Ibid., pp. 31–2.
31 Wroth, M. cited in Lamb, M.E. *Gender and Authorship in the Sidney Circle* (Wisconsin: University of Wisconsin Press, 1990), p. 160.
32 Stopes, C.C. *The Life of Henry, Third Earl of Southampton, Shakespeare's Patron* (Cambridge: Cambridge University Press, 1922), p. 236.
33 Nevile, J. 'Dance and the Garden: Moving and Static Choreography in Renaissance Europe', *Renaissance Quarterly*, 52 (1999), p. 822.
34 Ibid., p. 823.
35 Tongiorgi Tomasi, L. cited in Nevile, 'Dance and the Garden', p. 823.
36 'Orchestra Or a Poeme of Dauncing', in Krueger, *The Poems of Sir John Davies*, pp. 105–6.
37 An excellent account of the daily activities of women in the period is to be found in Mendelson, Sara Heller 'Stuart women's diaries and occasional memoirs', in *Women in English Society 1500–1800*, ed. Prior, M. (London and New York: Methuen, 1985), pp. 181–210.
38 Ibid., p.190.
39 Moody, J. (ed.) *The Private Correspondence of Jane Lady Cornwallis Bacon, 1613–1644* (London: Associated University Press, 2003), p. 91. The spending is recorded in Lord Braybrooke's edition of the letters. See Richard Braybrooke (ed.) *The Private Correspondence of Jane Lady Cornwallis Bacon, 1613–1644* (London, 1843).
40 Essex Record Office, Cornwallis-Bacon Papers, D/DBy C19 f.91v, 92r.
41 Daniel, S. 'To the Lady Lucie, Countesse of Bedford', lines 40–1 in *Samuel Daniel Poems and a Defence of Ryme*, ed. Sprague, A.C. (London: Routledge & Kegan Paul, 1950).
42 State Papers Venetian 1603–1607, ed. Brown, Horatio F. (London: HMSO, 1900), p. 71.
43 Massinger, P. and Field, N. *The Fatal Dowry* (London, 1632), sig. H3v.
44 Shakespeare, W. *Macbeth*, ed. Muir, K. (London and New York: Routledge, repr. 1991), I, v. l.41.

45 Florio, *A Worlde of Wordes*, sig. a4r.

46 Florio, J. *Florios Second Frutes* (New York: Da Capo Press, 1969 [facsimile of 1591 edition]), p. 173.

47 Ibid., p. 193.

48 Boutcher, 'Florio's Montaigne', p. 115.

49 Ibid., p. 116.

50 Roberts, J.A. (ed.) *The First Part of the Countess of Montgomery's Urania* (Binghamton, New York: Medieval & Renaissance Texts & Studies, 1995), p. 161.

51 McManus, C. *Women on the Renaissance Stage: Anna of Denmark and Female Masquing in the Stuart Court (1590–1619)* (Manchester and New York: Manchester University Press, 2002), p. 137.

52 Davies, J. *The Muses Sacrifice* (London, 1612), sig. ***2v.

Notes to Chapter 2: Marriage

1 English Law treated males and females differently. A female could legally engage in property transactions on her own behalf from the age of sixteen; a male had to wait until he was twenty-one.

2 State Papers Domestic, 1591–1594, ed. Green, M.A.E. (London: HMSO, 1867), p. 16.

3 London, Public Record Office, SP Domestic 12/233/71.

4 Cited in Stopes, *The Life of Henry*, p. 66.

5 *Oxford English Dictionary*.

6 Cowley, A. *Loves Riddle* (London, 1638), sig. D6r.

7 Donno, E.S. (ed.) *Sir John Harington's A New Discourse of a Stale Subject, Called The Metamorphosis of Ajax* (London: Routledge and Kegan Paul, 1962), p. 226.

8 London Metropolitan Archive, X024/068.

9 Spenser, E. *Epithalamion*, lines 315, 319–20, 349–50 in *The Yale Edition of the Shorter Poems of Edmund Spenser*, eds Oram, W.A., Bjorvand, E., Bond, R., Cain, T.H., Dunlop, A., Schell, R. (New Haven and London: Yale University Press, 1989).

10 Hannay, P. 'A Happy Husband', in *The Poetical Works of Patrick Hannay* (Hunterian Club, 1875), p. 169.

11 When the Duke of Buckingham organized a forced marriage between his underage niece and the son of the Marquis of Hamilton, the bride and groom were made to lie in King James's bedchamber in the presence of the King in order to give the marriage public proof. BL, MS Stowe 182, fol. 79.

12 Drayton, M. *Endimion and Phoebe* 'To the Excellent and most accomplish't Ladie: *Lucie* Countesses of Bedford', lines 1–2, 10 in Hebel, J.W. (ed.) *The Works of Michael Drayton*, 4 vols (Oxford: Basil Blackwell, 1931–33), I, 1931.

13 Brathwait, R. *Some Rules and Orders for the Government of the House of an Earle* (London: Benjamin Bensley, 1821).

14 Jeayes, I.H. (ed.) *Letters of Philip Gawdy* (London: J.B. Nichols and Sons, 1906), p. 77.

15 Collins, A. (ed.) *Letters and Memorials of State*, 2 vols (London, 1746), I, p. 357.

16 Ibid., I, p. 358.

17 Ibid., I, p. 358.

18 McClure, N.E. (ed.) *The Letters of John Chamberlain*, 2 vols (Philadelphia: American Philosophical Society, 1939), I, pp. 166, 178.

19 Peele, G. *Anglorum Feriae* (London, 1596), sig. B1r.

20 Ibid., sig. D2r.

21 Ibid., sig. E1r.

22 Du Maurier, D. *Golden Lads: A Study of Anthony Bacon, Francis and their Friends* (London: Victor Gollancz, 1975), pp. 144–45.

23 Ibid., p. 145.

24 Brathwait, *Some Rules and Orders*, p. 3.

25 Du Maurier, *Golden Lads*, p. 145.

26 Ibid., pp. 145–6.

27 Ibid., pp. 146–7.

28 Jonson, B. 'The Forrest', iii.ll.47–57 in Herford, C.H. and Simpson, P. (eds) *Ben Jonson*, 11 vols (Oxford: Clarendon Press, 1925–52), VIII (1947).

29 Ungerer, G. 'An Unrecorded Elizabethan Performance of Titus Andronicus', *Shakespeare Survey*, 14 (1961), p. 106.

30 Shakespeare, W. *Titus Andronicus*, ed. Maxwell, J.C. (London and New York: Routledge, repr. 1989), II, ii, ll. 1–3.

31 Ibid., II, I, ll. 1–4.

32 Ibid., II, iv, ll. 16–18, 22–24.

33 'Orchestra Or a Poeme of Dauncing', in Krueger, *The Poems of Sir John Davies*, p. 96.

34 McManus, *Women on the Renaissance Stage*, p. 38.

35 Cited in Boutcher, 'Florio's Montaigne', p. 216.

36 Collins, *Letters and Memorials of State*, II, p. 18.

37 Ibid., II, p. 22.

38 Ibid., II, p. 23.

39 HMC Salisbury (Cecil) Manuscripts (London: HMSO, 1895), VI, p. 100.

40 Collins, *Letters and Memorials of State*, II, p. 196.

41 Ibid., II, p. 26.

42 Ibid., II, p. 91.

43 HMC Salisbury (Cecil) Manuscripts (London: HMSO, 1899), VIII, p. 520.

44 Ibid., p. 520.

45 Collins, *Letters and Memorials of State*, II, p. 127.

46 Ibid., II, p. 127.

47 Ibid., II, p. 129.

48 Ibid., II, p. 129.

49 Woburn Abbey, 3rd Earl of Bedford's Papers.

50 Ibid.

51 Ibid.

52 Ibid.

53 Ibid.

54 Collins, *Letters and Memorials of State*, II, p. 201.

55 Lloyd, D. *State-Worthies* (London, 1670), p. 658.

56 Ibid., pp. 658-9.

57 Florio, J. *The Essayes or Morall, Politike and Millitarie Discourses of Lo: Michaell de Montaigne* (London, 1603), sig. A2v.

58 Ibid., sig. A2r.

59 Ibid., sig. A2r.

60 Ibid., sig. A3r.

61 Ibid., sig. A2r.

62 Ibid., sig. A3r.

63 Ibid., sig. A3r.

64 Gwinne, M. 'A reply vpon Maister Florio's answere to the Lady of Bedfords invitation to this worke, in a Sonnet of like terminations', in Florio, *Essayes or Morall, Politike and Millitarie Discourses*, sig. A7r. Gwinne signs the poem 'Il Candido'.

65 Florio, *Essayes or Morall, Politike and Millitarie Discourses*, sig. A7r.

66 Ibid., sig. A7r. The relationship between Lucy and Matthew Gwinne was sufficiently strong for him to include a tribute to her in the dedicatory verses of his play, *Vertumnus*. According to Gwinne she is '*excellens* Bedfordia Lucia, *cumen / Faemineum, Musis columen, patrona Poetae*'. Gwinne, M. *Vertumnus* (London, 1607), sig. B4r.

67 Jonson, B. Inscription 'To John Florio with a copy of the Quarto of *Volpone*, 1607', in Herford and Simpson, *Ben Jonson*, VIII.

68 Jonson, B. Inscription 'To Lucy, Countess of Bedford, in a gift-copy of *Cynthia's Revels*, 1601', lines 1-3, 5-6 in Herford and Simpson, *Ben Jonson*, VIII.

69 McClure, *The Letters and Epigrams of Sir John Harington*, p. 87.

70 Ibid., p. 87.

71 Ibid., p. 87.

72 State Papers Domestic, 1598-1601, ed. Green, M.A.E. (London: HMSO, 1869), pp. 459-60.

73 Frances Yates discusses the possibility that Florio was spying for Cecil and his activities at the French embassy in Yates, F.A. *John Florio: The Life of an Italian in Shakespeare's England* (Cambridge: Cambridge University Press, 1934).

74 HMC Salisbury (Cecil) Manuscripts (London: HMSO, 1906), vol. XI, p. 50.

75 Ibid., p. 51.

76 State Papers Domestic (1598-1601), p. 549.

77 State Papers Domestic (1598-1601), p. 548.

78 State Papers Domestic (1589-1601), pp. 557-58.

79 State Papers Domestic (1589-1601), p. 592.

80 Potter and Simpson, *The Sermons of John Donne*, II, p. 59.

81 Cited in Stopes, *The Life of Henry*, p. 236.

82 Cited in Byard, M.M. 'The Trade of Courtiership: The Countess of Bedford and the Bedford Memorials; a family history from 1585 to 1607', *History Today*, 29 (1979), pp. 20-28 at p. 26.

83 Woburn Abbey, 3rd Earl of Bedford's Papers.

84 Ibid.

85 Ibid.

86 Ibid.

87 Ibid.

88 HMC Salisbury (Cecil) Manuscripts (Dublin: HMSO, 1906), vol. XI, p. 119.

89 Ibid., p. 119.

Notes to Chapter 3: Courtier

1 McClure, *Letters of John Chamberlain*, I, p. 179.

2 Ibid., I, p. 179.

3 Cited in Newdigate-Newdegate, A.E. (ed.) *Gossip From a Muniment Room* (London: Ballatyne Press, 1897), p. 36.

4 Ibid., p. 38.

5 Clarendon, E. *The History of the Rebellion and Civil Wars in England* (Oxford: Oxford University Press, 1843), p. 24.

6 Ibid., p. 24.

7 Herford and Simpson, *Ben Jonson*, I, and II, p. 199.

8 Collins, *Letters and Memorials of State*, II, p. 262.

9 Ibid., II, p. 262.

10 Ibid., II, p. 262.

11 State Papers Venetian (1603–1607), p. 15.

12 Ibid., p. 16.

13 Daniel, S. *A Panegyrike Congratulatory Deliuered to the Kings most excellent maiesty at Burleigh Harrington in Rutlandshire* [London, 1603], sig. A3v, sig. A4r.

14 State Papers Venetian (1603–1607), p. 27.

15 Ibid., p. 26.

16 Ibid., p. 26.

17 Spedding, J. (ed.) *The Works of Francis Bacon*, 14 vols (London: Longmans & Co. 1862–75), VI (1870), p. 574.

18 Essex Record Office, Cornwallis-Bacon Papers, D/DBy C19 f.91v, 92r.

19 HMC Salisbury (Cecil) Manuscripts (London: HMSO, 1938), vol. XVII, p. 629.

20 Essex Record Office, Cornwallis-Bacon Papers, D/DBy C19 f.91r.

21 Birch, T. *The Court and Times of James the First*, 2 vols (London: Henry Colburn, 1849), I, p. 141.

22 Ibid., I, p. 141.

23 Nichols, J. *The Progresses, Processions, and Magnificent Festivities of King James the First*, 4 vols (London, 1828), I, p. 162.

24 Clifford, *Diaries of Lady Anne Clifford*, p. 23.

25 Master Burges Letter to the King's Majesty, in *A Sermon Preached before the late King James His Majesty, at Greenwich* (London: Thomas Brudenell, 1642), p. 26.

26 Clifford, *Diaries of Lady Anne Clifford*, p. 24.

27 State Papers Venetian (1603–1607), p. 74.

28 HMC Rutland Manuscripts (London: HMSO, 1911), vol. I, p. 392.

29 State Papers Venetian (1603–1607), p. 75.

30 Nichols, *Progresses, Processions, and Magnificent Festivities*, I, pp. 232–3.

31   Jeayes, *Letters of Philip Gawdy*, p. 35.

32   Clifford, *Diaries of Lady Anne Clifford*, p. 26.

33   Clifford, *Diaries of Lady Anne Clifford*, p. 26.

34   Harington, H. (ed.) *Nugae Antiquae*, 3 vols (London, 1792), II, p. 237.

35   Oman, C.M.A. *Elizabeth of Bohemia*, rev. ed. (London: Hodder and Stoughton, 1964), p. 24.

36   Daniel, S. *A Panegyrike Congratulatory* [1603], sig. Ar.

37   Cited in Schreiber, R.E. *The First Carlisle Sir James Hay, First Earl of Carlisle as Courtier, Diplomat and Entrepreneur, 1580–1636*, Transactions of the American Philosophical Society, Vol. 74, Part 7 (1984), p. 10.

38   Steen, S.J. (ed.) *The Letters of Lady Arbella Stuart* (Oxford: Oxford University Press, 1994), p. 192.

39   Cited in Chambers, E.K. *The Elizabethan Stage*, 4 vols (Oxford: Clarendon Press, 1923), III, p. 279.

40   Lindley, D. (ed.) *Court Masques: Jacobean and Caroline Entertainments 1605–1640* (Oxford: Oxford University Press, 1998), p. ix.

41   Ibid., p. x.

42   Rees, J. (ed.) 'The Vision of the Twelve Goddesses', in Bentley, G.E. (ed.) *A Book of Masques in Honor of Allardyce Nicoll* (Cambridge: Cambridge University Press, 1967), p. 30.

43   Cited in Brennan, M. *Literary Patronage in the English Renaissance: The Pembroke Family* (London and New York: Routledge, 1988), p. 109.

44   Rees, 'The Vision of the Twelve Goddesses', p. 27.

45   Ibid., p. 33.

46   Lee, M. Jnr. (ed.) *Dudley Carleton to John Chamberlain 1603–1624 Jacobean Letters* (New Brunswick, NJ: Rutgers University Press, 1972), p. 55. In the epistle which prefaced the text of the masque, Daniel noted that Pallas 'was the person her Majesty chose to represent', Rees, 'The Vision of the Twelve Goddesses', p. 27.

47   Lee, *Dudley Carleton to John Chamberlain*, p. 56.

48   Herford and Simpson, *Ben Jonson*, VII, p. 209.

49   Rees, 'The Vision of the Twelve Goddesses', p. 30.

50   Jeayes, *Letters of Philip Gawdy*, p.143.

51   Barroll, L. *Anna of Denmark, Queen of England: A Cultural Biography* (Philadelphia: University of Philadelphia Press, 2001), p. 49.

52   Cited in Barroll, *Anna of Denmark*, p. 49.

53   Nichols, *Progresses, Processions, and Magnificent Festivities*, I, p. 318.

54   Ibid., I, p. 318.

55   BL MS Add. 15914. f.76.

56   Cited in Wiffen, J.H. *Historical Memoirs of the House of Russell*, 2 vols (London: Longman, 1833), p. 86.

57   Essex Record Office, Cornwallis-Bacon Papers, D/DBy C19 f.97r.

58   Byard, 'The Trade of Courtiership', p. 28.

59   State Papers Venetian (1617–1619), p. 258.

60   Dekker, T. 'The Catch-pols Masque', in *A Strange Horse-Race* (London, 1613), sig. F1r.

61   Sawyer, E. *Memorials of Affairs of State in the Reigns of Q.Elizabeth and K.James I*, 3 vols (London, 1725), II, p. 40.

62   Ibid., II, p. 43.
63   Ibid., II, p. 43.
64   Herford and Simpson, *Ben Jonson*, VII, p. 177.
65   Ibid., VII, p. 178.
66   Gordon, D.J. 'The Imagery of Jonson's "The Masque of Blacknesse" and "The Masque of Beautie"', *Journal of the Warburg and Courtauld Institutes*, 6 (1943), p. 127.
67   Lee, *Dudley Carleton to John Chamberlain*, p. 68.
68   Herford and Simpson, *Ben Jonson*, X, p. 447.
69   Sawyer, *Memorials of Affairs of State*, II, p. 44.
70   Lee, *Dudley Carleton to John Chamberlain*, p. 68.
71   Jonson, B. *Eastward Hoe!*, IV, i, line 178, in Herford and Simpson, *Ben Jonson*, IV.
72   Ibid., III, iii. lines 41–42, 44.
73   Herford and Simpson, *Ben Jonson*, I, and II, p. 197.
74   Herford and Simpson, *Ben Jonson*, VII, p. 91.
75   *Nugae Antiquae*, II, p. 238.
76   Ibid., II, p. 239.
77   Chambers, *The Elizabethan Stage*, III, p. 379.
78   Newdigate, B.H. *Michael Drayton and his Circle* (Oxford: Basil Blackwell, 1941), p. 59.
79   Ibid., pp. 59–60.
80   Newdigate, *Michael Drayton and his Circle*, p. 65.
81   Lee, *Dudley Carleton to John Chamberlain*, p. 90.
82   *Nugae Antiquae*, II, p. 126.
83   Cited in Croft, P. *King James* (Basingstoke: Palgrave Macmillan, 2003), p. 56.
84   Scott-Warren, J. *Sir John Harrington and the Book as Gift* (Oxford: Oxford University Press, 2001), p. 188.
85   State Papers Venetian (1603–1607), p. 195.
86   Ibid., p. 236.
87   Massinger and Field, *The Fatal Dowry*, sig. D3v.
88   Roberts, *First Part of the Countess of Montgomery's Urania*, pp. 161–2.
89   Ibid., p. 162. In Wroth's work Lucenia attempts to seduce the character of Amphilanthus who is sometimes taken to represent Pembroke. However, it is possible that Wroth was thinking of Holstein as well because it is never possible to be totally confident of her representations. As Wroth's editor, Josephine Roberts, points out, 'Her [Wroth's] technique of including competing and often conflicting fictional representations of the same person necessarily leads to complexities of interpretation'. Roberts, *First Part of the Countess of Montgomery's Urania*, p. lxxi.
90   State Papers Venetian (1603–1607), p. 248.
91   Ibid., p. 248.
92   Essex Record Office, Cornwallis-Bacon Papers D/DBy C19 f.78r.

Notes to Chapter 4: Hermaphroditical Authority

 1   Cited in Carey, J. *John Donne: Life, Mind and Art* (London: Faber and Faber, 1981), p. 71.

2 Gosse, E. *The Life and Letters of John Donne*, 2 vols (London: William Heinemann, 1899), I, p. 110.

3 Mathew, A.H. (ed.) *The True Historical Relation of the Conversion of Sir Tobie Matthew* (London: Burns & Oates, 1904), p. 86.

4 Jonson, B. 'To Sir Henry Goodyere', LXXXV, lines 1–7, in Herford and Simpson, *Ben Jonson*, VIII.

5 Marcy North discusses the use of initials in North, M.L. *The Anonymous Renaissance Cultures of Discretion in Tudor-Stuart England* (Chicago and London: University of Chicago Press, 2003), pp. 67–75.

6 'The Vision of Matilda', lines 1–2, 4, 9–10, in Hebel, *Works of Michael Drayton*, I.

7 Donne, J. To the Countesse of Bedford ('Reason is our Soules left hand'), lines 9–12, in Milgate, *Donne: The Satires*.

8 HMC Salisbury (Cecil) Manuscripts (London: HMSO, 1938), vol. XVII, p. 629.

9 Ibid., p. 629.

10 Ibid., p. 630.

11 Ibid., p. 630.

12 Ibid., p. 630.

13 Ibid., p. 291.

14 Essex Record Office, Cornwallis-Bacon Papers D/DBy C19 f.105v. Lucy wrote to Jane about the death of Bridget Markham's daughter Frances: 'the newse whearof came to me yesterday, & brought me a great deale of sorrow … had shee [Frances] lived till alhallondtyde shee had died a wyfe, for I had concluded such a match for her as I had reson to beleive [sic] shee should have led contentedly'. Essex Record Office, Cornwallis-Bacon Papers D/DBy C19 f.60v.

15 Gosse, *Life and Letters of John Donne*, II, pp. 42–3.

16 Donne, J. To the Countesse of Bedford ('You have refin'd mee'), line 14, in Milgate, *Donne: The Satires*.

17 Gosse, *Life and Letters of John Donne*, II, p. 43.

18 *A Collection of Letters, Made by Sr Tobie Mathews Kt.* (London, 1660), p. 319.

19 Donne, J. To Mrs. M.H. ('Mad paper stay'), line 34, in Milgate, *Donne: The Satires*.

20 Ibid., line 41.

21 Ibid., line 42.

22 Gosse, *Life and Letters of John Donne*, II, p. 43.

23 Potter and Simpson, *The Sermons of John Donne*, II, p. 238.

24 Hooker, R. *Of the Lawes of Ecclesiasticall Politie* (London [n.d.]), V, p. 231.

25 Ibid., V, p. 234.

26 McClure, *The Letters of John Chamberlain*, II, p. 33.

27 Donne, J. Satyre IV, line 15, in Milgate, *Donne: The Satires*.

28 Donne, J. To Sir Henry Wotton ('Sir, more then kisses'), lines 59–62, in Milgate, *Donne: The Satires*.

29 Gosse, *Life and Letters of John Donne*, I, p. 219.

30 John Donne's marriage was declared valid on 27 April 1602.

31 Spedding, *Works of Francis Bacon*, VI, p. 574.

32 Strong, R. *The Renaissance Garden in England* (London: Thames and Hudson, 1998), p. 122.

33 Karen Hearn discusses this possibility. See Hearn, K. *Lucy Harington, Countess of Bedford as Art Patron and Collector* (MA diss., Courtauld Institute of Art, 1990).

34 John Taylor cited in Strong, *Renaissance Garden in England*, p. 122.

35 Essex Record Office, Cornwallis-Bacon Papers D/DBy C19 f.87r.

36 Ibid.

37 Dydymus Mountaine [Henry Dethicke] *The Gardeners Labyrinth* (London, 1577), sig. Aij r & v.

38 Ibid., sig. Llr.

39 Strong, *Renaissance Garden in England*, p. 75.

40 HMC Salisbury (Cecil) Manuscripts (London: HMSO, 1938), vol. XVII, p. 115.

41 Ibid., p. 114.

42 Arbella wrote to Gilbert Talbot: 'you know how we spend our time on the Queenes side[.] Whilest I was at Winchester theare weare certain childeplayes remembred by the fayre ladies. Viz. I pray my Lord give me a Course in your park. Rise pig and go … This exercise is most used from .10. of the clocke at night till .2. or .3. in the morning', in Steen, *The Letters of Lady Arbella Stuart*, pp. 192–3.

43 See for example Act II of Wroth's *Love's Victory* in Brennan, M.G. (ed.) *Lady Mary Wroth's Love's Victory: The Penshurst Manuscript* (London: The Roxburghe Club, 1988).

44 Schleiner, L. *Tudor and Stuart Women Writers* (Bloomington and Indianapolis: Indiana University Press, 1994), p. 109.

45 Ibid., p. 109.

46 Savage, J.E. (ed.) *The 'Conceited Newes' of Sir Thomas Overbury and His Friends* (Gainesville, FL: Scholars' Facsimiles & Reprints, 1968), pp. 230–1.

47 Ibid., pp. 233–4.

48 Jonson, B. 'Conversations with Drummond', in Herford and Simpson, *Ben Jonson*, I, and II, p. 150.

49 Jonson, B. 'An Epigram on the Court Pucell', lines 1–12, 35–36, in Herford and Simpson, *Ben Jonson*, VIII.

50 Schleiner, *Tudor and Stuart Women Writers*, p. 118. Schleiner has an excellent discussion of this based on a reading of Lady Southwell's correspondence and common-place book.

51 Essex Record Office, Cornwallis-Bacon Papers D/DBy C19 f.75v. Lady Roxburgh informed Anna that her husband had secretly obtained permission from James to become Chamberlain to Prince Charles. Anna was incensed that she had not been consulted in this decision and vowed to punish the perpetrators. Lady Roxburgh was duly sent to Scotland and never saw the Queen again.

52 Jonson, B. 'Conversations with Drummond', in Herford and Simpson, *Ben Jonson*, I, and II, p. 135.

53 *A Collection of Letters, Made by Sr Tobie Mathews Kt.*, p. 328.

54 Ibid., p. 328.

55 Ibid., p. 329.

56 Jonson, B. Epigram LXXXIIII 'To Lucy Countesse of Bedford', lines 1–4, in Herford and Simpson, *Ben Jonson*, VIII.

57 Grimble, I.N. *The Harington Family* (London: Jonathan Cape, 1957), pp. 152–3.

58 Ibid., p. 153.

59 Donne, J. *Letters to Severall Persons of Honour* (London, 1651), pp. 103–4.

60 Donne, J. To Sir Henry Wotton ('Sir, more then kisses'), lines 1–2, in Milgate, *Donne: The Satires*.

61 Potter and Simpson, *The Sermons of John Donne*, II, p. 179.

62 Gosse, *Life and Letters of John Donne*, II, p. 43.

63 Gosse, *Life and Letters of John Donne*, I, p. 194.

64 Ibid., I, p. 300. Curiously, in a letter about the lack of need for concerns about time, Donne does give a date.

65 Donne, J. 'The Sunne Rising', line 10, in Gardner, H. (ed.) *John Donne: The Elegies and The Songs and Sonnets* (Oxford: Clarendon Press, 1965).

66 Donne, J. To the Countesse of Bedford ('Reason is our Soules left hand'), lines 9–12, in Milgate, *Donne: The Satires*.

67 Ibid., lines 31–32.

68 Ibid., lines 33–34, 37–38.

69 *Oxford English Dictionary*.

70 Donne, J. To the Countesse of Bedford ('Reason is our Soules left hand'), lines 16–17, in Milgate, *Donne: The Satires*.

71 Scott-Warren, *Sir John Harington and the Book as Gift*, p. 64.

72 Ibid., p. 64.

73 Gosse, *Life and Letters of John Donne*, II, p. 73.

74 Gosse, *Life and Letters of John Donne*, I, p. 220.

75 Shuttleworth, *Life of Edward, First Lord Herbert of Cherbury*, pp. 100–1.

76 Ibid., p. 61.

77 Ibid., p. 62.

78 Ibid., p. 61.

79 Ibid., p. 60.

80 Ibid., p. 61.

81 Gosse, *Life and Letters of John Donne*, I, p. 167.

82 Ibid., I, p. 165.

83 Ibid., I, p. 165.

84 Ibid., I, p. 165.

85 Ibid., I, p. 166.

86 Ibid., I, p. 166.

87 Ibid., I, p. 178.

88 Ibid., I, p. 215.

89 Ibid., I, pp. 214–5.

90 Ibid., I, p. 215.

91 Ibid., I, p. 185.

92 Ibid., I, p. 188. Gosse assigns this letter to Sir John Harrington because the addressee's initials are 'I.H.' but as Roger Bennett points out this is probably erroneous and a result of tampering by Donne's son. The addressee is almost certainly Goodyer. See Bennett, R.E. 'Donne's Letters to Severall Persons of Honour', *PMLA* 56 (March 1941), pp. 120–40, at p. 121.

93 Potter and Simpson, *The Sermons of John Donne*, VII, p. 384.

94 Gosse, *Life and Letters of John Donne*, I, p. 189. The letter is headed 'To yourself' and Gosse has appended 'George Gerrard?' but Bennett argues that the letter was to Goodyer and that 'To your self' referred to the fact that it was sent in a packet with other materials. Bennett, 'Donne's Letters', p. 122.
95 Gosse, *Life and Letters of John Donne*, I, pp. 189, 191.
96 Donne, J. *Biathanatos*, ed. Sullivan, E.W. (London and Toronto: Associated University Press, 1984), p. 29.
97 Gosse, *Life and Letters of John Donne*, II, p. 124.
98 Ibid., II, p. 124.
99 Gosse, *Life and Letters of John Donne*, I, pp. 193, 194.
100 Essex Record Office, Cornwallis-Bacon Papers D/DBy C19 f.91r.
101 Ibid., f.91r, 62r.
102 Gosse, *Life and Letters of John Donne*, I, p. 195.
103 Pender, S. 'Essaying the Body: Donne, Affliction, and Medicine', in Colcough, D. (ed.) *John Donne's Professional Lives* (Cambridge: D.S. Brewer, 2003), p. 220.
104 Gosse, *Life and Letters of John Donne*, I, p. 197.
105 Ibid., I, p. 198.
106 Jonson, B. 'The Masque of Queenes', lines 655–7, in Herford and Simpson, *Ben Jonson*, VII.
107 McManus, *Women on the Renaissance Stage*, p. 131.
108 Gosse, *Life and Letters of John Donne*, I, p. 199.
109 Ibid., I, p. 199.
110 Donne, *Letters to Severall Persons of Honour*, sig. V1v.
111 Ibid., sig. V1v.
112 Essex Record Office, Cornwallis-Bacon Papers D/DBy C19 f.71v.
113 John Dowland dedicated his *Seconde Booke of Songs* to Lucy in 1600.
114 McClure, *The Letters and Epigrams of Sir John Harington*, p. 87.
115 Gosse, *Life and Letters of John Donne*, I, pp. 217–8.
116 Ibid., I, p. 220.
117 Ibid., I, p. 228.
118 Potter and Simpson, *The Sermons of John Donne*, II, p. 179.
119 Walton, I. *The Life of John Donne* (London, 1658), pp. 20–1, original italics.
120 Donne, J. To the Countesse of Bedford ('You have refin'd mee'), line 69, in Milgate, *Donne: The Satires*.
121 T. Wilson, *The Rule of Reason* (London, 1551), sig. Eijr.
122 Rogers, N. 'The Early History of Sidney Sussex College Library', in Beales and Nisbet, *Sidney Sussex College Cambridge*, p. 81.
123 Donne, J. 'Twicknam Garden', lines 1–9, in Gardner, *Donne: The Elegies*, p. 83.
124 Jonson, B. Epigram XCIIII, 'To Lucy, Countesse of Bedford, with Mr. Donnes Satyres', lines 1–4, 6–8, in Herford and Simpson, *Ben Jonson*, VIII.
125 Donne, J. Satyre IV, lines 2–8, in Milgate, *Donne: The Satires*.
126 Jonson, B. Epigram XCIIII, 'To Lucy, Countesse of Bedford, with Mr. Donnes Satyres', lines 11–12, in Herford and Simpson, *Ben Jonson*, VIII.
127 Ibid., lines 13–14.

128 'Occasioned by some person's impertinent exception', lines 9–14, in Jonson, B. *Epicene, or The Silent Woman*, ed. Dutton, R. (Manchester and New York: Manchester University Press, 2003).

129 Dutton, *Epicene, or the Silent Woman*, I, i, lines 72–87.

130 Jonson, B. Epigram LXXVI, 'On Lucy Countess of Bedford', line 13, in Herford and Simpson, *Ben Jonson*, VIII.

131 Spenser, E. *The Faerie Queene*, ed. Hamilton, A.C. (London and New York: Longman, 1977), p. 421.

132 Heywood and Brome associated hermaphrodites with hares and witches: 'Hares are like Hermaphrodites, one while Male, and another Female ... which some think to be the reason that witches take their shapes so oft', Heywood, T. and Brome, R. *The Late Lancashire Witches*, ed. Barber, L.H. (New York and London: Garland Publishing, 1979), p. 155.

133 Stubbes, P. *Anatomy of the Abuses in England* (London, 1593), p. 73.

134 McClure, *The Letters of John Chamberlain*, II, pp. 286–7.

135 See Roberts, J.A. 'An Unpublished Literary Quarrel Concerning the Suppression of Mary Wroth's "Urania" (1621)', in *Notes and Queries* New Series 24 (December 1977), 532–4, at p. 533.

136 HMC Salisbury (Cecil) Manuscripts (London: HMSO, 1971), vol. XXII, p. 161.

137 Mc Pherson, D. 'Ben Jonson's Library and Marginalia: An Annotated Catalogue', *Studies in Philology* 71, Texts and Studies (1974), p. 72.

138 Jonson, B. 'Conversations with Drummond', in Herford and Simpson, *Ben Jonson*, I, and II, p. 140.

139 Dutton, *Epicene, or the Silent Woman*, IV. iv. ll. 102–5, 109–12.

140 Ibid., III. iv. l.54.

141 Ibid., II. ii. ll. 101–2, 105–10, 115–9.

142 State Papers Venetian (1607–1610), p. 216.

143 Ironside, E. *The History and Antiquities of Twickenham* (London, 1797), p. 43.

144 Donne, J. 'Elegie on the Lady Marckham', lines 1–6, in Milgate, W. (ed.) *John Donne: The Epithalamions Anniversaries and Epicedes* (Oxford: Clarendon Press, 1978).

145 Sullivan, E.W. (ed.) *The First and Second Dalhousie Manuscripts Poems and Prose by John Donne and Others: A Facsimile Edition* (Columbia: University of Missouri Press, 1988), pp. 92, 94.

146 Gosse, *Life and Letters of John Donne*, I, p. 170.

147 Donne, J. 'To the Lady Bedford', lines 1–4, in Milgate, *Donne: The Satires*.

148 HMC De L'isle and Dudley (Sidney) (London: HMSO, 1942), vol. IV, p. 134.

149 Ibid., p. 134.

150 HMC De L'isle and Dudley (Sidney) (London: HMSO, 1936), vol. III, p. 140.

151 Gosse, *Life and Letters of John Donne*, I, p. 231.

152 Shuttleworth, *Life of Edward, First Lord Herbert of Cherbury*, p. 21.

153 Gosse, *Life and Letters of John Donne*, I, p. 217.

154 Jonson, B. 'Ungathered Verse IX. Epitaph', in Herford and Simpson, *Ben Jonson*, VIII, p. 372.

155 Ibid., p. 371.

156   Ibid., p. 371.

157   Perkins, W. *A salue for a sicke man* (London, 1615), sig. A2v.

158   Gosse, *Life and Letters of John Donne*, I, p. 232.

159   *The Poems of John Donne*, ed. Grierson, H.J.C., 2 vols (Oxford: Clarendon Press, 1912), I, pp. 422–3.

160   Essex Record Office, Cornwallis-Bacon Papers D/DBy C19 f.117r.

161   Donne, J. To the Countesse of Bedford ('T'have written then'), lines 67–70, in Milgate, *Donne: The Satires*.

162   Lucy, Southampton and Roe all at one time had interests in the Virginia Company.

163   J. Donne To the Countesse of Bedford ('T'have written then'), lines 1–4, in Milgate, *Donne: The Satires*.

164   Ibid., lines 6–8.

165   Ibid., lines 21–26.

166   Ibid., lines 75–76, 79, 87–90.

167   Sidney, M. 'Psalm 51', lines 4–5, 23–24, in *The Collected Works of Mary Sidney Herbert Countess of Pembroke*, eds Hannay, M.P., Kinnamon, N.J., Brennan, M.G., 2 vols (Oxford: Clarendon Press, 1998), vol. II.

168   'Of *Leda* that saies she is sure to be saued', lines 6–12, McClure, *The Letters and Epigrams of Sir John Harington*, p. 182.

169   Donne, J. To the Countesse of Bedford ('You have refin'd mee'), line 7, in Milgate, *Donne: The Satires*.

170   Donne, J. To the Countesse of Bedford ('T'have written then'), line 80, in Milgate, *Donne: The Satires*.

171   Sawyer, *Memorials of Affairs of State*, III, p. 180.

172   HMC De L'isle and Dudley (Sidney) (London: HMSO, 1924), vol. IV, p. 229.

173   Sidney, M. 'Psalm 58', lines 22, 23, in Wynne-Davies, M. (ed.) *Women Poets of the Renaissance* (London: J.M. Dent, 1998).

174   Essex Record Office, Cornwallis-Bacon Papers D/DBy C19 f.92v.

175   Ibid., f.76r.

176   Wroth, M. 'Pamphilia to Amphilanthanus', sonnet 35, lines 1–3, in *The Poems of Lady Mary Wroth*, ed. Roberts, J.A. (Baton Rouge and London: Louisiana State University Press, 1983).

177   Birch, *Court and Times of James the First*, I, p. 141.

178   Gosse, *Life and Letters of John Donne*, I, p. 284.

179   Ibid., p. 284.

180   Jonson, B. 'Conversations with Drummond', in Herford and Simpson, *Ben Jonson*, I, and II, p. 133.

181   Gosse, *Life and Letters of John Donne*, I, p. 302.

182   Gosse, *Life and Letters of John Donne*, I, p. 304.

183   Donne, J. To the Countesse of Bedford ('Though I be *dead*'), lines 7–12, in Milgate, *Donne: The Satires*.

184   Gosse, *Life and Letters of John Donne*, I, pp. 306–7.

185   Ibid., I, p. 310.

186   Ibid., I, p. 314.

187 Herbert, W., *Poems Written by the Right Honorable William Earl of Pembroke* (London, 1660), sig. Iv.
188 Woods, S. (ed.) *The Poems of Aemilia Lanyer* (New York and Oxford: Oxford University Press, 1993), p. xxii.
189 Ibid., pp. xxii–xxiii.
190 Ibid., p. 12.
191 Lanyer, A. 'To the Ladie *Lucie*, Countesse of Bedford', lines 1–3, in Woods, *Poems of Aemilia Lanyer*, p. 32.
192 BL. Harl. MS 7004 f.68.
193 Birch, *Court and Times of James the First*, I, p. 210.
194 Ibid., I, p. 211.
195 Ibid., I, p. 211.
196 Burges, J. *A Sermon Preached before the late King James His Majesty, at Greenwich* (London: Thomas Brudenell, 1642), p. 6.
197 Ibid., p. 24.
198 McClure, *Letters of John Chamberlain*, I, p. 517.
199 Ibid.
200 Birch, *Court and Times of James the First*, I, p. 262.
201 Potter and Simpson, *The Sermons of John Donne*, II, p. 239.
202 Harrington, J. 'Of an ill Physician for the body, that became a worse Surgeon for the soule', lines 30–31, in McClure, *The Letters and Epigrams of Sir John Harington*, p. 234.
203 Birch, *Court and Times of James the First*, I, p. 262.
204 Ibid.
205 Spedding, *Works of Francis Bacon*, XII, pp. 372–3.
206 Donne, J. To Sir Henry Wotton ('Here's no more newes'), line 19, in Milgate, *Donne: The Satires*.
207 Donne, J. 'A Nocturnall upon S. Lucies Day, being the shortest day', lines 1–5, in Gardner, *Donne: The Elegies*.
208 McClure, *Letters of John Chamberlain*, I, p. 422.
209 Essex Record Office, Cornwallis-Bacon Papers D/DBy C19 f.73r.
210 Sawyer, *Memorials of Affairs of State*, III, p. 421.
211 Birch, *Court and Times of James the First*, I, p. 262.
212 Potter and Simpson, *The Sermons of John Donne*, II, p. 343.
213 Ibid.

Notes to Chapter 5: Politician

1 Gosse, *Life and Letters of John Donne*, II, p. 16.
2 Gosse, *Life and Letters of John Donne*, I, p. 295.
3 Birch, *Court and Times of James the First*, I, p. 262.
4 Essex Record Office, Cornwallis-Bacon Papers D/DBy C19 f.62r.
5 The parliaments of 1621, 1624, 1626, see *Journals of the House of Lords*, vol. III.
6 John Harrington died 23 August 1613.

7   Pursell, B.C. *The Winter King Frederick V of the Palatinate and the Coming of the Thirty Years' War* (Aldershot: Ashgate, 2003), p. 18.

8   Ibid., p. 18.

9   Donne, J. 'Epithalamion at the Marriage of the Earl of Somerset', line 33, in Milgate, *Donne: The Epithalamions Anniversaries.*

10   Essex Record Office, Cornwallis-Bacon Papers D/DBy C19 f.60r.

11   Gosse, *Life and Letters of John Donne*, II, pp. 36–7.

12   John Harrington Jr. died in March 1614.

13   *Nugae Antiquae*, III, p. 158.

14   Ibid., pp. 158–9.

15   Tooke, G. *The Belides Or Eulogie and Elegie, Of that truly Honourable John Lord Harrington* (London, 1647), titlepage.

16   Ibid., sig. B3v.

17   Moody, *Private Correspondence*, p. 73.

18   Ibid., p. 73.

19   Donne, J. 'Obsequies to the Lord Harrington, brother to the Countesse of Bedford', lines 69–73, in Milgate, *Donne: The Epithalamions Anniversaries.*

20   Gosse, *Life and Letters of John Donne*, II, pp. 43–4.

21   Essex Record Office, Cornwallis-Bacon Papers D/DBy C19 f.60v.

22   Ibid., f.62v, 63r.

23   Ibid., f.62r.

24   Ibid., f.62r, 62v.

25   Ibid., f.60v, 61r.

26   Maclean, J. (ed.) *Letters from George Lord Carew to Sir Thomas Roe* (London: Camden Society, 1860), pp. 11–12.

27   Potter and Simpson, *The Sermons of John Donne*, II, pp. 248–9.

28   Cited in Wiffen, *Historical Memoirs*, II, p. 86.

29   Lockyer, R. *Buckingham: The Life and Political Career of George Villiers, First Duke of Buckingham 1592–1628* (London and New York: Longman, 1981), p. 16.

30   Lloyd, *State-Worthies*, p. 845.

31   W[eldon], A. 'Aulicus Coquinariae', in *Secret History of the Court of James the First*, 2 vols (Edinburgh: James Ballantyne and Co., 1811), II, p. 261.

32   Lloyd, *State-Worthies*, p. 844.

33   Ibid., pp. 769–70.

34   *A Collection of Letters, Made by Sr Tobie Mathews Kt.*, p. 311.

35   Cited in Barroll, *Anna of Denmark*, p. 137.

36   *Letters to Severall Persons of Honour*, sig. Aa2r.

37   Donne, J. 'Epithalamion at the Marriage of the Earl of Somerset', lines 171–2, in Milgate, *Donne: The Epithalamions Anniversaries.*

38   HMC Salisbury (Cecil) Manuscripts (London: HMSO, 1976), vol. XXIV, Addenda, p. 231.

39   *Letters to Severall Persons of Honour*, sig. V2v, V3r.

40   Ibid., Ff1v.

41   Gosse, *Life and Letters of John Donne*, II, p. 73.

42 Ibid., p. 73.

43 Byfield, N. *An Exposition Upon the Epistle to the Colosssians* (London, 1615), Epistle Dedicatory.

44 Ibid., Epistle Dedicatory.

45 Ibid., Epistle Dedicatory.

46 Gosse, *Life and Letters of John Donne*, II, p. 68.

47 Ibid., p. 68.

48 Ibid., p. 68.

49 Ibid., p. 68.

50 Cited in Barroll, *Anna of Denmark*, p. 146.

51 Lloyd, *State-Worthies*, p. 844.

52 Maclean, *Letters from George Lord Carew to Sir Thomas Roe*, pp. 16–17.

53 Essex Record Office, Cornwallis-Bacon Papers D/DBy C19 f.64r.

54 McClure, *Letters of John Chamberlain*, II, p. 1.

55 Ibid., II, p. 13.

56 Essex Record Office, Cornwallis-Bacon Papers D/DBy C19 f.71r, 71v.

57 Ibid., f.73r, 73v.

58 In 1619 Lucy was granted a thrity-one-year lease to collect 2d per chaldron on sea coal.

59 Spiers, W.L. *The Note-Book and Account Book of Nicholas Stone* (Oxford: Oxford University Press, 1919), p. 47.

60 Howarth, D. *Lord Arundel and his Circle* (New Haven and London: Yale University Press, 1985), p. 53.

61 McClure, *Letters of John Chamberlain*, II, p. 55.

62 Ibid., II, p. 55.

63 Jonson, B. *Lovers Made Men*, lines 117–19, in Herford and Simpson, *Ben Jonson*, VII, p. 457.

64 Burley eventually went to Buckingham.

65 Temple, W. *The Works of Sir William Temple*, 2 vols (London, 1720), I, pp. 185–6.

66 Essex Record Office, Cornwallis-Bacon Papers D/DBy C19 f.75r.

67 Ibid., f.78r.

68 Ibid.

69 'Cupid's Banishment', in Cerasano, S.P. and Wynne-Davies, M. (eds) *Renaissance Drama by Women: Texts and Documents* (London and New York: Routledge, 1997), p. 83.

70 'Cupid's Banishment', lines 40–41, in Cerasano and Wynne-Davies, *Renaissance Drama by Women*.

71 Harvey, P. (compiler) *The Oxford Companion to Classical Literature* (Oxford: Oxford University Press, 1984), p. 232.

72 Drayton, M. 'Endimion and Phoebe', lines 825–8, in Hebel, *Works of Michael Drayton*, I.

73 'Cupid's Banishment', lines 100–1, in Cerasano and Wynne-Davies, *Renaissance Drama by Women*.

74 'Cupid's Banishment', in Cerasano and Wynne-Davies, *Renaissance Drama by Women*, p. 77.

75 'Cupid's Banishment'; 'A Note of all the Masquers' Names', lines 139–46, in Cerasano and Wynne-Davies, *Renaissance Drama by Women*.

76   'Cupid's Banishment', in Cerasano and Wynne-Davies, *Renaissance Drama by Women*.

77   Clare Mc Manus discusses a range of possible meanings contained in the plants. See McManus, *Women on the Renaissance Stage*, pp. 192–5.

78   Essex Record Office, Cornwallis-Bacon Papers D/DBy C19 f.75v.

79   Potter and Simpson, *The Sermons of John Donne*, I, p. 236.

80   Ibid., p. 236.

81   Ibid., p. 243.

82   Ibid., p. 241.

83   Potter and Simpson, *The Sermons of John Donne*, II, p. 178.

84   London, Public Record Office, SP Domestic 14/140/95.

85   Essex Record Office, Cornwallis-Bacon Papers D/DBy C19 f.121v.

86   Cited in Barroll, *Anna of Denmark*, p. 172. For a comprehensive analysis of Anna's religious views see Leeds Barroll.

87   In addition to hearing Donne preach herself, Lucy would also have heard about him and the nature of his sermons from Anne Clifford with whom she was in regular contact. Anne's husband, Richard Sackville, 3rd Earl of Dorset, was a supporter of Donne. In 1617 Donne visited Knole, the country home of Anne and Richard, and preached in the local church. Anne recorded the visit in her diary: 'The 27th I went to Church (being Sunday), forenoon & afternoon, Dr Donne Preaching, and he & other strangers dining with me in the Great Chamber'. Clifford, *Diaries of Lady Anne Clifford*, p. 60.

88   Cited in Howarth, *Lord Arundel and his Circle*, p. 69.

89   Ibid., p. 69.

90   Essex Record Office, Cornwallis-Bacon Papers D/DBy C19 f.81v, 82r.

91   Ibid., f.82r.

92   The fresco was destroyed in a fire that swept through Whitehall Palace on 4 January 1698. Two seventeenth-century copies by Remigius Leemput exist, as does Hoblein's cartoon for the left-hand section of the fresco.

93   Potter and Simpson, *The Sermons of John Donne*, II, p. 238.

94   Roe, T. *The Negotiations of Sir Thomas Roe, in his Embassy to the Ottoman Porte* (London, 1740), p. 584.

95   London, Public Record Office, SP Domestic 84/103/213.

96   Lloyd, *State-Worthies*, p. 791. Along with the Countess of Arundel and other ladies of the court, Lucy made a point of going to the Star-Chamber where the trial was held to show her support for Lady Exeter.

97   London, Public Record Office, SP Domestic 14/103/50.

98   Ibid., SP Domestic 14/103/50.

99   Essex Record Office, Cornwallis-Bacon Papers D/DBy C19 f.87v.

100 Ibid., f.105v.

101 McClure, *Letters of John Chamberlain*, II, pp. 187–8.

102 Ibid., p. 224.

103 Ibid., p. 237.

104 Essex Record Office, Cornwallis-Bacon Papers D/DBy C19 f.93r.

105 Gosse, *Life and Letters of John Donne*, II, p. 127.

106 McClure, *Letters of John Chamberlain*, II, p. 189.

107 Sloan, A.W. *English Medicine in the Seventeenth Century* (Durham: Durham Academic Press, 1996), p. 158.

108 Jonson, B. 'An Epigram to the small Poxe', lines 1–3, 13–14, in Herford and Simpson, *Ben Jonson*, VIII.

109 Woburn Abbey, 3rd Earl of Bedford's Papers.

110 Ibid.

111 McClure, *Letters of John Chamberlain*, II, p. 250.

112 Ibid., pp. 244–5. Anne Clifford recorded that: 'my Lady Bedford had the Small-pox and had them in that extremity that she lost one of her Eyes'. Clifford, *Diaries of Lady Anne Clifford*, p. 78.

113 McClure, *Letters of John Chamberlain*, II, p. 245.

114 Carmichael, A.G. and Silverstein, A.M. 'Smallpox in Europe before the seventeenth century: virulent killer or benign disease?' *Journal of the History of Medicine*, 42 (1987), pp. 147–68.

115 Cited in Parker, G. (ed.) *The Thirty Years' War*, 2nd ed. (London and New York: Routledge, 2006), p. 50.

116 Cited in Adams, S.L. 'Foreign Policy and the Parliaments of 1621 and 1624', in Sharpe, K. (ed.) *Faction and Parliament Essays on Early Stuart History* (Oxford: Clarendon Press, 1978), p. 147.

117 McClure, *Letters of John Chamberlain*, II, pp. 263–4.

118 Ibid., II, p. 291.

119 Potter and Simpson, *The Sermons of John Donne*, II, p. 335.

120 Ibid., p. 346.

121 HMC Salisbury (Cecil) Manuscripts (London: HMSO, 1971), vol. XXII, p. 117.

122 McClure, *Letters of John Chamberlain*, II, p. 336.

123 Hannay, 'A Happy Husband', p. 190.

124 Adams, 'Foreign Policy and the Parliaments of 1621 and 1624', p. 140.

125 Essex Record Office, Cornwallis-Bacon Papers D/DBy C19 f.95r. Anne Harrington died 25 May 1620.

126 Ibid., f.95v.

127 BL MS Landsdowne 498. f.80.

128 Woburn Abbey, 3rd Earl of Bedford's Papers.

129 Burton, R. *The Anatomy of Menancholy*, eds Faulkner, T.C., Kiesslilng, N.K., Blair, R.L., 6 vols 1989–2000 (Oxford: Clarendon Press, 1989), I, pp. 378–9.

130 Burton, *The Anatomy of Melancholy*, II, p. 106.

131 Potter and Simpson, *The Sermons of John Donne*, III, p. 187.

132 Ibid., p. 187, original italics.

133 Burton, *The Anatomy of Menancholy*, II, p. 118.

134 Furdell, E.L. *The Royal Doctors 1485–1714: Medical Personnel at the Tudor and Stuart Courts* (Rochester, NY: University of Rochester Press, 2001), p. 104.

135 Cited in Furdell, *The Royal Doctors 1485–1714*, p. 104. Essex Record Office, Cornwallis-Bacon Papers D/DBy C19 f.123r.

136 Burton, *The Anatomy of Menancholy*, I, p. lxii.

137 London, Public Record Office, SP Domestic 14/122/156.

138   Ibid., SP Domestic 14/122/156–57.

139   London, Public Record Office, SP Domestic 14/130/20.

140   Cited in Morgan, F.H. 'A Biography of Lucy Countess of Bedford, The Last Great Literary Patroness' (unpublished DPhil., University of Southern California, 1956), p. 251.

141   Hannay, P. 'Sheretine and Mariana', in *The Poetical Works of Patrick Hannay* (Glasgow: Hunterian Club, 1875), p. 91.

142   London, Public Record Office, SP Domestic 14/140/95.

143   Cited in Adams, 'Foreign Policy and the Parliaments of 1621 and 1624', p. 144.

144   HMC Salisbury (Cecil) Addenda (1605–1668), vol. XXIV, pp. 235–6.

145   London, Public Record Office, SP Domestic 14/176/95.

146   Essex Record Office, Cornwallis-Bacon Papers D/DBy C19 f.117r.

147   Ibid., f.117v.

148   Ibid., f.122v.

149   Ibid., f.117v.

150   HMC Mar and Kellie, *Supplementary Reports* (London: HMSO, 1930), p. 227.

151   *A Collection of Letters, Made by Tobie Mathews Kt.*, pp. 58–60.

152   Roe, *Negotiations of Sir Thomas Roe*, p. 583.

153   Ibid., p. 583.

154   Hearn, K. 'A Question of Judgement: Lucy Harington, Countess of Bedford, as Art Patron and Collector', in Chaney, E. (ed.) *The Evolution of English Collecting: Receptions of Italian Art in the Tudor and Stuart Periods* (New Haven and London: Yale University Press, 2003), pp. 221–39, at p. 230.

155   This interpretation of the medal is pointed out by Karen Hearn who also provides a detailed and illuminating analysis of the coin and the likely conditions of its manufacture.

156   Topsell, E. *The Historie of Serpents* (London, 1608), p. 18.

Notes to Chapter 6: Post Mortem

1   Moody, *Private Correspondence*, p. 158.

Bibliography

Adams, S. (ed.) *Household Accounts and Disbursement Books of Robert Dudley, Earl of Leicester, 1558–1561, 1584–1586*, Camden Fifth Series Volume 6 (Cambridge: Cambridge University Press, 1995).

Alumni Cantabrigiensis (Cambridge: Cambridge University Press, 1922).

Bald, R.C. *John Donne: A Life* (Oxford: Clarendon Press, 1970).

Barroll, L. *Anna of Denmark, Queen of England: A Cultural Biography* (Philadelphia: University of Philadelphia Press, 2001).

Beales, D.E.D. and Nisbet, H.B. (eds) *Sidney Sussex College Cambridge Historical Essays* (Suffolk: The Boydell Press, 1996).

Bennett, R.E. 'Donne's Letters to Severall Persons of Honour', *PMLA* 56 (March 1941), pp. 120–40.

Birch, T. *The Court and Times of James the First*, 2 vols (London: Henry Colburn, 1849).

Boutcher, W.V. 'Florio's Montaigne: Translation and Pragmatic Humanism in the Sixteenth Century' (unpublished DPhil., Cambridge, 1991).

Brathwait, R. *Some Rules and Orders for the Government of the House of an Earle* (London: Benjamin Bensley, 1821).

Braybrooke, R. (ed.) *The Private Correspondence of Jane Lady Cornwallis Bacon, 1613–1644* (London, 1843).

Brennan, M. *Literary Patronage in the English Renaissance: The Pembroke Family* (London and New York: Routledge, 1988).

Brennan, M.G. (ed.) *Lady Mary Wroth's Love's Victory: The Penshurst Manuscript* (London: The Roxburghe Club, 1988).

Burges, J. *A Sermon Preached before the late King James His Majesty, at Greenwich* (London: Thomas Brudenell, 1642).

Burton, R. *The Anatomy of Menancholy*, eds Faulkner, T.C., Kiesslilng, N.K., Blair, R.L., 6 vols 1989–2000 (Oxford: Clarendon Press, 1989).

Byard, M.M. 'The Trade of Courtiership: The Countess of Bedford and the Bedford Memorials; a family history form 1585 to 1607', *History Today*, 29 (January 1979), pp. 20–28.

Byfield, N. *An Exposition Upon the Epistle to the Colosssians* (London, 1615).

Carey, J. *John Donne: Life, Mind and Art* (London: Faber and Faber, 1981).

Carmichael, A.G. and Silverstein, A.M. 'Smallpox in Europe before the seventeenth century: virulent killer or benign disease?' *Journal of the History of Medicine*, 42 (1987), pp. 147–68.

Cerasano, S.P. and Wynne-Davies, M. (eds) *Renaissance Drama by Women: Texts and Documents* (London and New York: Routledge, 1997).

Chambers, E.K. *The Elizabethan Stage*, 4 vols (Oxford: Clarendon Press, 1923).

Clarendon, E. *The History of the Rebellion and Civil Wars in England* (Oxford: Oxford University Press, 1843).

Clifford, D.J.H. (ed.) *The Diaries of Lady Anne Clifford* (Gloucestershire: Alan Sutton Publishing, 1990).

Collins, A. (ed.) *Letters and Memorials of State*, 2 vols (London, 1746).

Collinson, P. *The Elizabethan Puritan Movement* (London: Jonathan Cape, 1967).

—*English Puritanism* (London: The Historical Association, 1983).

Cowley, A. *Loves Riddle* (London, 1638).

Croft, P. *King James* (Basingstoke: Palgrave Macmillan, 2003).

Daniel, S. *A Panegyrike Congratulatory Deliuered to the Kings most excellent maiesty at Burleigh Harrington in Rutlandshire* (London, Edward Blount, 1603).

Davies, J. *The Muses Sacrifice* (London, 1612).

Dekker, T. *A Strange Horse-Race* (London, 1613).

Desainliens, C. *Campo di Fior* (London, 1583).

Donne, J. *Letters to Severall Persons of Honour* (London, 1651).

—*Biathanatos*, ed. Sullivan, E.W. (London and Toronto: Associated University Press, 1984).

Donno, E.S. (ed.) *Sir John Harington's A New Discourse of a Stale Subject, Called The Metamorphosis of Ajax* (London: Routledge and Kegan Paul, 1962).

Du Maurier, D. *Golden Lads: A Study of Anthony Bacon, Francis and their Friends* (London: Victor Gollancz, 1975).

Dutton, R. (ed.) *Epicene, or the Silent Woman* (Manchester and New York: Manchester University Press, 2003).

Dydymus Mountaine [Henry Dethicke] *The Gardeners Labyrinth* (London, 1577).

Florio, J. *A Worlde of Wordes* (London, 1598).

—*The Essayes or Morall, Politike and Millitarie Discourses of Lo: Michaell de Montaigne* (London, 1603).

Furdell, E.L. *The Royal Doctors 1485–1714: Medical Personnel at the Tudor and Stuart Courts* (Rochester, NY: University of Rochester Press, 2001).

Gardner, H. (ed.) *John Donne: The Elegies and The Songs and Sonnets* (Oxford: Clarendon Press, 1965).

Gordon, D.J. 'The Imagery of Jonson's "The Masque of Blacknesse" and "The Masque of Beautie"', *Journal of the Warburg and Courtauld Institutes*, 6 (1943), pp. 122–41.

Gosse, E. *The Life and Letters of John Donne*, 2 vols (London: William Heinemann, 1899).

Grierson, H.J.C. (ed.) *The Poems of John Donne*, 2 vols (Oxford: Clarendon Press, 1912).

Grimble, I.N. *The Harington Family* (London: Jonathan Cape, 1957).

Gwinne, M. *Vertumnus* (London, 1607).

Hannay, P. *The Poetical Works of Patrick Hannay* (Glasgow: Hunterian Club, 1875).

Hannay, M.P., Kinnamon, N.J. and Brennan, M.G. (eds) *The Collected Works of Mary Sidney Herbert Countess of Pembroke*, 2 vols (Oxford: Clarendon Press, 1998).

Harington, H. (ed.) *Nugae Antiquae*, 3 vols (London, 1792).

Harvey, P. (compiler) *The Oxford Companion to Classical Literature* (Oxford: Oxford University Press, 1984).

Hearn, K. *Lucy Harington, Countess of Bedford as Art Patron and Collector* (MA diss., Courtauld Institute of Art, 1990).

—'A Question of Judgement: Lucy Harington, Countess of Bedford, as Art Patron and Collector', in Chaney, E. (ed.) *The Evolution of English Collecting: Receptions of Italian Art in the Tudor and Stuart Periods* (New Haven and London: Yale University Press, 2003), pp. 221–39.

Hebel, J.W. (ed.) *The Works of Michael Drayton*, 4 vols (Oxford: Basil Blackwell, 1931–33).

Herbert, A.L. 'Oakham parish library', *Library History*, 6 (1982–84), pp. 1–11.

Herbert, W. *Poems Written by the Right Honorable William Earl of Pembroke* (London, 1660).

Herford, C.H. and Simpson, P. (eds) *Ben Jonson*, 11 vols (Oxford: Clarendon Press, 1925–52).

Heywood, T. and Brome, R. *The Late Lancashire Witches*, ed. Barber, L.H. (New York and London: Garland Publishing, 1979).

HMC Rutland Manuscripts (London: HMSO, 1911), vol. I.

HMC Salisbury (Cecil) Manuscripts (London: HMSO, 1895), vol. VI.

HMC Salisbury (Cecil) Manuscripts (London: HMSO, 1899), vol. VIII.

HMC Salisbury (Cecil) Manuscripts (Dublin: HMSO, 1906), vol. XI.

HMC Salisbury (Cecil) Manuscripts (London: HMSO, 1938), vol. XVII.

HMC Salisbury (Cecil) Manuscripts (London: HMSO, 1971), vol. XXII.

HMC Salisbury (Cecil) Manuscripts (London: HMSO, 1976), vol. XXIV, Addenda.

Hooker, R. *Of the Lawes of Ecclesiasticall Politie* (London [n.d.]).

Howarth, D. *Lord Arundel and his Circle* (New Haven and London: Yale University Press, 1985).

Ironside, E. *The History and Antiquities of Twickenham* (London, 1797).

Jeayes, I.H. (ed.) *Letters of Philip Gawdy* (London: J.B. Nichols and Sons, 1906).

Krueger, R. (ed.) *The Poems of Sir John Davies* (Oxford: Clarendon Press, 1975).

Lamb, M.E. *Gender and Authorship in the Sidney Circle* (Wisconsin: University of Wisconsin Press, 1990).

Lee, M. Jnr. (ed.) *Dudley Carleton to John Chamberlain 1603–1624 Jacobean Letters* (New Brunswick, NJ: Rutgers University Press, 1972).

Lindley, D. (ed.) *Court Masques: Jacobean and Caroline Entertainments 1605–1640* (Oxford: Oxford University Press, 1995).

Lloyd, D. *State-Worthies* (London, 1670).

Lockyer, R. *Buckingham: The Life and Political Career of George Villiers, First Duke of Buckingham 1592–1628* (London and New York: Longman, 1981).

Maclean, J. (ed.) *Letters from George Lord Carew to Sir Thomas Roe* (London: Camden Society, 1860).

Massinger, P. and Field, N. *The Fatal Dowry* (London, 1632).

Mathew, A.H. (ed.) *The True Historical Relation of the Conversion of Sir Tobie Matthew* (London: Burns & Oates, 1904).

Mathews, T., *A Collection of Letters, Made by Sr Tobie Mathews Kt.* (London, 1660).

McClure, N.E. (ed.) *The Letters and Epigrams of Sir John Harington* (Philadelphia: University of Pennsylvania Press, 1930).

—(ed.) *The Letters of John Chamberlain*, 2 vols (Philadelphia: American Philosophical Society, 1939).

McManus, C. *Women on the Renaissance Stage: Anna of Denmark and Female Masquing in the Stuart Court (1590–1619)* (Manchester and New York: Manchester University Press, 2002).

McPherson, D. 'Ben Jonson's Library and Marginalia: An Annotated Catalogue', *Studies in Philology*, Vol. LXXI Texts and Studies (1974), pp. 1–106.

Mendelson, S.H. 'Stuart women's diaries and occasional memoirs', in Prior, M. (ed.) *Women in English Society 1500–1800* (London and New York: Methuen, 1985).

Milgate, W. (ed.) *John Donne: The Satires, Epigrams and Verse Letters* (Oxford: Clarendon Press, 1967).

—*John Donne: The Epithalamions Anniversaries and Epicedes* (Oxford: Clarendon Press, 1978).

Moody, J. (ed.) *The Private Correspondence of Jane Lady Cornwallis Bacon, 1613–1644* (London: Associated University Press, 2003).

Morgan, F.H. 'A Biography of Lucy Countess of Bedford, The Last Great Literary Patroness' (unpublished PhD diss., University of Southern California, 1956).

Nevile, J. 'Dance and the Garden: Moving and Static Choreography in Renaissance Europe', *Renaissance Quarterly*, 52 (1999), pp. 805–36.

Newdigate, B.H. *Michael Drayton and his Circle* (Oxford: Basil Blackwell, 1941).

Newdigate-Newdegate, A.E. (ed.) *Gossip From a Muniment Room* (London: Ballatyne Press, 1897).

Nichols, J. *The Progresses, Processions, and Magnificent Festivities of King James the First*, 4 vols (London, 1828).

Norden, J. *Speculum Britanniae* (London, 1593).

North, M.L. *The Anonymous Renaissance Cultures of Discretion in Tudor-Stuart England* (Chicago and London: University of Chicago Press, 2003).

Oman, C.M.A. *Elizabeth of Bohemia*, rev. ed. (London: Hodder and Stoughton, 1964).

Oram, W.A., Bjorvand, E., Bond, R., Cain, T.H., Dunlop, A., Schell, R. (eds) *The Yale Edition of the Shorter Poems of Edmund Spenser* (New Haven and London: Yale University Press, 1989).

Parker, G. (ed.) *The Thirty Years' War*, 2nd ed. (London and New York: Routledge, 2006).

Peele, G. *Anglorum Feriae* (London, 1596).

Pender, S. 'Essaying the Body: Donne, Affliction, and Medicine', in *John Donne's Professional Lives*, ed. Colclough, D. (Cambridge: D. S. Brewer, 2003).

Perkins, W. *A salue for a sicke man* (London, 1615).

Plat, H. *The Garden of Eden* (London, 1659).

Potter, G.R. and Simpson, E.M. (eds) *The Sermons of John Donne*, 10 vols (Berkeley and Los Angeles: University of California Press, 1953–62).

Pursell, B.C. *The Winter King Frederick V of the Palatinate and the Coming of the Thirty Years' War* (Aldershot: Ashgate, 2003).

Rees. J. (ed.) 'The Vision of the Twelve Goddesses', in Bentley, G.E. (ed.) *A Book of Masques in Honour of Allardyce Nicoll* (Cambridge: Cambridge University Press, 1967).

Roberts, J.A. 'An Unpublished Literary Quarrel Concerning the Suppression of Mary Wroth's "Urania" (1621)', *Notes and Queries* New Series 24 (December 1977), pp. 532–4.

—(ed.) *The Poems of Lady Mary Wroth* (Baton Rouge and London: Louisiana State University Press, 1983).

—(ed.) *The First Part of the Countess of Montgomery's Urania* (Binghamton, New York: Medieval & Renaissance Texts & Studies, 1995).

Roe, T. *The Negotiations of Sir Thomas Roe, in his Embassy to the Ottoman Porte* (London, 1740).

Savage, J.E. (ed.) *The 'Conceited Newes' of Sir Thomas Overbury and His Friends* (Gainesville, FL: Scholars' Facsimiles & Reprints, 1968).

Sawyer, E. *Memorials of Affairs of State in the Reigns of Q.Elizabeth and K.James I*, 3 vols (London, 1725).

Schleiner, L. *Tudor and Stuart Women Writers* (Bloomington and Indianapolis: Indiana University Press, 1994).

Schreiber, R.E. *The First Carlisle Sir James Hay, First Earl of Carlisle as Courtier, Diplomat and Entrepreneur, 1580–1636*, Transactions of the American Philosophical Society Vol. 74, Part 7 (1984).

Scott-Warren, J. *Sir John Harington and the Book as Gift* (Oxford: Oxford University Press, 2001).

Shakespeare, W. *Titus Andronicus*, ed. Maxwell, J.C. (London and New York: Routledge, repr. 1989).

—*Macbeth*, ed. Muir, K. (London and New York: Routledge, repr. 1991).

Sharpe, K. (ed.) *Faction and Parliament Essays on Early Stuart History* (Oxford: Clarendon Press, 1978).

Shuttleworth, J.M. (ed.) *The Life of Edward, First Lord Herbert of Cherbury written by himself* (London: Oxford University Press, 1976).

Sidney, P. *A Defence of Poetry*, ed. Van Dorsten, J.A. (Oxford: Oxford University Press, 1984).

Sloan, A.W. *English Medicine in the Seventeenth Century* (Durham: Durham Academic Press, 1996).

Spedding, J. (ed.) *The Works of Francis Bacon*, 14 vols (London: Longmans & Co. 1862–75).

Spenser, E. *The Faerie Queene*, ed. Hamilton, A.C. (London and New York: Longman, 1977).

Spiers, W.L. *The Note-Book and Account Book of Nicholas Stone* (Oxford: Oxford University Press, 1919).

Sprague, A.C. (ed.) *Samuel Daniel Poems and a Defence of Ryme* (London: Routledge & Kegan Paul, 1950).

State Papers Domestic 1591–1594, ed. Green, M.A.E. (London: HMSO, 1867).

State Papers Domestic 1598–1601, ed. Green, M.A.E. (London: HMSO, 1869).

State Papers Venetian 1603–1607, ed. Brown, H.F. (London: HMSO, 1900).

State Papers Venetian 1607–1610, ed. Brown, H.F. (London: HMSO, 1904).

State Papers Venetian 1617–1619, ed. Hinds, A.B. (London: HMSO, 1909).

Steen, S.J. (ed.) *The Letters of Lady Arbella Stuart* (Oxford: Oxford University Press, 1994).

Stewart, A. *The Cradle King: A Life of James VI and I* (London: Chatto & Windus, 2003).

Stopes, C.C. *The Life of Henry, Third Earl of Southampton, Shakespeare's Patron* (Cambridge: Cambridge University Press, 1922).

Strong, R. *The Renaissance Garden in England* (London: Thames and Hudson, 1998).

Stubbes, P. *Anatomy of the Abuses in England* (London, 1593).

Sullivan, E.W. (ed.) *The First and Second Dalhousie Manuscripts Poems and Prose by John Donne and Others: A Facsimile Edition* (Columbia: University of Missouri Press, 1988).

Temple, W. *The Works of Sir William Temple*, 2 vols (London, 1720).

Tooke, G. *The Belides Or Eulogie and Elegie, Of that truly Honourable John Lord Harrington* (London, 1647).

Topsell, E. *The Historie of Serpents* (London, 1608).

Ungerer, G. 'An Unrecorded Elizabethan Performance of Titus Andronicus', *Shakespeare Survey*, 14 (1961), pp. 102–9.

Walton, I. *The Life of John Donne* (London, 1658).

W[eldon], A. 'Aulicus Coquinariae', in *Secret History of the Court of James the First*, 2 vols (Edinburgh: James Ballantyne and Co., 1811).

Woods, S. *Lanyer: A Renaissance Woman Poet* (Oxford: Oxford University Press, 1999).

—(ed.) *The Poems of Aemilia Lanyer* (New York and Oxford: Oxford University Press, 1993).

Wiffen, J.H. *Historical Memoirs of the House of Russell*, 2 vols (London: Longman, 1833).

Wilson, T. *The Rule of Reason* (London, 1551).

Wright, J. *The History and Antiquities of the County of Rutland* (London, 1684).

Wynne-Davies, M. (ed.) *Women Poets of the Renaissance* (London: J.M. Dent, 1998).

Yates, F.A. *John Florio: The Life of an Italian in Shakespeare's England* (Cambridge: Cambridge University Press, 1934).

Index

Ingram Content Group UK Ltd.
Milton Keynes UK
UKHW020043110723
424901UK00003B/115